PALGRAVE STUDIES IN THEATRE AND PERFORMANCE HISTORY is a series devoted to the best of theatre/performance scholarship currently available, accessible, and free of jargon. It strives to include a wide range of topics, from the more traditional to those performance forms that in recent years have helped broaden the understanding of what theatre as a category might include (from variety forms as diverse as the circus and burlesque to street buskers, stage magic, and musical theatre, among many others). Although historical, critical, or analytical studies are of special interest, more theoretical projects, if not the dominant thrust of a study, but utilized as important underpinning or as a historiographical or analytical method of exploration, are also of interest. Textual studies of drama or other types of less traditional performance texts are also germane to the series if placed in their cultural, historical, social, or political and economic context. There is no geographical focus for this series and works of excellence of a diverse and international nature, including comparative studies, are sought.

The editor of the series is Don B. Wilmeth (EMERITUS, Brown University), Ph.D., University of Illinois, who brings to the series over a dozen years as editor of a book series on American theatre and drama, in addition to his own extensive experience as an editor of books and journals. He is the author of several award-winning books and has received numerous career achievement awards, including one for sustained excellence in editing from the Association for Theatre in Higher Education.

Also in the series:

Lady Macbeth in America

From the Stage to the White House

Gay Smith

palgrave
macmillan

LADY MACBETH IN AMERICA
Copyright © Gay Smith, 2010.

First published in 2010 by
PALGRAVE MACMILLAN®
in the United States—a division of St. Martin's Press LLC,
175 Fifth Avenue, New York, NY 10010.

Where this book is distributed in the UK, Europe and the rest of the world,
this is by Palgrave Macmillan, a division of Macmillan Publishers Limited,
registered in England, company number 785998, of Houndmills,
Basingstoke, Hampshire RG21 6XS.

Palgrave Macmillan is the global academic imprint of the above companies
and has companies and representatives throughout the world.

Palgrave® and Macmillan® are registered trademarks in the United
States, the United Kingdom, Europe and other countries.

ISBN: 978–0–230–62288–3

Library of Congress Cataloging-in-Publication Data

Smith, Gay, 1943–
    Lady Macbeth in America : from the stage to the White House /
Gay Smith.
        p. cm.—(Palgrave studies in theatre and performance history)
    Includes bibliographical references.
    ISBN 978–0–230–62288–3 (alk. paper)
        1. Shakespeare, William, 1564–1616.—Characters—Lady
Macbeth. 2. Shakespeare, William, 1564–1616. Macbeth.
3. Shakespeare, William,1564–1616.—Stage history. 4. Acting.
5. Presidents' spouses—United States—History. 6. Politics and
literature—United States—History. I. Title.

PR2823.S545 2010
822.3'3—dc22   2009022732

A catalogue record of the book is available from the British Library.

Design by Newgen Imaging Systems (P) Ltd., Chennai, India.

First edition: February 2010

10 9 8 7 6 5 4 3 2 1

Printed in the United States of America.

Transferred to Digital Printing in 2011

Contents ❧

Illustrations ❧

Acknowledgments ❧

R ecognizing the libraries and museums and their staffs for their assistance, I especially appreciate the following: American Philosophical Society Library, Philadelphia; Beinecke Rare Book and Manuscript Library, and the Lewis Walpole Library, Yale University; Bibliothèque Historique de la Ville de Paris; Bibliothèque Nationale, Paris; Boston Public Library; Derry Public Library, Ireland; Edinburgh Central Library; Ellen Terry Museum, Smallhythe Place, Kent; Free Library, Philadelphia; Houghton Library, Harvard University; Huntington Library, San Marino; Linen Library, Belfast; Maîson Jean Vilar, Avignon; Massachusetts Historical Society; National Library, Dublin; New York Historical Society Library; New York Public Library; Rare Book and Manuscript Library, University of Pennsylvania; Special Collections, University of California Library, Santa Barbara; University of Edinburgh; Victoria and Albert Museum; Library of Congress; Trinity College Library, Dublin; Wesleyan University Libraries, Special Collections and Archives, Davison Art Center and Humanities Center.

Likewise I gratefully acknowledge the acumen and support of my editor, Don Wilmeth, the assistance of the editorial staff at Palgrave Macmillan; and the many and various contributions of colleagues and friends: Patricia Beaman, Mary Bosakowski, Lorna Brown, Virginia Crosby, Judy Dunbar, John Elmore, Jim and Anne Gould, Jeff Hatcher, Paul Horton, Gertrude Reif Hughes, Noah Isenberg, James Manifold, Sean McCann, Skip Mercier, Elizabeth Milroy, Betsy Morgan, Alain and Rosemary Munkittrick, Jean-Claude and Micheline Patau, Jason Poston, Melanie Rehak, David Schorr, Mark and Greta Slobin, Richard Slotkin, William Stowe, Andy Szegedy-Maszak, Suzy Taraba, Tula Telfair, Karin Trainer, Thomas Wickman, Allynn Wilkinson; the late Phil Bosakowski, August Coppola, Ellen D'Oench; my students at Wesleyan University, Remy Auberjonois and Michael Twist for their Macbeth and Lady Macbeth, and honors' thesis students Daniel Poliner, Jake Robinson, and Jessica Smith; British actor Timothy Dalton and director Terence Knapp for their production of *Macbeth* at the University of Hawaii featuring two alternating Lady Macbeths that sparked this investigation into the role of Shakespeare's Lady Macbeth in America.

Previous Publications by the Author ∾

as Gay Smith Manifold:

George Sand's Theatre Career

George Sand's Gabriel, Introduction, Translation, and Adaptation

as Gay Smith:

Plays by Phil Bosakowski, Edit and Introduction

Introduction ∿

Perceived as iconic, and experienced as a mythic type haunting America's cultural memory, Shakespeare's Lady Macbeth migrated from the stage to the White House. This study tracks that migration. Lady Macbeth has no more than half an hour upon the stage in a play that takes two and a half hours to perform. Yet the character appears to dominate, at least initially. Whether at first to goad her husband to action or later in the play to try to subdue him, Lady Macbeth's efforts on behalf of Macbeth's ambitions remain a textual imperative. An actor playing Lady Macbeth may vary her manner and means, play her as a mother figure, scornful or tender or both, or as a sensual and seductive youth, warm and loving or cold and critical. But no matter what the variations, they serve as means or at least attempts to persuade and promote her husband's advancement to commander in chief and ruler of the country. Performances of Shakespeare's Lady Macbeth have provided American audiences with protean images of a political wife able to influence her husband, as the couple climbs to the pinnacle of political power, precariously holds fast to it, and ultimately falls. In *Macbeth* they do so by criminal means; but Shakespeare has scored their characterizations in such a way that they need not be reduced to melodramatic villains, entirely evil. The script allows for actors to elicit sympathy, even empathy, for their characters, for example, playing Macbeth as a noble warrior, a military officer, propelled into criminal actions by outside forces as well as by his own ambition. Less sympathetic toward Lady Macbeth, audiences tend to blame the wife for the husband's errant ways, an impetus for dramatic plots since the ancient Greeks staged stories about Medea and Clytemnestra, but especially prevalent in American attitudes toward political wives, and particularly when the country is at war.

To see how Shakespeare's Lady Macbeth entered American politics and eventually the White House, this investigation will focus on who the actresses prominent in the role have been, how they performed Lady Macbeth, and to what effect. Running parallel with the theatre history of each actor is an account of the First Lady whose influence over the president resembles Lady Macbeth's over Macbeth. Their parallel paths converged in the late twentieth century when a decade-long attempt to vilify First Lady Hillary Clinton as a Lady Macbeth in the White House succeeded in making "Lady Macbeth Hillary Clinton" all one name, not just in right-wing journals and papers, but mainstream media as well (chapter 1). But Shakespeare's Lady Macbeth entered politics from the moment of her creation. The playwright based his character on an eleventh-century Scottish queen, vanquished and succeeded by ancestors of King James I, the ruling monarch when Shakespeare premiered *Macbeth*. By entering Lady Macbeth in the public debate over whether women can be trusted with political power and influence, Shakespeare made the character resonate with his audience. This debate intensified among Puritan dissenters, founders of New English nationalism in America, in their denunciation of strong women as unnatural and the devil's minions. With a copy of Shakespeare's *Macbeth* and books on how to ferret out witches, Cotton Mather led his congregation in a dramatic exorcism to drive Catholic devilry from a bewitched girl, and proceeded to hang neighbors as witches in America's first, but not last, infamous witch-hunt. Back in the motherland, with the theatre and monarch restored, new versions of *Macbeth* played to a new generation of actors and audiences, supplying the less theocratic American colonies with their first professional actress in the role of Lady Macbeth (chapter 2).

John Adams found the image of Lady Macbeth horrifying, and his wife Abigail denounced the character as "detestable." But they both greatly admired Shakespeare's plays, and during their years in Paris and London they eagerly attended the theatres. Back in the States, they never lost their New English sense of superiority and intolerance of non-English immigrants, made manifest when John Adams became vice president and then the president in the 1790s. American theatres in Philadelphia and New York housed all classes and cultures, and became sites for audiences to play out their political differences in public. Major conflicts between Adams' Federalists and Jefferson's Democratic-Republicans went beyond their competing songs and badges, spilling into the newspapers and out into the streets. Pro-English Federalists applauded First Lady Abigail Adams' use of the theatre to propagandize support for her husband, and her mongering for war against the French and the expulsion from the country of immigrant "calumniators," especially the Irish. The Jeffersonians judged hers and her party's hammering for the Alien and Sedition legislation a "Season of Witches" (chapter 3).

Playing Lady Macbeth before revolutionaries on both sides of the Atlantic, and socializing with Ben Franklin in Paris, Irish-Catholic Charlotte Melmoth became an American citizen, an inspiring teacher in New York, and the definitive Lady Macbeth to a generation of Americans. With her lovely singing voice and eloquent speech, characteristic of enlightenment oratory and romanticist passion, Melmoth's Lady Macbeth drew Americans' attention to the artistry of the performance. She had more in common with First Lady Dolley Madison than with Abigail Adams. Up until now, little has been written about Charlotte Melmoth and her forty-year career on the stage, with no notice of her starring in Ireland for a dozen years before coming to the States. Because she developed her Lady Macbeth at a time of intense interest in the art of acting, when Diderot developed his theory about an inherent paradox in accomplished acting, and then as she became a teacher as well as performer, later mentoring younger actors in Shakespearean roles, Melmoth receives a longer treatment than the other, better known Lady Macbeths (chapter 4).

The Lady Macbeth of muscular, square-jawed, Boston-born Charlotte Cushman dominated the Civil War stage. A young protégé of Junius Booth earlier in the century, she later overpowered his sons Edwin and John Wilkes Booth on the stage, schooling John Wilkes in his first appearance in *Macbeth*. Cushman put her art on the line for the Union during the Civil War, playing Lady Macbeth to raise funds for the Sanitary Commission, a precursor of the Red Cross. President Abraham Lincoln and First Lady Mary Todd Lincoln attended one of those performances in Washington, D.C. (chapter 5). During their tenure in the White House, with the country divided and theatres in the North and the South frequently producing *Macbeth*, Lincoln identified his war-torn world, "steeped in blood" with *Macbeth*, his favorite Shakespeare play. And he affectionately called his wife his "partner in greatness" as Macbeth does Lady Macbeth. Not until his death, assassinated by an actor, did the public identify Lincoln as Duncan, and John Wilkes Booth as the Macbeth who assassinated him. Little sympathy was accorded to the grieving First Lady, and the circumstances surrounding her death inspired Lincoln's hagiographer, Carl Sandburg, to damn Mary Todd Lincoln with images that resonate with Lady Macbeth's sleepwalking scene (chapter 6).

Wives of World War I President Woodrow Wilson and World War II Franklin D. Roosevelt provoked controversy and condemnation for their assuming power as First Ladies: Mrs. Wilson when she acted as "Mrs. President" while her husband recovered from a stroke, and Eleanor Roosevelt for her liberal activism. Leading up to World War I, English actress Ellen Terry and French Sarah Bernhardt shaped divergent images of Lady Macbeth, suggestive of the character's exhortation to "Be the innocent flower" in outward show, Terry's loving-wife approach, but the "serpent within," Bernhardt's sensual dominatrix. Terry's docile, "dove-like" Lady Macbeth conformed to Victorian expectations of a political wife, while Bernhardt's "pretty monster" challenged them. Edith Wilson seemed to incorporate both the flower and the serpent in her behavior when she became First Lady and then took command of the White House and the presidency (chapter 7).

The "G.I. Lady Macbeth" of World War II, Australian-born Judith Anderson, prevailed as America's Lady Macbeth for much of the twentieth century, making a lasting impression on stage, film, television, sound and video recordings. Anderson's performance of Lady Macbeth, like her horror film, Medea and Clytemnestra roles, confirmed Brooks Atkinson's observation, that, "She is at home with the Furies. By instinct and temperament, she acts on their plane."[1] Her World War II director of *Macbeth*, Margaret Webster, observed that Anderson's acting caught the sensational aspects of Lady Macbeth that fed into the zeitgeist of the 1950s witch-hunt era, but failed to plumb the depths of the character, as she, Webster, is reported to have done when she played the part herself. Webster, an outspoken proponent for liberal causes, resembled First Lady Eleanor Roosevelt. But while the acting career of the apolitical Dame Judith Anderson continued on the upswing, and the widow Mrs. Roosevelt became ambassador to the United Nations, Webster's career as the leading female director of Shakespeare's plays in America suffered collapse under the witch-hunts of McCarthyism. The definitive moment of her hearing occurred at the same time as the electrocution of "monster wife" Ethel Rosenberg. Even Arthur Miller, in *The Crucible* and his autobiography, blamed the ills of the times on the wives, his as well (chapter 8).

How Shakespeare's creation of Lady Macbeth arrived on the American stage and became an American bogey I investigate through theatre history, political history insofar as *Macbeth* invites debate about a wife's role in her husband's ambition for power. Arguments as to the psychological, sociopolitical and religious constructs of Shakespeare's Lady Macbeth that scholars continue to clarify, I wish to supplement with interpretations of the principal actresses who have performed Lady Macbeth in America during times of war when presidents' wives have come under attack. Phyllis Rackin gives an especially comprehensive and concise account of changes in feminist interpretations of Lady Macbeth in her book *Shakespeare and*

Women. She recommends Janet Adelman's *Suffocating Mothers* as an "excellent feminist psychoanalytic study of *Macbeth*," however, without considering Lorraine Helms' essay, "Acts of Resistance," that posits Adelman's "reading" of Lady Macbeth, "theatrically inert," in which "femininity comes to seem almost universally demonic." Helms observes that feminist revaluations of Lady Macbeth "have shown less hostility" to the character than Adelman, and for an example, gives Sinead Cusack's performance of Lady Macbeth (Royal Shakespeare Company 1986), that caught the character in a "domestic" struggle, the "destruction of a marriage."[2] Catherine Belsey discounts psychological unity in the character, for in the language of Lady Macbeth's first scene, when she calls to "spirits that tend on mortal thoughts" to unsex her, Belsey identifies the "spirits" as the grammatical subject of the speech, setting up a "discontinuity." "The speech concludes with the opposition between heaven and hell, reproducing the morality pattern of the human being as a battleground between cosmic forces, autonomous only to the point of choosing between them."[3] This interpretation of Lady Macbeth as an allegorical site for opposing forces, fighting for good or evil, aligns with Racken's point that, "Religion was a far more important issue than gender" to Shakespeare's audience.[4] Cristina León Alfar argues that the politics of gender and religion operate equally, if not inseparably, to the construction of the ideology that placed male power as rightful and powerful women as evil.[5] Alan Sinfield encourages his readers, "literary intellectuals," to interpret "across the grain of customary assumptions and, if necessary across the grain of the text, as it is customarily perceived," interpretations he calls "oppositional analyses."[6] As to whether *Macbeth* is about evil, "we might draw a more careful distinction: between the violence which the State considers legitimate and that which it does not."[7] Shakespeare's characterization of Lady Macbeth provokes just such distinctions about the legitimacy of a wife's role in fostering her husband's political ascent. Even the widely held view that Lady Macbeth's actions are motivated by overweaning ambition, Ellen Terry called into question with "oppositional analysis"—motivating the character by love alone.

Since Coleridge and the romanticists, literary historians and critics writing about Shakespeare's Lady Macbeth have decried stage performances as inferior to their private ruminations inspired by reading the script as literature. In his book, *The Shakespeare Revolution*, J.L. Styan observes that as late as 1900 "readers turned to the scholar to elucidate the plays," but that by 1970 "scholarship seems suspect and the stage seems to be more in touch with [the plays'] spirit"; in the twentieth century "the initiative in recovering Shakespeare shifted to the theatre." Styan's ground-breaking book, which begins by surveying Victorian performances of Shakespeare and ends with Peter Brook's productions, tracks how the revival in England of Elizabethan and Jacobean non-illusionist, presentational staging freed the plays from psychological realism and the expectation of a message or moral to the story. The gist of Styan's book, he explains, "has been to suggest that to stop short at the text is now a kind of surrender, for the text will not tell us much until it speaks in its own medium....Actor and scholar will teach each other, not what Shakespeare 'means,' but what his possibilities are beyond logic."[8] Now, over thirty years later, Shakespeare scholarship, while still dependent on reading and interpreting the text's language, has made strides in studying the play's action in performance. Other scholars writing the cultural history of Shakespeare and the import of his plays in his own time, such as Stephen Greenblatt, James Shapiro, and Stephen Orgel, have vastly extended the boundaries of Shakespeare studies. Indebted to them for their insights and inspiration, I have undertaken to search with a narrower lens focused on one of Shakespeare's characters, specifically to see how his Lady Macbeth crossed the Atlantic to America, to enthrall American audiences and reflect their fears of a political wife—how Lady Macbeth has haunted America and continues to do so.

1. Lady Macbeth in the White House ✒

MacBird, the 1966 antiwar play, portrays Lyndon Johnson and Lady Bird Johnson as Macbeth and Lady Macbeth. Begun in Berkeley, California, as a protest to the Vietnam War, Barbara Garson's trenchant satire went on to become a full-length play running for 386 performances at the Village Gate in New York before touring the country. The play daringly shows how from one administration to the next, presidents make the same blunders and repeat the same excuses in launching wars. Garson's characters parallel those in *Macbeth*. She gives them speeches that parody Shakespeare's iambic pentameter blank verses by filling them with the clichéd rhetoric employed by commanders in chief promoting war. The mixture of lexicons produces a comic disjuncture and strips the heavy-handed chauvinism of any eloquence, as, for example, in this speech delivered by John Ken O'Dunc (Kennedy as Shakespeare's Duncan):

> Let every nation know, both weak and mighty
> That we'll pay any price, bear any burden,
> Meet any hardship, challenge any foe
> To strengthen, to secure and spread our system.[1]

Ken O'Dunc qualifies how America will use its force: "We shall not force small nations to their knees," but "only force them to be free."[2] This last line chillingly reverberates down the four decades that separate America's invasion of Vietnam from the one into Iraq.

The year *MacBird* played in New York City, Lady Bird Johnson received the George Foster Peabody Award for the television program "A Visit to Washington with Mrs. Lyndon B. Johnson on Behalf of a More Beautiful America," one of many awards she received for her work in promoting beautification of the country. Garson places Lady Bird and her preoccupation with flowers in a scene suggestive of Lady Macbeth's sleepwalking scene with its "out, out damned spot, out!" But instead of the scent of a murdered king's blood on her hands, she smells the odor of her foul husband, the president. The stage direction reads: "*Enter LADY MACBIRD followed by her two daughters. LADY MACBIRD is carrying a giant bouquet of flowers. She is distraught. The daughters carry aerosol cans. LADY MACBIRD sniffs around the room, gasping at a foul odor.*"[3] Stopping at the side of her husband, MacBird, the First Lady says, "Here's the smell. Out, out damned odor, out!" And the daughters press their air fresheners. Lady MacBird continues wandering around the room, "Flowers by the roadside... plant these flowers... Let all the land be lined with living blooms," more like Ophelia than Lady Macbeth in this her last of two scenes in Garson's play. She has to be escorted out of the Oval Office and is seen no more.

Garson gives Lady MacBird only two scenes, as the play aims more specifically on the warmongering and bumbling presidents. In contrast to the last, the first of Lady MacBird's scenes shows her in full command. Here, parallel to Lady Macbeth's first scene in Shakespeare's play, Lady MacBird reads her husband's account of how the witches have prophesied he will become president. Lyndon Johnson's colloquialisms and voice echo through the lines.

(*A room on the MacBird ranch. LADY MACBIRD is seated at her desk and reading aloud from a letter.*)

LADY MACBIRD: ...and these weird critters had no sooner slithered out when in strides Bobby, the punky younger brother, trumpeting out their very words. 'Hail MacBird, Vice-president thou art.' I don't know what the devil they are but I reckon it's something mighty deep. So now it's two down and one to go. I'll be home straight from here and we can puzzle out these strange happenings together. I just wanted you to know right away, my dearest little pardner, what we have and what's been promised. Be seeing you real soon, *your loving Bird.*[4]

While the comedy of this scene prevails for 1966, its reference to Bobby Kennedy horrifies in light of his assassination in 1968. After reading aloud the letter, Lady MacBird does none of the conjuring given to Lady Macbeth by Shakespeare but in a matter-of-fact manner immediately sets about making plans and arrangements for her husband's rise to the presidency. She complains that she has had to do all the work and gets none of the credit, "How often in the past have I arranged to have the right connections come your way, myself performing all the devious acts so you receive the bounty graciously." Even so, and however begrudgingly, she puts into effect the plan to have President Ken O'Dunc come to Texas. She will organize a big procession in his honor, one that will not only attract his "faithful followers," but also *"Expose* [Garson's emphasis] him to the fury of his foes." Then, ominously, she uses Lady Macbeth's exact words: "He that's coming must be provided for, and you shall put the day's great business into my dispatch which shall to all our days and nights to come give solely sovereign sway and masterdom."[5] The illustrator for the play's publication, Lisa Lyons, has made amusing cartoons of Lady MacBird, showing the character's different attitudes in the two scenes in which she appears. In the first one, as organizer and perpetrator, Lady MacBird has a firm hold over her rather hapless-looking husband. In the second, she appears mad as a hatter, with LBJ now clearly in control.

Shakespeare's archetypal war play about leaders who wage war and commit assassinations to augment their own power and position provided Garson with the ammunition to warn how the country was in danger of being led into an ever more deadly war, first by Jack Kennedy and then by Lyndon Johnson. Neither the first nor the last to pillage and parody Shakespeare's play to satirize contemporary politics, Garson's play surpasses most others in both length and quality. Trying to imitate it, a silly and ugly little piece called "MacDeth" appeared in the extreme right-wing journal *American Spectator* as part of that magazine's efforts to vilify President Bill Clinton and First Lady Hillary Rodham Clinton, one of its many attempts at character assassination during the Clinton administrations. The author wants "MacDeth" to wage a culture war on the side of the arch conservatives. This short skit that appeared in the August 1994 issue, two years into the first Clinton administration, burlesques Bill Clinton in the role of "MacDeth" and Hillary as a Lady Macbeth character named simply "Hillary." As the boss in the White House who uses up and spits out powerful men, "Hillary" parodies Lady Macbeth's first appearance in Shakespeare's play, reading her husband's letter and conjuring dark forces to assist them: *"Mister* President! First Lady, I?/Say rather Empress, partnered with a drone. / ...O come, /Ye Wellesley-spawned Eumenides of spite, / Unsex me here!" The title "Empress" in the second line will be seen to recall how right-wing opponents of Franklin D. Roosevelt characterized his wife, Eleanor Roosevelt, Hillary's role model. The three Weird Sisters of *Macbeth* are characterized in "MacDeth" as "but antecedents of the pronoun s/he-three Deans of Gender Studies." Unworthy of stage performance, humorless and mean spirited, the doggerel dies on the page. While it does not achieve effective dramatic satire, "MacDeth" did contribute to the persistent hammering at Hillary Clinton as a Lady Macbeth. Whatever nuance and eloquence exists in Shakespeare's character, however much depth and complexity actresses have brought to performances of Lady Macbeth, the iconic figure manhandled by hacks devolved into crude comic-book clap-trap. These efforts did not achieve their goal of preventing the Clintons from winning the presidency, but they did add weight to the pressures on Hillary to change her name to her husband's, quit her high-paying job, and bake more cookies. The opposition may not have kept her from achieving the status of First Lady or New York senator, but it kept her influence over President Clinton and his policies under vigilant and hostile scrutiny. The comparison with Lady Macbeth, so persistently repeated, stuck.

In the summer of 1992, in the final months of Bill and Hillary's cam-paigning for the presidency, an article appeared in *American Spectator* that more persuasively superimposed an idea or image of Lady Macbeth onto Hillary Clinton. The strategy harkens back to the kind of dirty tricks that worked for Richard Nixon when he ran against Helen Gahagan Douglas for Congress: link the opponent's name with someone or something odi-ous to Americans and repeat it until it rings true and sounds like fact to the voters. "Pinko" and "Commy" worked to bring down Nixon's opponent. "Lady Macbeth" could work to defeat Hillary and her husband. Simple: make up or exaggerate parallels between Hillary and Macbeth's smart but evil wife, keep repeating the epithet, and get Hillary on the defensive. The advertising of Hillary as a Lady Macbeth, intending to spur voters' fear of an intelligent and ambitious wife of a political enemy, got underway with the *American Spectator*'s long article entitled "The Lady Macbeth of Little Rock."[6] Before getting down to the business of making comparisons with Lady Macbeth, the author investigates Hillary's past. He even examines her undergraduate papers, written while she was a student at Wellesley College, in order to map out characteristics and accomplishments sure to make the magazine's conservative readers bristle. He portrays Hillary as overeducated and implies that she is a lesbian and that she has formed a partnership with Bill that is "non traditional," an "open" marriage of convenience. These attacks on the First Lady's personal life would con-tinue throughout the 1990s, exacerbated by the president's dalliance, lie, and subsequent impeachment proceedings. Dislike for Hillary as a profes-sional woman, an accomplished lawyer, expressed in the article, stems in part from her having served on the independent counsel that investigated Richard Nixon's wrongdoings in the Watergate scandal, an investigation that continues to grate with Nixon's defenders. By dint of his description of Hillary's involvement, the author of "Lady Macbeth of Little Rock" clearly intends that his readers hold Hillary partly responsible for the humiliation of Nixon and the Republican Party. He does not mention Hillary Rodham's astute legal maneuvers and nationwide lobbying that thwarted the Reagan administration's efforts to dismantle the Legal Services Corporation.[7] The references to Hillary Clinton as a Lady Macbeth rely heavily on innuendo and implication, rather than fact. "Lady Macbeth of Little Rock" involves its readers in making the comparison, as if reporting their thoughts, rather than admitting it is trying to shape them. *"The image of Mrs. Clinton that has crystallized in the public consciousness, is, of course that of Lady Macbeth"* [my emphasis]. But claiming this to be so does not make it so, not without some tricky prose and much repetition. "The image of Mrs. Clinton that has crystallized in the public consciousness is, of course, that of Lady Macbeth: consuming ambition, inflexibility of purpose, domination of a pliable husband, and an unsettling lack of tender human feeling, along with the affluent feminist's contempt for traditional female roles."[8] Four of these descriptive phrases relate to Shakespeare's characterization of Lady Macbeth in some fashion or another. The fifth phrase, "the affluent feminist's contempt for traditional female roles," is wholly of our times rather than Shakespeare's, reflecting the sensibilities of the editorial staff of the *American Spectator* and its readers, mostly male, affluent, sexist, and to the far right politically. The word "feminist" would effectively raise a red flag on its own, but a *rich* feminist who can thumb her nose at "traditional female roles" conjures up a woman hard to control, defiant of the male-dominated world and a threat to its power.

The other four phrases, which do connect in some way to Lady Macbeth's lines in Shakespeare's play, attribute to Hillary Clinton the author's impression of Lady Macbeth as an overly ambitious, inflexible, domineering woman who lacks tenderness. These phrases point to two especially riveting images created in Lady Macbeth's dialogue from her earlier scenes in the play, *Macbeth*. Offstage, at the end of the first act, Macbeth has left his dinner table where the king and other guests are dining. He comes onstage and reconsiders, alone, his resolve to murder Duncan. Lady Macbeth hurries in after him, worried that his absence will be noted by the king. He tells her he has changed his mind, they will proceed no further in the business of assassinating the king. She won't stand for it. Demonstrating her powers of persuasion, she first equates his waffling with a lack of love for her, and then attributes it to cowardice and squeamishness, which has the desired effect of making Macbeth angry: "I dare do all that may become a man." Good. She uses the anger to change tactics and tells him that if he were a man then he would dare to do it and that he will be even more of a man upon doing it—a rhetorical persuasion that has no basis in fact, as the course of the play will show. But it sounds good in the moment. And more to the point, it goads him on. Finally, and here it is, Lady Macbeth calls forth an image of such brutality that like a sting ray it transfixes her husband:

> I have given suck, and know
> How tender 'tis to love the babe that milks me;
> I would, while it was smiling in my face
> Have pluck'd my nipple from his boneless gums,
> And dasht the brains out, had I so sworn
> As you have done to this. (I, vii, 63–68)

She invokes an inversion of her nature, from maternity to violent infanticide—a boast to spur him on. Stunned and transfixed, Macbeth can only utter: "If we should fail?" She has him. Now quickly and businesslike, Lady Macbeth sets out the plan, step by step, for the next thirteen lines. They can't possibly fail. Finding his footing and impressed by her strategy, Macbeth exclaims, "Bring forth male children only/ For thy undaunted mettle should compose/Nothing but males." Macbeth stands in awe of Lady Macbeth's masculine mind. The writer for the *American Spectator* is "unsettled" and chooses to ignore Lady Macbeth's tactics and take at face value her infanticide image as a demonstration of her lack of tender human feelings.

Another image from the play, two scenes later, provides "Lady Macbeth of Little Rock" with more fuel. Moments after he has murdered the king, Macbeth returns to the stage unhinged in body and spirit. Seeing this, Lady Macbeth knows she must take action herself. Macbeth stares off distractedly talking about sleep and how voices told him he has murdered sleep, how he will sleep no more. Lady Macbeth scolds him, he mustn't unbend himself "by thinking so brainsickly on things." Like a mother, she orders him to go "wash the filthy witness from his hand," only to discover that in his distraction he has carried the daggers back with him. They must stay in Duncan's room. She commands him to take them back. Oh, no, he'll not look upon that again. He dares not. So Lady Macbeth grabs the daggers from his hands with these words and utters the key phrase:

> Infirm of purpose:
> Give me the daggers: the sleeping, and the dead,
> Are but as pictures: 'tis the eye of childhood,
> That fears a painted devil. (II, ii, 66–69)

With a summary slight of hand, the author of "Lady Macbeth of Little Rock" transposes Lady Macbeth's line *"infirm* of purpose" to Hillary's "*inflexibility* of purpose." With syllogistic logic he reasons that if Macbeth is "infirm of purpose," then it follows that Lady Macbeth must be "inflexible of purpose" and so then must Hillary be too. But back in the world of the play, which interests the author only for what he can use against Hillary (like quoting scripture), Lady Macbeth needs to quell her own fears as well as her husband's, especially as she puts the bloody daggers in her hands and proceeds to the dead king's chamber. With, "the sleeping, and the dead/ Are but as Pictures: 'tis the Eye of Childhood/ That fears a painted Devil" and blanching like a child, she must be the mother to herself as well as to her husband to brace herself for what will be a horrible sight of the still bleeding cadaver. She overcompensates with bravura and goes off to return the daggers, bathe her hands in Duncan's blood, and then smear his grooms so that it will look like they have done the murder. The weaker the husband the stronger the wife must be, but at what cost to her psychic health. The image of dashing out the brains of her nursing child that Lady Macbeth fabricates to get what she wants, and the image of her bathing her hands in the blood of the dead king, which she does by default, both are part of Shakespeare's rhetoric of persuasion. But for the author of "Lady Macbeth of Little Rock," they become appeals to his readers' worst fears of a kind of monster mom and wife who might take over the White House. The polemic intends to crystallize in the public consciousness only Lady Macbeth's bravura performance, not her struggle or suffering. But however incomplete and misguiding "Lady Macbeth of Little Rock" may be, the taunts do affirm that the appellation of Lady Macbeth can evoke images of prowess that serve propagandists to make readers wary of a strong, smart wife close to the seat of power.

The large amounts of money and energy devoted to vilifying Hillary Rodham Clinton and her husband led to a chain of publicity stunts that gave the name-calling significant public exposure. Right after the article appeared in print, its author, Daniel Wattenberg, appeared on television to discuss Hillary as a Lady Macbeth with his host, Ted Koppel, thus reaching a much wider audience than the magazine could initially. But by buying subscriptions of the magazine for public libraries, a device similar to how right-wing propagandists produce and then buy up their books in bulk to make them best sellers, the article gained wider recognition. The wealthy influence peddler supporting the magazine, Richard Mellon Scaife, an Alcoa, Gulf Oil, and Mellon Bank heir, and vice chairman of the board for the Heritage Foundation in 1992, helped to finance the library subscriptions and other ploys. He gave hundreds of millions of dollars to the Heritage Foundation, the Hoover Institution, the Cato Institute, and the Federalist Society, and to publications including *American Spectator* and *Human Events*. His several "educational" funds—the Allegheny, Carthage, Scaife Family, and Sarah Scaife Foundations—funneled the money. His millions made it possible for the *American Spectator* to hire writers and "witnesses" to damn the Clintons. But in 1998 when the magazine and its editor, Emmett Tyrell, came under close scrutiny for misallocation of funds and tax violations, Scaife gave up on the *Spectator* and withdrew his support. Later, ironically, Scaife backed Hillary Clinton's bid for the presidency in 2008.

Around the same time Scaife stopped financing the *American Spectator*, one of the magazine's hired guns, David Brock, revealed that he had fabricated the articles he wrote alleging that Governor Clinton used his state troopers to solicit sex. Brock apologized to President Clinton and made a public retraction in *Esquire*. But his initial stories inspired a columnist of the *Washington Times*, a neoconservative newspaper, to write that the president must be allowed his Gennifer Flowers and Paula Jones because "the devil in Miss Hillary made him do that," thus accusing Hillary of being sexually unforthcoming to her husband and holding her responsible for driving her husband to other women for satisfaction. To exorcise the devil in the First Lady, the Republicans came up with a voodoo doll. A rag doll representing Hillary Rodham Clinton was on sale at the Republican convention during Bill Clinton's 1996 presidential campaign for reelection. Garry Wills observed first hand that "Hillary Hate is a large-scale psychic phenomenon." He saw there a "dismemberment doll" for sale: "For twenty dollars you could buy a rag-doll Hillary with arms and legs made to tear off and throw on the floor." Demonstrating by tearing off the arms and legs, the seller "with furious rending" then pulled off the head, telling Wills, "you can dash it down, or eat it, or burn it, or whatever."[9] The "entrepreneur" may have been laughing as he tore the doll apart, toying rather than actually harming anyone, but it contributed to an ongoing campaign to make Hillary a bewitched Lady Macbeth.

Half way through Clinton's second term of office, in January of 1998, Hillary in "battle mode" faced the television cameras—her husband, his presidency, and their partnership were under attack. He had just given a public denial of any sexual relations with his White House intern. His wife covered for him by reiterating the strength of their conjugal relationship. She used the word "husband" twenty-two times and twice stated that she and Bill had been married twenty-two years. Perhaps, like the Queen in *Hamlet*, she protested too much. To many who knew the First Lady, and to many observers who didn't, it appeared that Hillary actually believed her husband, making her onscreen defense sincere. Hillary projected an image of confidence in her husband, in their marriage, and in his ability to govern—an image that favorably impressed many. But the First Lady's television defense of her husband raised again the Lady Macbeth bogey. A self-styled theatre critic, Charles Spencer, writing about the First Lady's "performance" in Britain's *Daily Telegraph*, a paper well connected with the *American Spectator*, relates how he experienced "a chilling hint of the Lady Macbeths [*sic*] about the American First Lady." Haunted by her "immaculate" dress and bearing, he found "something faintly spooky about the whole performance." He concludes that her motive is power "rather than unconditional love" (January 28, 1998). A day later, reporting in the *Scotsman*, Annette Witheridge calls Hillary Clinton's "performance" "more like a president than the president himself" and harkens back to the 1992 article that promoted Hillary as a Lady Macbeth: "Once cruelly nicknamed the Lady Macbeth of Little Rock, Hillary comes into her own in a crisis." But Witheridge does not negate the comparison. She actually reinforces it by adding "a power-crazed Valkyrie" to the epithets. Hillary is a warrior woman, engaged in war; she "rallies the troops" and "takes up the battle cry for her husband." But "she sends out conflicting messages," deliberately so, Witheridge adds. In one moment she can be performing the "little woman" and in the next "a power-crazed Valkyrie who will put up with everything to keep the White House crown…Never before has a woman been the power behind the throne so much as Hillary Rodham Clinton." Witheridge's concluding paragraphs compare Hillary Clinton to Hillary's proclaimed role model, Eleanor Roosevelt: "She knows that the latter also suffered a lackluster marriage and that work for both of them became a substitute for love."

Months after this television appearance, with the outing of the intern affair and trumped up accusations of financial misdeeds in Whitewater real estate transactions, politicians and journalists joined in a "feeding frenzy" of scandal mongering. Hillary Clinton received pity and compassion from those who believed her to have been truly deceived by her husband's lie. But not from the Hillary-Haters who continued to publish more cartoons and caricatures of her as a devilish Lady Macbeth. Even mainstream *Time* magazine (March 18, 1996) did a cover of Hillary Clinton that editors privately confided was deliberately doctored "to look like a Lady Macbeth." The picture shows Hillary baring her teeth and her eyes looking to the side rather than directly at the camera. Against a black background, and showing her wearing black, so that Hillary's head looks as if it is emerging from the darkness, the editors have made her face whiter, her lipstick redder, and her eyebrows darker. Half her face is in shadows, the other half glaringly overexposed with light. The image, a kind of cultural memory, corresponds with the "vampira" Lady Macbeth created by actress Judith Anderson that predominated in twentieth-century perceptions of a Lady Macbeth on the stage, television, and film.

In the final weeks of Hillary's own campaign for senator from New York, journalists trumpeted out the now old and established comparison of the First Lady with Lady Macbeth. A Conservative MP remonstrated against the British prime minister's wife that she should beware the "Hillary syndrome...an unaccountable cross between first lady and Lady Macbeth" (*New York Times* September 7, 2000). And a week later, in a report on the debate between the rival candidates for the New York Senate, the *Times* again brought up the bogey, "Mrs. Clinton who had to show she wasn't Lady Macbeth stuck to substance" (September 15, 2000). The article "Lady Macbeth Comes to N.Y.," which appeared in the July 21, 1999 *New York Post*, makes a longer attack on Hillary reminiscent of "Lady Macbeth of Little Rock," and is written with the same aim of keeping Mrs. Clinton from political power. It claims that "Hillary Clinton can no more leave the White House with clean hands than Lady Macbeth could leave Dunsinane Castle innocent of her husband's crimes.... She wants to step virgin-clean from the years of corruption and abuse of power which she and her husband have shared in Little Rock and Washington." While the corruption and crimes go unspecified and unsubstantiated, the references to Shakespeare's play are more specific. The "clean hands" recalls Lady Macbeth trying to wash blood from her hands in the famous Act V sleepwalking scene. And Dunsinane Castle is indeed the location for the last act of the play. But Shakespeare's Lady Macbeth does not leave Dunsinane Castle, in the play she dies there, to the wailing of women and the profound grief of her husband: "She should have died hereafter,/ there would have been a time for such a word,/ To-morrow and to-morrow and to-morrow..." A destiny for First Lady Hillary in the White House comparable to Lady Macbeth's in Dunsinane Castle might have been the journalist's darkest desire. With or without contradictions, he had hoped his murky metaphors and his patched up parallels between Hillary and Lady Macbeth would agitate New York voters not to vote for the outgoing First Lady. But despite such efforts, Hillary Clinton came out of the White House alive and well and won the Senate seat. She exited the White House with no blood on her hands, only mud at her feet from the mudslingers, and maybe a little egg on her face from being overcredulous and overzealous in defending her husband. Becoming a political leader herself, rather than the wife of one, should have made any comparison to Lady Macbeth moot—but it didn't. During Hillary's run for the presidency in the 2008 primaries, she received advice on reading material from writers John Irving and Lorrie Moore. Irving cautioned that were Hillary to read or see the play *Macbeth*, self-comparisons with Lady Macbeth could prove too close for comfort: "Clinton might find 'Macbeth' a challenge—namely, to somehow read or see the play and not take the character of Lady Macbeth personally." Moore recommends that Hillary read the play as a warning: "The timeless tale of how untethered ambition and early predictions may carry a large price tag."[10]

Why Lady Macbeth? How did a historical eleventh-century Scottish queen arrive as a character in Shakespeare's "timeless tale of untethered ambition" to become an American bogey applied to presidents' wives?

2. From Shakespeare's Stage to America's ❧

Like a series of engravings in a morality tale, Lady Macbeth's nine of *Macbeth*'s twenty-five scenes depict the stations of her passion's progress. Faced with a choice between heaven and hell, Lady Macbeth makes a Faustian bargain with dark forces and chooses hell. Shakespeare has constructed the character's actions in such a way, and indicated in the dialogue such stage properties to be used by the actor playing Lady Macbeth, that she performs her own excommunication and damnation—with bell, book, and candle. In Catholic excommunication, the priest expels one accused of witchcraft, by pronouncing her excluded from the Church, judging her "condemned to eternal fire with Satan...so long as she will not burst the fetters of the demon, do penance and satisfy the Church." He closes the book, rings a bell as a symbol of death, and extinguishes a candle, throwing it down as if casting the reprobate down to hell. Shakespeare's Lady Macbeth acts as her own priest, propelling herself away from the protection of a human community and banishing herself to murky hell. She reads (from a letter), she rings a bell (alerting her husband that all is ready for the murder of the king), and extinguishes her candle (when she kills herself), condemning herself to "murky hell." Macbeth echoes, "She should have died hereafter....Out, out brief candle."

Excommunication is not the same as exorcism, in the same way that the practitioner of witchcraft is not the same as a victim possessed. But the ceremonies of excommunication and exorcism resemble one another as practiced by both Catholic priests and Puritan ministers in the seventeenth century to purge their communities of the devil and his minions. Stephen Greenblatt examines Shakespeare's characters that fake an exorcism, for example, in *Twelfth Night* and *King Lear*. In considering only imposter characters in support of his statement that theatre performance destroys the sacred, Greenblatt denies theatre's potential to investigate both sacred and secular ritual. But Lady Macbeth's self-induced excommunication and invitation to be possessed by dark forces she performs in all seriousness, not as an imposter. Shakespeare opens up an examination of the sacred by inverting it, not destroying it.[1]

Lady Macbeth first appears on the stage alone, in her room, reading. The audience pays more attention to what she is reading than the fact that she *is* reading. While Shakespeare's public audience for *Macbeth*'s premier at the Globe in 1606 generally had a high degree of complexity in oral language (evidenced by Shakespeare's wordplay addressed to the ear), the majority could not read. This scene of Lady Macbeth reading her husband's letter, and later in the play when her gentlewoman describes how she sits at her desk, takes out paper, and writes (a naked Lady Macbeth performs this vignette in Polanski's film), show that Macbeth's wife is literate and educated. The stage picture works on certain half-buried concerns about a smart, educated, solitary woman left alone to her own devices. The audience looks in on Lady Macbeth with mounting misgivings about what she is doing in there. It cannot be good. The script calls for Lady Macbeth to play upon such suspicions, increasing and intensifying them as she performs a masturbatory incantation, seizing her breasts and invoking murderous angels of dark night to come to them and unsex her, to turn her milk to gall, to fill her with "direst cruelty," to squelch all conscience and mercy in herself and her husband, to assure success as they plot to assassinate the king and seize the throne.

In their first scene together, before any crime has been committed, in untrammeled exuberance as "partners in greatness," their passion for power hangs in the balance with their amorous passion for each other. The passions cannot coexist for long, and following the murder of Duncan, Macbeth leaves his wife alone. She's given nothing to say at their coronation. She begs him to come to bed throughout the play, even with her last words, "To bed, to bed," spoken to the empty air as she wanders through the darkness lit only by her candle, hallucinating the night's dark deed that has brought her to this hell. Her husband's final soliloquy serves as her funeral oration. On being told that the queen is dead, Macbeth responds, "She should have died hereafter, there would have been a time for such a word. Tomorrow." Actors and directors debate the intent and emotion with which Macbeth responds to the news of his wife's death. Is he struck with sorrow and grief for the death of his wife that he had called his "partner in greatness" and "dearest chuck"? Or is he angrily dismissing her death, no longer capable of caring for her or anyone else? Or, moment by moment, do his emotions and thoughts war within him as he delivers the famous monologue? How the actor performs the speech determines the answer. Just as whether the audience takes Malcolm's line, the last reference in the play to Lady Macbeth, when he calls her a "fiend-like queen," to be Shakespeare's judgment of the character or Malcolm's alone. That, too, depends on how the actors play Malcolm and Lady Macbeth.[2]

The same season of plays at the Globe Theatre in 1606 in which *Macbeth* premiered, also included Shakespeare's *Antony and Cleopatra*. And if Garry Wills is correct, the beautiful young actor, John Rice, played both Lady Macbeth and Cleopatra. (This "boy actor" who played women's roles well into mid-life, later became a clergyman.)[3] The future performers of Lady Macbeth, women mostly, seem to divide up between those who play both Lady Macbeth and Cleopatra, and those who play both Lady Macbeth and Medea. Seeing Rice play both roles in the same season, the audience could connect Lady Macbeth with Cleopatra as having similar characteristics— both characters are powerful women having strong influence over their mates, but whose circumstances and choices create contrasting scenarios. It is as if Shakespeare has set up the two plays to test what happens when like characters choose opposite actions, the one sacrifices love for power, the other sacrifices power for love. In suggesting that Shakespeare consciously composed *Macbeth* and *Antony and Cleopatra* as a pair of plays, I offer as evidence a comparison of scenes from the two plays, when Macbeth and Antony arm for their final battles. Macbeth, isolated and alone in his castle, calls for his armor with only his servant Seyton (pronounced *Satan*) to do his bidding. But when Seyton tries to put it on him, Macbeth pushes him away, throwing the armor back and commanding Seyton to carry it off after him. Macbeth has no love, as he says, just mouth honor. His thanes desert him. His partner, Lady Macbeth, dies alone in her bed, offstage. Contrast this with Antony's arming scene. The audience sees the couple in bed together, in the rising light of dawn. Cleopatra begs her lover to sleep a little longer, like Juliet to her Romeo. Cheerfully, Antony rises and calls to his servant *Eros* to come bring him his armor, and when he does, indulges Cleopatra who insists upon helping Eros put the armor on him. He tells her that she is the true armor (amour) of his heart, this other, material stuff, false. Antony's soldiers enter with hearty greeting and mutual good cheer, eager to follow their general into battle. They have all come earlier than Antony had commanded, out of love. "To business that we love we rise betime/And go to't with delight." Love, playfulness, good cheer, companionship and respect—all this directly contrasts with the Macbeths' dark and loveless isolation. In the end they all die, these are tragedies. But Macbeth and Lady Macbeth die apart from one another, with no one to mourn them. Cleopatra ascends her bright monument where the dying Antony is lifted up to his lover for a last kiss. Cleopatra follows him in death delivering to the audience an apotheosis rich with love poetry evocative of the "Song of Songs." Traditionally, critics have held Cleopatra's sensuality and Lady Macbeth's powers of persuasion responsible for the downfall of their men.[4] The tradition continues. "The threat posed by daunting, emasculating women in [Shakespeare's] great tragedies is thus symptomatic of a larger disorder. Order is restored to Scotland in *Macbeth* only when the threatening maternal presence embodied in Lady Macbeth and the Weird Sisters is expunged."[5] Debate over traditional interpretations continues as well, not only as to whether Shakespeare intended one interpretation over another, but also as to whether speculation regarding a playwright's intentions has merit. The play in performance provides arbitration.

Many of Shakespeare's plays study leaders' succession to power. *Macbeth* dramatizes a contest between rival monarchs and rival cultures somewhat parallel to what the playwright was witnessing in his own lifetime. Set in the eleventh century when the Celtic Queen Gruoch Macbeth and her second husband ruled over Scotland (1040–1057), the play capitalizes on that moment in history at the end of the Macbeths' reign when English forces joined with an exiled Scottish prince to invade Scotland and seize the throne by killing the king and chasing away the queen. Gruoch apparently had no children by Macbeth. For when a few of Malcolm's henchmen ambushed and beheaded Macbeth near a well at Lumphanan, his stepson, Gruoch's son by an earlier marriage, succeeded him to the Scottish throne. Briefly. Months later Lulach met the same fate near Essie and the Water of the Bogie. Surviving her husband and son, Gruoch retreated farther north into the Grampian Mountains, where two rivers from Glens Rinnes and Fiddich join and flow into the River Spey. The Scots buried the Macbeths on the sacred Island of Iona, the last of a long line of Celtic rulers to be interred there. Queen Margaret, an Anglo-Saxon princess, replaced Gruoch Macbeth, and Scottish royalty shifted from matrilineal to patrilineal succession. Malcolm and Margaret moved the royal seat to Edinburgh, closer to England. Together with Turgot, the priest on assignment from the Pope who served Margaret as secretary and confessor,[6] they abolished the local Culdee Christian practices (such as allowing priests to marry), in favor of official edicts from Rome. Margaret was educated, and Turgot witnessed how the illiterate Malcolm would sit at his wife's knee to hear her read aloud to him.[7] Such changes in the succession of Scottish royalty from a Celtic warrior Queen to a domestic Anglo-Saxon one, from Culdee Christianity to Roman Catholicism, from Gaelic to English, changes brought about by wars and murders, reflect the struggle in Shakespeare's own lifetime between Catholic

Mary, Queen of Scotland, and Protestant Elizabeth, Queen of England. Born when the two young queens had begun their reigns, Shakespeare as a young man launched his theatre career in London about the time Elizabeth had Mary beheaded. Sixteen years later, with Shakespeare in his prime as a playwright, his theatre company became the King's Men under the newly crowned King James I of England, Protestant James the Sixth of Scotland—and son of Catholic Mary Queen of Scots. On her deathbed, the old, unmarried, and childless English Queen named James her successor—Mary's son by her second husband, Elizabeth's cousin. When James was yet an infant and his mother still reigning Queen of Scotland, the man who became Mary's third husband orchestrated the murder of her second, James's father. Mary's third marriage lasted only weeks before the Scottish lords pursued the royal couple, suspecting them of having orchestrated the assassination. Mary escaped and sought sanctuary in England, where her cousin, Queen Elizabeth, put her under house arrest and confined her for many years. In 1587 the Protestant Queen, under pressure from her advisors who feared Catholic designs on the crown, finally consented to have the Catholic Queen executed.

These circumstances complicate the widely held view that Shakespeare wrote *Macbeth* in large part to flatter King James, by creating a heroic portrayal of Banquo, the king's mythic ancestor, and by showing a long line of Stuart royal progeny conjured by the witches in the cauldron scene.[8] For while King James never knew his mother, it is unlikely that he would have sat comfortably watching how in some ways the Macbeths' actions in the play resemble those of his mother and her third husband, implicated in the killing of James' father.[9] Mary gave him birth. But Elizabeth gave him the throne. How would the king sort out, much less resolve, such conflicting loyalties and emotions? Such a dilemma may account for the mixed reception of *Macbeth* in James' court. The religious strife that had existed between the Catholic and Protestant queens and their followers continued to plague James' realm, at one point almost destroying the King and his entire government. Shakespeare alludes to that near-disaster and its aftermath in the Porter's scene, when the drunken doorman pretends to escort into hell an equivocator, a reference to one of the Jesuit conspirators in the Gunpowder Plot. That aborted attempt to blow up the Parliament House, with the King and Parliament sitting in session, occurred in 1605, the year before *Macbeth* premiered.[10]

The question here, then, is not so much whether Shakespeare's Lady Macbeth owes more to Mary (or Elizabeth), than to Gruoch, but how the character's actions resonate with his audiences' attitudes toward powerful female rulers. Shakespeare and his contemporaries debated the subject of women's power primarily on religious and political grounds, Protestants arguing against the legitimacy of Catholic monarchs, and Catholics against the Protestants. Each side claimed their religion as the chosen one, with the monarch ruling by divine right over both church and state. Rebellion was not only treason but considered to be witchcraft as well. Queen Elizabeth I, to avoid religious battles, banned religious plays and religious subjects from the theatre. She authorized her Master of Revels to examine and censor all plays (a government authority that remained in effect until the 1960s). Shakespeare's plays circumvented censorship without sacrificing topicality, just as the playwright may have secretly remained loyal to the Catholic faith of his parents, while worshipping at the official Anglican Church.[11] And, so Shakespeare created a play performance drawn from an eleventh-century conflict in the British Isles between the Scots and the English that enabled an investigation, however indirect, into similar conflicts and crises in his own times. His creation of Lady Macbeth focused his audience's attention on the question of a wife's role in promoting her husband's ambitions, and her own, and in so doing made her relevant to future audiences in similar circumstances.

Opposed to the theatre, Puritan dissenters formed a third party in England's religious conflicts, in addition to official Anglicans and the outlawed Catholics. Severely restrained in England, waves of Puritan "pilgrims" left for New England, some returning later in the century during the Puritan Commonwealth under Oliver Cromwell, only to leave again when the monarchy was restored to England. Associating powerful women with Satan's workers, and Catholicism with witchcraft, the pilgrims set out to purge their city on the hill of all such devilry. They agreed with the railings of Calvinist firebrand John Knox, leader of the Protestant reformers who laid waste Catholic churches and monasteries in Scotland, and who argued against powerful women on religious grounds in his essay "The First Blast of the Trumpet Against the Monstrous Regiment of Women." The young Elizabeth, crowned Queen of England the same year that Knox's essay first appeared, 1558, took great exception to the polemical tract's thesis: "To promote a Woman to beare rule, superioritie, dominion, or empire above any Ralme, Nation, or citie, is repugnant to Nature; contumelie to God, a thing most contrarious to his reveled will and approved ordinance; and finallie, it is the subversion of good Order, of all equitie and justice." Because Elizabeth was a Protestant ruler and not a Catholic, Knox later softened his language against the English queen, but continued railing against Catholic queens, specifically Mary, Queen of Scots: "Scotland hath dronken also the enchantment and venom of Circes, let it be so to their owne shame and confusion." "[W]here a Woman reigneth and Papistes beare authoritie,...there must nedes Satan be president of the counsel."[12] In fabricating the Macbeth royal couple from old chronicles and contemporary conflicts, Shakespeare put to the test another of Knox's denouncements, that "men subject to the counsel or empire of their wyves [are] unworthy of all public office."[13]

Discovering Lady Macbeth-like women among the fold, women who could read, write, and speak persuasively even on knotty theological matters, the Puritan ministers accused them of consorting with dark and evil powers, and exiled them from their community. Anne Hutchinson, a well-educated immigrant to New England who dared to challenge the Puritan ministers' authority and argue theology with them, suffered banishment from the colony. Daughter of an English clergyman, Anne, with her husband and children, joined a wave of Puritan dissenters leaving England in the 1630s. In Boston she held regular and open meetings in her home to teach and discuss religious matters, and ran into trouble when her parlor became more popular than the church pulpit, her insights more influential than those of the ministers. And apparently she backed the losing side in a rivalry between Boston's male theocrats. To silence her, the authorities arrested, imprisoned, and tried her for heresy, blasphemy, and lewd behavior. Convicted and sentenced to eternal exile from the colony, Anne moved with her husband, children, and some followers to the more tolerant Rhode Island, and eventually to Long Island where, tragically, her farm lay in the path of avenging Indians who slaughtered her and her family, save one daughter. The preachers back in Massachusetts gloated that Anne's end was God's punishment for her wayward ways. A generation later fiends appeared in New England as birds of prey shadowing mostly pre-pubescent little girls whose parents, encouraged to report to their minister anything out of order in the community, accused neighbors of bewitching their daughters. As more girls fell sick, or "possessed," more women were accused of witchcraft. And because the Bible states that no witch is to be allowed to live, dozens of Puritans, mostly women, were hanged in homage to this scriptural authority.

The maverick religious preachers who governed the New England colony, some of them Cambridge and Oxford educated, brought to the New World their most treasured books: the King James Bible (translated from the Greek and Hebrew by a team of scholars as commanded by the king), King James' book on *Daemonology* (in which he took a greater interest), and other authoritative texts on how to identify witches—and, at least in the case of Cotton Mather, Shakespeare's *Macbeth*. Cotton would admit a familiarity with the text of the play, but his governance would not allow its performance. "The northern-most colonies were populated by psalm-singing Puritans and governed by blue laws as repressive as ever were on the books in Cromwell's Commonwealth."[14] One Puritan minister denounced plays as having been "sucked out of the Devil's teats to nourish us in idolatrie, heathenrie, and sinne." William Prynne's 1000-page *Histriomastix* (1633) lays out the Puritans' objections to theatre performances. While allowing for the writing and reading of plays, Prynne condemns the effects he believed live performance could have on its audience, such as making men effeminate, encouraging sodomy, and inciting fornication or adultery. He claims that theatre, "a temple of the infidel," posed a rival to the church for the worshippers' attention, where dissipated actors performed plays that contained heretical and seditious ideas, and housed thieves and prostitutes amongst its audience.[15] Such fears of theatre's effects on their congregations led New England's theocrats to ban all live performances.

Of all the Puritan ministers to shepherd their New England flocks, three generations of Mathers predominated: Richard Mather, his son Increase Mather, and grandson Cotton Mather. When the power of the ministers was threatened by England's restrictions on their authority, Increase Mather returned to "motherland" England to lobby for the old charter that had protected their colony's theocracy from outside influences and exempted it from reporting to a board of governors in England, as the other colonies were required to do. After spending six years in England, Increase succeeded in bringing back to the colony a new charter that restored some of the old privileges, but not all. The new charter disbanded the Bay Colony's Dominion status, yet retained the rights of Anglicans to worship and vote in Massachusetts. It also gave the English colonial governor veto power over colonial governance, in effect permanently diminishing theocratic rule. And British soldiers garrisoned in Boston could continue performing their amateur theatrics. Upon his return to New England in 1692 Increase Mather found his own authority diminished due to his having made too many concessions. Adding to his woes, the aging minister arrived home in time to see his son, the Rev. Cotton Mather, caught up in the hysteria of the Salem witch-hunts.

Cotton Mather stood out as a leader of the fight against what he identified as "fiends" and "hellish harpys." He knew the play *Macbeth*, and even knew about a staging device for one of its scenes, the cauldron scene, when the witches terrify Macbeth with visions of bloody babies rising out of the boiling pot, and call forth ghost-like figures reflected in a mirror. Cotton writes about it in one of his religious tracts, how the use of the mirror onstage makes the appearances of Banquo's royal descendants, King James' ancestors, seem to go on ad infinitum. "Shakespeare has shown his art in not suffering more than eight kings to appear in the procession, the rest being shown only on the mirror."[16] Was he able to make this statement based solely on his reading of the play in his own edition of Shakespeare's plays?[17] Or did Cotton's father see or hear about William Davenant's version of *Macbeth* on the London stage during his six-year sojourn in England? Davenant's adaptation of Shakespeare's *Macbeth*, "central to the repertoire throughout the Restoration and the English Enlightenment,"[18] premiered in 1663. Trimming out "coarse" words and characters such as the Porter, Davenant added new scenes, one to make Lady Macduff a major player and moralizing voice, and another to show Lady Macbeth haunted by Duncan's ghost and trying to get Macbeth to repent. Even in those speeches of Lady Macbeth that follow most closely the 1623 Folio edition, the Davenant version makes significant word changes. For example, in Lady Macbeth's opening monologue, where she considers those characteristics of her husband's that might make him recoil from assassinating Duncan, Davenant's addition of "effeminacy" is remarkable:

Davenant:
    Oh haste thee hither
That I may pour my spirits in thy ear
And chastize with the valor of my tongue
Thy too effeminate desires[19]

Shakespeare:
    High thee hither,
That I may powre thy Spirits in thine Eare,
And chastise with the valour of my Tongue
All that impeides thee from the Golden Round[20]

In his most spectacular and enduringly entertaining addition, Davenant multiplied the number of witches to form a large chorus that would sing, dance, and fly through the air using the new stage machinery from France and Italy. Politically as well as artistically, Davenant's adaptation suited the times, "evoking in its premiere the usurpation and murder of Charles I and the recent restoration of his progeny." This version would continue to celebrate English power, representing "the successful invasion of a northern wilderness country by heroic yet benevolent English forces in alliance with progressive local tribes.... [culminating] with the usurpation of the tyrant Macbeth and the reclamation of peace founded on dynastic legitimacy and the rule of law"[21]—until 1744 when it would be replaced by another revision, somewhat closer to Shakespeare's.

If Increase Mather had attended a performance of *Macbeth* in London, he would have seen the first female actor ever to perform Lady Macbeth. Highly regarded for her good character as well as her fine acting and sweet voice, Mary Saunderson Betterton performed the role in Davenant's version that premiered in 1663, and continued playing it until her retirement at the end of the century. She also coached younger actresses in the role and tutored the royal princesses in the art of acting. Colly Cibber, an actor manager of the next century who saw Mrs. Betterton in her old age perform Lady Macbeth, compares her favorably with a younger actress in the role: "She was so great a Mistress of Nature that even Mrs. Barry, who acted the Lady Macbeth after her, could not in that Part, with all her Superior Strength and Melody of Voice, throw out those quick and careless Strokes of Terror from the disorder of a guilty mind, which the other gave us with a Facility in her Manner that render'd them at once tremendous and delightful." Cibber testifies to her good character as helpmate to her husband, Thomas Betterton, the famous actor and teacher who played her Macbeth: "When she quitted the stage [1694] several good Actresses were the better for her Instruction. She was a Woman of an unblemish'd and sober life, a faithful companion to her husband and his fellow laborer for five and forty years."[22]

But across the Atlantic where the play existed as reading matter, Cotton Mather conflates the effluvia of the witches' cauldron in Shakespeare's play with apparitions conjured by women accused of witchcraft. He aims to locate and destroy these "Hellish Harpyes." And he finds them in Catholic ritual. Ironically, to expel Catholic devilry from his flock, Mather performs excommunications and exorcisms not unlike his enemy's. In his essay "A Brand Pluck'd from the Burning," Cotton Mather documents such an exorcism in his treatment of the tormented young woman, Mercy Short, giving a detailed account of how he and fifty of his followers crammed themselves into Mercy's bedroom where she lay in bed, to all appearances bewitched. Surrounding the bed, with Mather at the head, the congregation prayed aloud and sang psalms for several days in their attempts to rid the girl of the fiend. Seventeen years old in 1692, Mercy Short years before had been taken captive during an Indian raid and marched to French Canada where she was housed in a Catholic convent and given religious instruction. In one of several ongoing exchanges of captives brokered by British and French colonial officials, the orphaned teenager was returned to New England and placed in a Puritan household as a domestic servant. There her torment became acute. Towards the end of his narration, Mather directly attributes

Mercy's bewitchment to the Catholic education she received in Canada. He gives as testimony one of the "Executed at Salem for Witchcraft" who confessed, "That at their Cheef Witch-meetings, there had been present some French Canadiens, and some Indian Sagamores, to concert the methods of ruining New England." Regarding Mercy's travails, Cotton learns that:

> French Canadiens and Indian Sagamores sho'd Mercy a Book, out of which they said they took their Directions for the Devotions perform'd at their Meetings.... It was a Book that indeed came from Canada; a French Book of Idolatrous Devotions, entitled, *Les Saints Devoirs de L'Ame Devoté. Avec L'Office de La Vièrge, pour tous Les Temps De L'Année: Et L'Office des Morts, de La Croix, et Autres; reformez au Saint Concile de Trente.*[23]

Another book, said to be used at the devil's diabolical meetings and shown to Mercy, was *L'Office de La Semaine Sainte, et de L'Octave de Pasque, à L'usage de Rome, et du Diocèse de Paris.* Both books provide ritual observances for Catholic worshippers. Mather exclaims that:

> These Things very Naturally Raised in mee, a Contemplacion of the proper *Enchantments* whereby Popery was at first Begun, and has been Maintain'd and of the Confusion with which the Divels may probably bee cast, from an Apprehension of the Total Dissolution that is quickly to bee given unto all the Charms, which have hitherto Intoxicated the Nations in that Superstition.[24]

In writing about the captivity, exile, and reintegration of Mercy Short, a return to the Puritan community effected by a ceremony resembling both a religious exorcism and a theatrical performance, Cotton Mather makes his city on the hill distinct and separate from the native Americans, the French, and the English across the Atlantic. "The French—and during the revolutionary period, the English—posed a threat to the English [New English] character. The temptations of religious conversion, in the first case, and of treason, in the second, could sever the individual's connection to home and community just as permanently as going native."[25] Cotton Mather contributed to New England's formation of "New World nationalism," by writing about the colonial experience while at the same time incorporating references to Old World texts, even Shakespeare's *Macbeth*.

Mather's copy of Shakespeare's play appears as an oddity amongst the collection of his ministerial books.[26] Pursuant to Puritan ideology and the practices of the Protestant Reformation, Catholic pictures, icons, and statues, so plentiful before the Reformation, could not be shown in these books, or in churches or homes. Of the few illustrations permitted in the Puritan canon is an image

Figure 1   The Witch of Endor, in Joseph Glanvil, Saducismus Triumphatus: or, *Full and Plain Evidence Concerning Witches and Apparitions*. London: Collins, 1681. By permission of Special Collections & Archives, Wesleyan University Library.

of the Witch of Endor whose story appears in the Old Testament, an image printed and reprinted to illustrate the cautionary tale and Jehovah's command that no witches should be allowed to live. Curiously, this picture resembles Lady Macbeth's sleepwalking scene: both women carry a large candle, it gets

Figure 2 Lady Macbeth, engraved by François Gravelot from an ink and wash drawing by Francis Hayman for *The Works of Shakespear.* 6 vols. Ed. Thomas Hanmer. Oxford: University Press, 1744. 5:478. Courtesy of Special Collections & Archives, Wesleyan University Library.

placed on a table, and witnesses watch the woman enact her ritual whether it be the Witch of Endor's conjuration or Lady Macbeth's sleepwalking.

Offsetting this male-dominated purview of books and pictures, female New Englanders could have a totally different list of books of interest.

When a "Mrs. H" came to buy from a Boston bookseller in 1686, she appeared to him as more like a painted actress playing a queen than a respectable Puritan housewife, one reticent to laugh for fear of cracking her makeup: "She looks high and speaks in a Majestic Tone, like one acting the Queen's Part in a Play.... She paints and to hide her painting dares hardly laugh." But the bookseller's appreciation of profit tempers his critique of Mrs. H. He is only too willing to place orders to English publishers for the books of her choice: "She was a good customer to me.... The chief Books she bought were Plays and Romances; which to set off the better she would ask for *Books of Gallantry*."[27] Here's evidence of religious Puritans becoming pragmatic Yankees. But it would be a full century before the likes of Mrs. H. could see any of her plays performed in New England. In the 1790s, Boston opened its doors to theatre. But in colonies farther south, by mid-century, audiences had professional players acting Shakespeare's plays in their own theatres. Dependent on England for publications, the English colonies were kept up-to-date on the plays and theatrical news from London. By 1730 political interpretations of Shakespeare's plays had become common practice in England. "What was new from the 1730s onwards was the political appropriation of Shakespeare outside the theatre."[28] Soon Lady Macbeth in America would leave the page for the stage, and proceed to play a role in conflicts inside and outside the theatre, between rival rulers, forms of governments, and cultures in an age of revolutions.

Sarah Hallam Douglass performed Lady Macbeth in the first recorded professional production of *Macbeth* in America on October 26, 1759 in Philadelphia,[29] and thereafter in a long career that had begun in Britain in the 1740s and ended in Jamaica at the start of the American Revolution.[30] She may have played the part as soon as she arrived in Williamsburg, Virginia, in 1752, where the young military officer, George Washington, would be a frequent audience member. A founding member of the company of strolling players that later became known as the American Theatre Company, Sarah, along with her first husband, Lewis, and the Hallams' children, arrived in the New World supplied with trunk loads of costumes and stage properties. Lewis' brother William remained behind in London to serve as the company's agent and supplier. The actors' paraphernalia brought from England to Virginia included not just old, but new and newly revised play scripts, and, less tangibly, traditions and recent innovations in the art and craft of acting. When just beginning her career in London in the 1740s, Sarah must have witnessed and participated in the theatre reforms and innovations made by her more famous contemporaries, principally Peg Woffington in the role of Lady Macbeth, and David Garrick, Thomas Sheridan, and Charles Macklin playing Macbeth. Sarah certainly would have seen, and might well have brought to America the script of *Macbeth* that David Garrick introduced to the London stage in 1744, printed and reprinted in London, Edinburgh, and Dublin for another generation at least. It reformed the seventeenth-century Davenant adaptation by restoring much of Shakespeare's original text for the play as first printed in 1623.

Though generally attributed to Garrick alone, the new version of *Macbeth* arose out of his collaboration with Peg Woffington, Charles Macklin, and Thomas Sheridan. These four actors were colleagues, and close friends for a time in the early 1740s, when Woffington and Garrick were lovers,[31] performing with Sheridan in Dublin, and sharing lodging and expenses in London with Macklin. In London, with their housemate Macklin coaching them, Garrick and Woffington introduced their version of *King Lear* in the spring of 1742, a performance that gave Garrick his start, and a salaried engagement at Drury Lane. In Dublin Woffington played Ophelia to Garrick's Hamlet, and Lady Anne to his Richard III. The more experienced Woffington had already played Ophelia in Dublin in 1737, her first great success in a Shakespearean role. The lovers returned to London for a busy season at Drury Lane. But in 1743 Macklin and Garrick fell out over a strike against Drury Lane management, with Macklin holding out against, and Garrick giving in to the manager. In disgust, Macklin left. Woffington, too, left Garrick in 1744.[32] It was during these heady days with Woffington, Sheridan, and Macklin that Garrick worked on his version of the *Macbeth* script. "What had been for too long the plaything of enterprising machinists and fustian-spouting actors was now restored, for the most part, in form and spirit as a supreme human expression."[33] First performed in 1744, and as published in Bell's *Shakespeare* in 1773, Garrick's version nevertheless made concessions to popular taste and Davenant's "machinist" version. No Porter with his bawdy drunkenness interrupts the tragic tone. And Garrick like Davenant cut the murder of Lady Macduff and her children on the assumption that the public would find it too violent to behold. Davenant's opera-like scenes featuring a bevy of singing and dancing witches also appear in Garrick's script. And Garrick added a long dying speech for Macbeth.[34] As for Lady Macbeth, the script continues the recent practice of deleting Lady Macbeth's faint from the scene when the castle is awakened to Duncan's murder. In fact, she does not appear in that scene at all in Garrick's script, so that there was no "Look to the Lady!" moment. One explanation given for this deletion is that the actress needed time offstage to make an elaborate costume change for her upcoming coronation scene. Then, too, Lady Macbeth's absence from the scene may have resulted from an incident earlier in the century, during a performance that had included the fainting scene, and the actress performing the faint provoked the audience to laugh at her "hypocrisy." But many of Shakespeare's lines for Lady Macbeth that the 1660s Davenant script had changed or cut, the 1744 Garrick script restored, as in Lady Macbeth's first appearance in the play, reading the letter from Macbeth. "In Davenant the coldness and wintry harshness of Lady Macbeth's words are reduced somewhat by the substitution of smooth meters and refined images.... the raven's voice is musical, not harsh, and heaven perhaps peeps through 'the Curtains of the dark.'" With the new script, the "hoarse raven" returns, along with "the blanket of the dark." The Garrick script adds a new stage direction, more appropriate to Woffington's Lady Macbeth than Garrick's rebound Lady Macbeths, the direction that Lady Macbeth and Macbeth "embrace" at the end of their first scene together, a gesture of genuine affection not often practiced.

Without Peg Woffington performing in the 1744 production, this new script did not immediately succeed, as Garrick's replacement for her in the part of Lady Macbeth "appears to have lacked the kind of sensibility and skill that would make Shakespeare's character believable."[35] Not until Hannah Pritchard assumed the role in 1748 did Garrick find his Lady Macbeth, for Pritchard "presented the image of a mind 'insensible to compunction and inflexibly bent to cruelty,'" a cruelty that permitted Garrick's Macbeth to show, by contrast, more sensitivity.[36] An audience member observed Pritchard in the banquet scene rise from her seat and seize Macbeth by the arm, "and with a half whisper of terror, [say] 'Are you a Man!' [with] a look of such anger, and contempt, as cannot be surpassed." Pritchard's Lady Macbeth was "an angry Hecate."[37] Known neither for intelligence nor sensitivity, but rather for her clear enunciation, Pritchard would prepare for her role by reading only her own lines from a play's script, never the whole play.[38] That suited Garrick who played Macbeth only when Mrs. Pritchard performed Lady Macbeth, and with the exception of one performance, stopped playing Macbeth when Pritchard retired in 1768.[39]

Peg Woffington and Thomas Sheridan probably used a text similar to Garrick's, rather than Davenant's, for their three seasons of playing the two leads in *Macbeth* at Dublin's Smock Alley in the 1750s. Working with Sheridan, Woffington became the only woman to be a member and honorary president of his Beefsteake Club. Sheridan, renowned teacher of oratory and elocution, considered Woffington one of the best Lady Macbeths of her day. However, when in 1749 Woffington made her first appearance as Lady Macbeth, a command performance in London for the Prince and Princess of Wales, she played opposite the "old school" actor, James Quin, who may have retained the familiar Davenant script. One wonders if on that occasion Woffington had to perform Davenant's addition to Act One, a scene in which "Lady Macbeth consoles Lady Macduff, who pines for her husband off at the wars" in long and moralizing speeches.[40] After the Irish beauty's death in 1760, Sheridan played Macbeth opposite Mrs. Pritchard at Drury Lane Theatre in 1761, and there, under Garrick's management, the text would have been Garrick's. It would be the same script Sheridan's son, Richard Brinsley Sheridan, used when he succeeded Garrick as manager of Drury Lane and engaged future American actress and citizen, the Irish actress Charlotte Melmoth, to play Lady Macbeth in 1776.[41] Drury Lane retained the promptbook of Garrick's *Macbeth* for both Garrick's management (1747–1776) and R.B. Sheridan's (1776–1780), and most likely until 1794, when Sarah Siddons played Lady Macbeth opposite her brother, John Kemble, and they performed his version.

In addition to their newly revised script, the "Young Turks" of the 1740s, Woffington, Garrick, and Thomas Sheridan, together with the older, but indomitable Macklin (who outlived them all), developed a more natural acting style, with a wider range of expression and more freedom of movement than previously practiced. "In Peg Woffington, Garrick saw the lifelike way of acting for which his soul thirsted. He beheld her, 'all grace and bright nature, moving like a goddess among the stiff puppets of the scene.' "[42] Woffington played both comedy and tragedy, elegant in high-ranking characters, and vulgar in lower ones; and showed no aversion to making her face ugly or old to fit the character. She emphasized visual elements in her creation of a character: movement, gesture, and facial expression, in relation to stage properties, costume, and set design. Her one drawback as an actress was an unlovely voice, said to be scratchy. Graced with intelligence, wit, that some regarded as impudence, a beautiful face, and shapely figure, noted for her good legs in transvestite roles, Peg Woffington created a bold and passionate Lady Macbeth. Rising from her origins as a Dublin street urchin, becoming a child actress in Madame Violante's Lilliputian company in Dublin, Woffington became internationally recognized as both an accomplished actress and a female rake.[43] In 1748 she made a trip to France to study with the actress Marie Dumesnil, who introduced Woffington to Voltaire. Then in his prime, Voltaire gave the Irish beauty his play, *Mahomet*, which she took back to Dublin's Smock Alley Theatre, unwittingly visiting a disaster upon her good friend and fellow actor, the theatre's manager, Thomas Sheridan.[44] From France Woffington also brought back with her the fencing and riding master, Angelo, who became King George's master of horse and fencing, and, along with his family, part of the circle of friends surrounding Sheridan and Woffington in their country houses just outside London, Sheridan at Kingston and Woffington at Teddington, where, together, they hosted their fellow Irish exiles.

The oldest of these mid-eighteenth-century "naturalist" actors, Charles Macklin (1699–1797), had already broken new ground in producing Shakespeare's plays before lodging with Woffington and Garrick. In 1741 he reinterpreted Shylock in *Merchant of Venice*, rendering the character more natural in both appearance and speech.[45] Years later, in 1773, well into his seventies, Macklin revolutionized *Macbeth* by applying the same attention to detail and more natural acting. Macklin's script eliminates Lady Macduff entirely, a radical cut sustained by nineteenth-century productions in both Britain and America that makes the focus on Lady Macbeth all the more glaring. A letter printed in the *London Evening Post* attributed the performance of a "thinking Lady Macbeth," "her manner of speaking" to the "intelligence she had received" from Macklin. For the music, Macklin added bagpipes to the traditional fifes and drums.[46] And he moved the actors into the stage scenery, where painted drops, realistic stage properties, and working doors were replacing the old perspective wing system. "Inside of the Castle—every room should be full of bad pictures of warriors, sword, helmet, target and the dirk—Escutchions—and the Hall, bores stufft, wolves—and full of Pikes and broadswords."[47] (Did the "bad" pictures suggest that the Macbeths had "bad" taste?) Macklin put the actors in historical costumes, "dresses and decorations, proper to the time, place and action... of a sort hitherto unknown to an English audience." For his first scene Macklin's Macbeth appeared in an "old highland military habit," and not only Macbeth, but his escort were to be dressed similarly in "the long plaid, tartan stockings and tunic" resembling "dress worn in the highlands of Scotland in the late sixteenth century," Shakespeare's era.[48] Macklin and his 1773 London audience's interest in "habits of the time" demonstrated "how the historical appeal, traveling northwards and forming an alliance with Scots' patriotic sentiment, created something entirely new."[49] It also demonstrated that the English government no longer prohibited the wearing of Highlander plaids, as was the case during the Jacobean uprising when the 1744 script went into production and Garrick wore the red-coat and breeches of the English.[50]

Woffington's longtime friend and theatre colleague, Thomas Sheridan, focused on the voice—sounds and articulation, and especially how speech can and must express both emotions and ideas. His contemporaries remarked on his "mellow and expressive voice," "his deep tones...and the vehemence of his action" so "well adapted to the turbulent and gloomy passions," calling him "a master of the human passions."[51] Sheridan writes in his *Lectures on Elocution*: "The finest artificial tones in the world, and the most musical cadences, can never stand in the place or answer the ends, of such as are natural, or appear so by being always used in discourse."[52] He proved to be highly successful as an actor/manager/director by raising the standards of performance and the salaries of his actors, and insisting on proper rehearsals.[53] And he founded a school in Dublin in the 1750s with a curriculum based on rhetoric and oratory, and wrote several books on the subjects, including a phonetic dictionary "to establish a standard of Pronunciation." Later in England and Scotland he lectured at all the major universities, gave public readings and private lessons, and continued writing about the importance of communication through speech, gesture, and movement. Father of playwright and parliamentarian Richard Brinsley Sheridan, Thomas himself wrote plays, at least one comedy *The Brave Irishman*, and his wife Frances wrote both novels and plays that received much acclaim and influenced their more famous son's works. Among Thomas Sheridan's several publications is his biography of Jonathan Swift, his godfather, whose complete works he edited as well. Thomas Sheridan played Macbeth for many years and opposite several actresses in the role of Lady Macbeth. And when he himself no longer performed Macbeth to all the leading actresses playing Lady Macbeth, he coached the new ones, including the young actress Charlotte Melmoth who first performed the role at Drury Lane Theatre in 1776, and who would become America's leading Lady Macbeth by the end of the century. Later Sheridan mentored Sarah Siddons during her apprenticeship in Bath, who, in turn, would become England's leading Lady Macbeth starting in 1785, the year future First Lady Abigail Adams saw her perform the role in London.

Of the many eighteenth-century pictures representing Lady Macbeth, popular on both sides of the Atlantic, those created by Swiss artist Henry Fuseli evoke the most striking and haunting images of Shakespeare's "fiendish queen." Elegant, erotic, and Gothic, both in accord and in conflict with eighteenth-century sensibility, Fuseli's art reveals a kind of cohabitation of religion with art in his obsessive painting of theatre characters, especially those from Shakespeare's *Macbeth*. This became all too apparent when, in the 1770s while residing in Rome, he painted several studies of *Macbeth* characters in a series of scenes sized to fit the ceiling of the Sistine Chapel! In his teens in his native Zurich, Switzerland, Fuseli had already become obsessed with Shakespeare's *Macbeth*, making his own translation of the play into German before being forced to leave Zurich for having publicly accused a magistrate of corruption. Abandoning the vocation of Zwinglian minister for that of artist, and leaving Switzerland, the twenty-one-year-old ordained minister set out on a series of peregrinations that eventually led to London, where, as a frequenter of the theatre he saw Pritchard and Garrick perform in *Macbeth*. Fuseli's 1760 drawing of them served as the basis for a full painting he made six years later that now hangs in the Zurich Kunsthaus. It shows Lady Macbeth in the full-skirted gown, fashionable when Fuseli made his first trip to England. She leans slightly backward, her face in profile, the right hand outstretched toward Garrick in the moment when she demands "Give me the daggers." The left hand's forefinger is at her lips, whether to silence Macbeth's ravings or to draw attention to herself as the one who would shame to wear a heart so pale, or both, is uncertain. Garrick's Macbeth, in wig, breeches, and buckles on his shoes, has eyes wide and frightened, in clear contrast to the frowning eyebrow of his wife. He holds the daggers, one in each hand, pointed toward Lady Macbeth, yet rearing back from her with his weight on his back right leg, as if trying to get away from her. With this realistic portrayal, where even the screen, stage curtains, and floor covering are depicted, Fuseli reveals that cruelty in Lady Macbeth that Garrick prized in Pritchard's interpretation.

The memory of that scene stayed with Fuseli for years. He painted it again, or rather transformed it with a new style he had developed during a decade of working in Italy. In this later treatment, gone are the realistic details of contemporary clothes, décor, and architecture of the castle room. Gone are the individualized portraits of Garrick and Pritchard. Though similarly positioned in terms of spatial relationship, their postures have changed, becoming more energized and dynamic, less "staged"—Lady Macbeth especially. Now she lunges forward clearly on the offensive. Her body is almost skeletal, the boney knee and foot of her downstage left leg straining under her stretched skirts, the way Martha Graham dancers move in fabric. Now it is the upstage right hand that has her finger at her lips. This Lady Macbeth appears more witchlike. With the exception of her left arm outstretched behind her, all movement lunges forward, in profile: foot, knee, breasts, right arm, pointed nose, dark eyebrow, even a tuft of hair on her forehead. By contrast the Macbeth figure retreats backward, framed in a doorway too short for him that presses down on his head. Now the daggers are pointed downward and away from Lady Macbeth. Instead of Garrick's costume, the body is stripped of clothing revealing the contours of his anatomy, curves, in contrast to Lady Macbeth's sharp edges. The movement of the two players in Fuseli's later picture of this "Give me the daggers" scene has that dancer-like quality attributed to Garrick, and closely resembles the violent choreography of modern-day Pina Bausch.

But it is Fuseli's painting of Lady Macbeth sleepwalking that strikes the viewer as most representative of the wild and more sensual interpretation acted by Peg Woffington and later the young Charlotte Melmoth, preceding Sarah Siddons' more stately performance. Fuseli's painting (now in the Louvre) was first exhibited in London a year before Sarah Siddons' London premier in the role. Painted about the same time as his famous "Nightmare" (1781) with its monster seated on the breast of a sleeping woman vulnerably spread out over her fainting couch, the life-size Lady Macbeth sleepwalking was shown at the Royal Academy of Art's annual exhibition in January of 1784, and immediately reproduced in J.R. Smith's engraving and put on sale.[54] Horace Walpole took one look at the exhibited painting of this deranged and disheveled sleepwalker and pronounced it "execrable."[55] London's *Morning Chronicle* (May 8, 1784) makes up a word for the painting no more enlightening than Walpole's: "Fuzel-issima—that is the manner." The identity or identities of the model for Fuseli's "Lady Macbeth Walking in her Sleep" is unknown—maybe not an actress, or even one model alone, but a composite. It cannot have been the actress Sarah Siddons as has been claimed, since that actress did not achieve notoriety as Lady Macbeth until her London debut in February of 1785, over a year after Fuseli's painting was exhibited. Before that the actress herself stated how she was averse to playing the role, claiming that the parts of Lady Macbeth and Medea were not for her, "she did not look on them as female characters."[56]

Fuseli has painted a commanding life-sized figure of Lady Macbeth sleepwalking. Dressed in a pale yellow night dress, her red hair unbound flies in the same direction as the windswept flame of the large candle she holds in her right hand, while the visible dangling earring darts out in the opposite direction, suggesting a jerk of the head. Again, the movement is dynamic, almost frantic, as if she is running rather than walking, her staring gaze focused inward. Smith's engraving clearly shows one rosary crisscrossing her out-stretched left forearm, its cross perhaps under her curled fingers. Another lies on the floor, dropped at her running feet, one slipper on and

Figure 3 Lady Macbeth, engraved by John Raphael Smith, from the painting by Henry Fuseli exhibited in London and engraved in 1784. Courtesy of Davison Art Center, Wesleyan University.

one off. Almost as voyeurs, the characters of the Doctor and Gentlewoman lurk in the background watching Lady Macbeth's every move. Gary Wills points out that the candle is a penitent's candle, an extra large one used to light the sinner's barefoot pilgrimage to a holy shrine of forgiveness. That may or may not have been Fuseli's intent. What the artist does paint clearly is the physical strength and power of Lady Macbeth's body, set loose. This is a wild Lady Macbeth bearing no resemblance to the boney witch-like one of Pritchard, or the stately dignity of Sarah Siddons.[57]

Fuseli's Lady Macbeth springs out of the new era of *sturm und drang* and romanticism, but also builds on past imagery. For, just as the setting in Gravelot's engraving of Lady Macbeth in Hayman's 1744 edition of Shakespeare resembles the picture of the Witch of Endor used to illustrate seventeenth-century books on how to identify witches, Fuseli makes a similar leap in his own work by employing one of the witches from his 1773 *Macbeth* cauldron scene to depict his 1777 painting of the Witch of Endor. Fuseli's portraiture of the three witches in *Macbeth*, cartoonists appropriated to identify and satirize political figures, exemplifying the pictorial process, in tandem with the words and performances of Shakespeare's play, by which Lady Macbeth came to haunt America.[58]

3. "Politicianess" ᴄ

An image of Lady Macbeth horrified John Adams. A decade before the American Revolution, and while still loyal to the English crown, Adams took exception to a comparison made between his mother country and Lady Macbeth. To rebellious colonists who accused the English government of being a cruel Lady Macbeth, the young Boston lawyer had this to say in his 1765 "Essay on Canon and Feudal Law":

> Let me intreat you to consider, will the mother be pleased, when you represent her as deaf to the cries of her children?...When you resemble her to Lady Macbeth in Shakespear, (I cannot think of it without horror) Who "had given suck, and knew/How tender 'twas to love the babe that milk'd her." But yet, who could "Even while 'twas smiling in her face/Have pluck'd her nipple from the boneless gums/And dash'd the brains out."...[B]anish for ever from our minds...all such unworthy ideas of the King, his Ministry, and Parliament.[1]

While defending England on the grounds that the character in Shakespeare's play is far more terrible—"detestable" is the word his wife Abigail would use for Lady Macbeth—he nevertheless, acknowledges the potency of the figure by admitting that he cannot think of the character without horror. Already, at the nation's founding, Lady Macbeth has entered the public sphere as a figure of speech, a bogey in political contests.

Abigail Adams shared with her husband a strong recognition of Shakespeare's characters, using them to identify qualities within herself. About the time John was writing about the comparison of Mother England with Lady Macbeth, the young and as yet unmarried Abigail Smith wrote to her future husband a most curious love letter (April 20, 1764). She describes her longing to see him, as if possessed by tormenting spirits, not unlike those "hellish harpys" of the previous century believed to have bewitched Abigail's New England predecessors.

> Why may not I visit you a Days as well as Nights? I no sooner close my Eyes than some invisible Being, swift as the Alborack of Mahomet, bears me to you.

I see you but cannot make myself visible to you. That tortures me, but it is still worse when I do not come for I am then haunted by half a dozen ugly Sprights. One will catch me and leep me into the Sea, an other will carry me up a precipice (like that which Edgar describes to Lear) then toss me down,... —an other will be pouring down my throat stuff worse than the witches Broth in Macbeth.—Where I shall be carried next I know not, but I had rather have the small pox by inoculation half a dozen times, than be sprighted about as I am. What say you can give me encouragement to come?[2]

As a reader of Shakespeare's plays, might not young Abigail have chosen images for her love letter from Shakespeare's love stories and comedies rather than *King Lear* and *Macbeth*? "Haunted by ugly Sprights," she draws her sentiments instead from the darkest tragedies, as if forced to drink "stuff worse than the witches Broth in Macbeth." Later, married to the Bostonian lawyer, Abigail Adams claimed *Julius Caesar* as her favorite Shakespeare play. She identified so closely with the wife of Brutus in the play that she took her name for her own as both a pen name and a nick name—that of "Portia." Not to be confused with the Portia of *Merchant of Venice*, this Portia, wife of the assassin, Brutus, stabs herself in the thigh to prove to her husband her reliability in keeping a secret. Like the wife of Brutus, a serious and determined Abigail devoted herself to her husband's ambitions and course of action—not unlike Lady Macbeth.

Daughter of a Puritan preacher, Abigail was born in Massachusetts in 1744, a half century after the Salem witch trials. Well into middle age when she became America's First Lady in 1796, she made her New England heritage an important part of her political positions. She supported the abolition of slavery and formal education for girls. But she could not tolerate religions other than her own—she hated Catholicism. Likewise, she was dismissive if not outright hostile toward nationalities and cultures other than her own and that of her English forebears—she disliked the French and detested the Irish. Eventually her self-righteousness in combination with Lady Macbeth-like ambition would broach no argument, and led to her estrangement from former friends such as Mercy Otis Warren and Thomas Jefferson. As much a political animal as her husband, Abigail, too, was plagued with what her husband referred to as his "fiendish" ambition. So driven, she threw her bonnet into the arena of partisan politics, keeping abreast of all the ins and outs, and giving advice if not orders to her mostly obliging husband who, throughout his career, valued her opinions more than anyone else's. For all their travel and urban living, Abigail and John Adams remained moralistic, ambitious Puritan Yankees. In a letter to Abigail on October 29, 1775, John writes to Abigail of his "overweening prejudice in favour of New England": "The People are purer English Blood, less mixed with Scotch, Irish, Dutch, French, Danish, Sweedish & c. than any other; and descended from Englishmen too who left Europe in purer Times than the present and less tainted with corruption than those they left behind them."[3] John Adams was short on generosity toward his political colleagues. Reflecting on George Washington after his death, Adams summed up his former boss as "more an actor than a leader, brilliant at striking poses 'in a strain of Shakespearean... excellence at dramatic exhibitions.'"[4] Displaying little stage presence or dramatic flare himself, Adams was more expressive in his copious and didactic writing. Studious and perfectionist, he found Washington's spelling appalling. And the fact that America's first president relied on others to write his speeches Adams judged a stain on the image of Washington as "father of the country," a title John—and Abigail—felt Adams deserved.

Abigail's interest in drama began with her reading of plays. But in mid-life, during the years 1784–1785, she became an active audience member in the theatre, and thereafter while her husband served as vice president and then one term as president. Her theatre attendance began neither in New England, where the ban on theatres stayed in effect until the 1790s, nor elsewhere in America during the Revolution when American officials outlawed theatre performances. She may have heard about the British troops staging *Macbeth* in New York City during their seven-year occupation of the city, but certainly would not have attended such a performance. No, the New England matron and manager of the Adams' Massachusetts farm expanded her cultural education when she attended live theatre performances in Paris and London. With her husband in Paris working with, and more often against Ben Franklin on the final treaty negotiations to end the American Revolution, Abigail and her teenage daughter, also named Abigail, crossed the Atlantic to join him. This would be the future First Lady's only trip to Europe, somewhat edifying for the New England matron, but from her point of view more of a reinforcement of her superiority, and grist for her critical bent of mind. Mrs. Adams tempered her enjoyment of living in a palatial mansion and five acres of gardens and woods just outside Paris with complaints about the easy manners of the French, especially the French women. The aristocratic women, who pleased Ben Franklin with their cultured minds and affectionate gestures, offended Abigail with their dirty skirt hems and arms about men's shoulders at the dinner table.[5] However, once she moved to London the following summer, when her husband was appointed to serve as ambassador there, she found things to praise about the French in comparison to the English. This was especially so when it came to the subject of theatre.

The French National Theatre had moved into the Odeon Theatre, a beautiful neoclassical structure with a spacious marble lobby and the latest refinements in staging and audience seating, built in 1782 just two years before Abigail's visit. There Ben Franklin, Abigail and her husband, and Thomas Jefferson, all on various occasions witnessed the play partly inspired by the American Revolution that would be hailed as a clarion call warning the French aristocracy of an impending revolution of their own—the controversial *Marriage of Figaro*, in which the middle-class heroes, Figaro and Suzanne, outwit the arrogant aristocrat Count Almaviva. The playwright, Beaumarchais (Pierre-Augustin Caron), had been instrumental in securing French aid in arms, supplies, and money that won the Battle of Saratoga for the American revolutionaries and changed the course of the war. Having personally gone into debt to do so, Beaumarchais never received thanks or reimbursement from a begrudging American Congress that for the most part has remained anti-French to this day. John Adams, too, begrudged recognition of France's role in winning the Revolution. Even so, the Adams family enjoyed Beaumarchais's play in 1784.

Another play, that opened early that same year at Versailles and was possibly attended by Franklin and the other American commissioners, was a French version of Shakespeare's *Macbeth*. The actress Mme Vestris starred in the key role of Lady Macbeth, or Fredegonde, as renamed by the play's adaptor, J.F. Ducis. If *Figaro* can be considered the comedy of revolution, particularly foreshadowing the French Revolution, then *Macbeth* can be considered the tragedy of revolution, with Ducis's version playing throughout the French Revolution and its aftermath, just as the British had played Shakespeare's *Macbeth* throughout the American Revolution (that they called a Civil War), and its aftermath. Ducis named his Lady Macbeth "Fredegonde" after an especially cruel Dark Ages' queen of the Franks, whose string of murders included her husband in order to further her son's ascent to power. And while Shakespeare's Lady Macbeth has echoes of Medea in her threat that she *could* kill her own child, Ducis's character *is* a Medea who *does* kills her children. But like Agave in *The Bacchae*, Fredegonde is out of her mind when she does it, only coming to her senses when the deed has been done. Recognizing with horror the body of her son, Fredegonde stabs herself, a suicide that takes place on the stage, rather than off, as in the case of Shakespeare's Lady Macbeth.[6]

The actress Mme Vestris interpreted Fredegonde for Ducis' premier and all subsequent performances of his *Macbeth* up until her last before

Napoleon and Josephine in 1798. Françoise Marie Rosette Gourgaud (not to be confused with the later Mrs. Vestris, actress/manager in Britain), Ducis described in his 1790 preface to *Macbeth*, as being of superior intelligence, suppleness, and vigor. "She rendered the burning ambition, the infernal invocation and the execrable firmness of that character." Playing the sleepwalking scene, "upon which the strength of the work depends," Vestris stunned her audience into immobility, terror, and silence.[7] In 1792, during the French Revolution, Vestris, at forty-nine, played Fredegonde/Lady Macbeth opposite the twenty-nine-year-old François-Joseph Talma, as he made his debut in the role of Macbeth. The artist François Boucher designed the set. Vestris and Talma formed part of the troupe that broke away from the Comédie française to start their own revolutionary theatre. But by 1798, when Talma and Vestris performed *Macbeth* for Napoleon, Vestris had lost her powers and her audience, and would not repeat the role ever again, whereas Talma's star was still on the rise. This night (April 22, 1798) the audience booed Madame Vestris, "an extinguished candle," performing with "trivial gestures…false inflexions," "a pantomime of the role that she once played so brilliantly."[8] On this eve of Napoleon's departure for Egypt, the general invited Ducis into his theatre box after the performance of *Macbeth*. A politically savvy playwright, Ducis had carefully excised from his script any reference to the former monarchy, and he changed the coronation of Macbeth to one in which the character puts his hand on a law book and swears that as a citizen he is nothing without the law.[9] Note that Napoleon did not proclaim himself emperor until 1800, and vestiges of the democratic ideals of the Revolution still lingered. After Napoleon declared himself emperor, Ducis condemned Napoleon's court as "*un sabbat à la Macbeth*,"[10] and made further changes to the script as political circumstances warranted. The monarchy was restored in 1815, with Ducis, a year before his death at age eighty-three, receiving the plaudits of his early patron, now King of France. After 1827, with Talma's departure, the French *Macbeth* lost its appeal. However in the history of Lady Macbeth, Ducis' version contributed to Verdi's operatic character (1847), one almost as cruel and murderous as Fredegonde. The last recorded appearance of Ducis' Fredegonde/Lady Macbeth, in a Dutch translation performed at The Hague, coincides with the 1848 revolutions that swept across Europe, resulting in the overthrow of the monarchy in France and the rise of another emperor, Napoleon's nephew.

No doubt Abigail Adams would have agreed with Ducis' assessment of Napoleon's imperial reign as "*un sabbat à la Macbeth*," a metaphor she might have liked to apply more generally to France as a whole when, as an embittered partisan she was trying to get her husband as the president of the United States to declare war on France in the late 1790s. But earlier, while residing near Paris and Versailles for a year, 1784–1785, while the French hosted treaty negotiations between America and Britain, the middle-aged Abigail formed her opinions less on prejudice and more on observation. And her estimation of France improved, however temporarily, in proportion to her disapproval of England, where she took up residence as wife of the newly appointed American ambassador to the Court of St. James. Within weeks of arriving in London from Paris in the summer of 1785, Abigail commented on the differences between the two cities in terms of their theatre performances and audiences. She admires the actors and audiences at the Comédie française, and finds London theatre wanting by comparison. She observes how English audiences applaud action, while the French applaud "judgment" and "sentiment." Recognizing the relevance of Sheridan's satire of the English in his play *The School for Scandal*, even likening it to some of her own satirical sketches, Abigail tells her sister in a letter home how she misses the refinement of the French plays and audiences:

> I think the People, generally, do not discover so much judgment at the Theatres here as in Paris. In seeing a good Tragedy acted at the Comedy Francaise [*sic*] you will hear every good sentiment applauded highly, even by the Partarre [cheap seats], but here it is the action rather than the sentiments which they applaud. (Abigail Adams to Lucy Cranch, June 23, 1785)

Two months later, in a letter to Thomas Jefferson she expands on the same comparison, remarking how "cold, heavy and uncouth" the English theatre is, and with what "ease and grace" the French perform (August 12, 1785). The Adams' daughter, writing from Paris the previous year, makes a similar observation with regard to fashion: "Dress of the Ladies here [in France] is more agreeable than in either England or America. We in America coppy the English. There is more taste more variety, and more ease here than in England . . . very little trimming, if any, and the people of highest rank dress least" (to E. Cranch, December 10, 1784). Her mother has occasion to remark again on how scandal represents English manners in a letter to her son, when the rest of her family went to see another performance of Richard Brinsley Sheridan's *The School for Scandal* while she stayed at home in their London residence writing letters and "darning socks" (Abigail Adams to John Quincy, April 24, 1786): "Scandle is the *fort* of this [English] nation and a school in which they have arrived at great experience. That and lyeing make the greater part of their daily publications, as their numerous gazetts fully testify."[11]

The first time Abigail saw Sarah Siddons on the stage, the actress was playing Desdemona in Shakespeare's *Othello*, and the experience proved an uncomfortable one for the New England matron. She confesses in a September 18, 1785, letter to her sister, Cranch, how revolted she was when "the More" touched "the fair Desdemona." She tries to explain a prejudice she can only partially understand: "Whether it arises from the prejudices of Education or from a real natural antipathy I cannot determine, but my whole soul shuderd when ever I saw the sooty More touch the fair Desdemona. I wonder not that Brabantio thought Othello must have used Spells and magick to have won her affections." However she acknowledges that the character of Othello is "merry open generous and noble." And she wishes to appear tolerant of all nations and "complexions": "There is something I dare say esteemable in all and the liberal mind regards not what nation or climate it spring up in, nor what coulour or complxion the Man is of."[12] She struggles with her prejudices. Abigail was especially eager to see Siddons perform Lady Macbeth, the talk of London town ever since the actress debuted in the role at Drury Lane on February 2, 1785. She complains that getting a box at the theatre to see Siddons is comparable to the corruption of the English court where bribery is the ticket of admission. "You must make as much interest here, to get a Box when she plays, as to get a place at Court, and they are usually obtained in the same Way. It would be very difficult to find the thing in this Country which money will not purchase, provided you can bribe high enough." But when she finally does attend a performance, she is not pleased. Crediting Siddons with acting the part with "propriety" (a word current in newspaper reviews by theatre critics), Abigail nevertheless dislikes the performance because she dislikes the character. "I saw Mrs. S—a few Evenings ago, in Macbeth a play you recollect full of horrour. She supported her part with great propriety, but She is too great to be put in so detestable a Character."[13] She takes Shakespeare to task: "Much of Shakspears language is so uncouth that it sounds very harsh. He has beauties which are not equald, but I should suppose they might be rendered much more agreeable for the Stage by alterations." Abigail prefers Siddons in more likeable roles: "I have been pleased with her since [Desdemona] in several other characters particularly in Matilda in the Carmelite, a play which I send you for your amusement." And she approves of the actress' moral standing because Siddons performs the more "sensitive roles" (by this she apparently means romantic or erotic roles) with her brother, John Philip Kemble, thus protecting her reputation as a married woman with five children. "The virtuous part of the audience can see them in the tenderest scenes without once fearing for their reputation." As for

Siddons' husband, Abigail peremptorily adds, "he bears a good character, but his Name and importance is wholly swallowed up in her Fame."[14]

While in London, John and Abigail visited with John Jebb and his wife, Ann, who wrote her newspaper columns under the name of "Priscilla." An important liberal and Unitarian, or "radical dissenter" as the Unitarians were first called, the Dublin-born Dr. Jebb corresponded with Benjamin Franklin and Joseph Priestly; and, along with his activist wife, wrote and spoke persistently on behalf of Catholic emancipation in Ireland and in support of the French Revolution. The Jebbs and Adamses had in common their fervor for the abolition of slavery and other matters of social and political reform. (Slavery was not abolished in Britain until 1807, with trading in slaves continuing long after that.) The Adams' daughter writing to her brother about one such visit between her parents and the Jebbs, refers to both Abigail and Priscilla as "great politicianesses": "Dr. Jebb, who has visited your father several times since we arrived, and who is of his opinions I believe in Politics, brought his Lady to see Mamma this morning. She is also a great Politiciness, which consequently pleased Mamma." Ann Jebbs' involvement in politics, particularly her efforts to reform the electoral system in 1784, subjected her to public ridicule, stimulating "a formal debate at Coachmakers Hall on the topic: 'Is it consistent for the female sex to interfere at elections?'" Following her husband's early death in 1786, Ann Jebbs continued their reform efforts in her own writings, "she supported her husband's opinions with a force of argument that made his antagonists quail." But lest his reader get the wrong impression, her eulogizer qualifies by saying, "She had a delicacy of mind which admitted no compromise with that masculine boldness in which some females of a highly cultivated intellect have at times indulged."[15] While Abigail appreciated the Jebbs' spirit of reform, she "was led to describe Jebb as 'an Irishman,' and found herself dining at the Jebb household with two Irish visitors." Their being Irish was not at all to her liking, a prejudice accentuated later on, during Adams' presidency.[16]

Shakespeare's *Julius Caesar* had provided Abigail Adams with her pen name of "Portia." But in 1793 she stopped signing her letters "Portia," at the same time as her husband stopped addressing her as Portia in his letters. Was Portia too minor a character for Abigail now that her husband was vice president and aspiring to become the next president? Or did John and Abigail stop identifying with Brutus and Portia when they recognized that their political opponent, Governor George Clinton of New York, son of an Irish immigrant, the Jeffersonian candidate running against Adams for vice president, called himself "Brutus"? Though she would not have accepted the comparison to Lady Macbeth, Abigail was becoming more and more like a Lady Macbeth in her striving for the destruction of her political enemies, and for power and position for her husband. As First Lady, at the end of the decade she became an active "politicianess," and pushed against both the Irish and French by exerting pressure on her husband to declare war against France, and political war in the form of Alien and Sedition Acts against those immigrant reformers and revolutionary exiles who had come to America. She found the theatre useful to promote her political ideology. Aware of her outspoken behavior, sharp tongue, and ready opinions, Abigail approached the position of First Lady with some self doubt, expressed in a backhanded compliment to Martha Washington:

> Whether I have patience, prudence, discretion sufficient to fill a Station so unexceptionably as the Worthy Lady who now holds it [Martha Washington], I fear I have not.... I have been so used to a freedom of sentiment that I know not how to place so many guards about me, as will be indispensable, to look at every word before I utter it, and to impose a silence upon my self, when I long to talk (to John Adams February 20, 1796).

She satisfied her longing to talk by addressing her opinions and advice in frequent letters to her husband when parted from him, and in person when together with him in the country's capital of Philadelphia, and then, briefly, in the White House when Washington, D.C. became the seat of the federal government in 1800. Contemporary observers of Abigail's influence over the president called her husband's administration "a petticoat government," and viewed the Adams as overly fond of English aristocracy, facetiously calling Abigail's husband "His Serene Highness" and the First Lady "excellente wife of the excellent President." Abigail buttressed the appropriateness of such epithets when she referred to her fellow Federalist, American-born Congressman Griswold, as "Noble British Griswold," and to his Jeffersonian opponent, Irish-born Congressman Matthew Lyon, as "the beastly transported Lyon."[17] Adams identified the rebels of the Whiskey Rebellion in western Pennsylvania as Irish: "The Members of Congress begin to see the Danger of receiving Foreigners with open Arms, and admitting them into our Legislatures so easily as we have done. The Western Insurgents are almost all Irish white Boys, and Peep O Day Boys &c, imported and many of them sold since the Peace."[18]

Partisan politics fired up to fever pitch between Adams' pro-English anti-immigration Federalists and Jefferson's pro-French Democratic-Republicans during the "Season of Witches" that enthralled the nation's capital of Philadelphia in the spring of 1798. The First Lady, whether residing in the President's House in Philadelphia or running the farm in Massachusetts, pressed her indomitable energies to the service of her husband's ambitions, advising and bolstering him, and attacking those she perceived as his enemies. Her letters reveal how she showed signs of Macbeth-like paranoia:

> French emissaries are in every corner of the union sowing and spreading their Sedition. We have renewed information that their System is to calumniate the president, his family and administration until they oblige him to resign, and then they will Reign triumphant, headed by the Man of the People [Jefferson]. It behooves every pen and press to counteract them. We are come to a crisis too important to be languid, too dangerous to slumber. (Abigail Adams to her sister, March 20, 1798)[19]

The Federalists' agenda had as its priorities pushing for war against France, for the expulsion of aliens or "foreigners," and for the suppression of newspaper publishers and writers critical of the Adams' administration—all of which led up to the government's passing Alien and Sedition Acts in the summer of 1798. In the wake of this divisive atmosphere, in late summer and early autumn, came one of Philadelphia's major plagues of yellow fever that swept away many of the contestants.

Abigail's wish for pen and press to counteract her husband's calumniators was fulfilled by two Philadelphia newspapers, *Gazette of the United States* and *Porcupine Gazette,* pro-Federalist party newspapers that targeted their most vicious attacks on writer and publisher of the pro-Jeffersonian *Aurora* newspaper, Benjamin Franklin Bache, grandson of his namesake. In his *Porcupine Gazette*, William Cobbett vilified Bache as a seditionist, and even after the *Aurora* publisher's untimely death, continued his diatribes until Thomas Jefferson became president in 1800, after which the cantankerous Englishman returned to England and took up his pen to cudgel the pro-Irish member of England's parliament, playwright Richard Brinsley Sheridan. A case study demonstrating the political mood swings of the times, Cobbett later changed his stripes, became a convert to American democracy, returned to the United States, then went back to England for good with the remains of Thomas Paine in his suitcase. Benny Bache, an articulate thinker, writer, and printer like his grandfather, founded the *Aurora* in 1792, not long after Ben Franklin's death. Bache's paper countered Federalists agitating for war against France by bringing the Adams' government to task for violating the alliance with France his grandfather had forged, one that had enabled America to win its revolution.

> The advocates for a war with France [say]...that our national honor hath been insulted...Those who speak...seem to forget that the existence of the United States as a nation is but of yesterday.... The alliance of France...saved us from perdition. Have we forgotten the mission to France...to present our distress, the relief we obtained, and its consequences. (*Aurora*, April 4, 1798)[20]

Bache would be arrested under the Federalists' Sedition Law that was made law on July 14, 1798 (Bastille Day), his trial set for October 1798. But before that could happen, the "young lightening rod," not yet thirty, died on September 10, 1798, prey to the epidemic of Yellow Fever that decimated the city of Philadelphia. Bache's widow, Peggy Markoe Bache, barely delivered of their fourth child when her husband died, took charge of the *Aurora*, writing for the paper as well as publishing it. She later married one of the paper's writers, Irish immigrant William Duane.

To protect Adams and his party, a militia of young Philadelphians formed, recognized by the wearing of a black ribbon, or "cockade," upon their hats, after the fashion of the English. By day they marched and sang songs. At night, after several drinks at their local tavern, they roamed the streets of Philadelphia, threatening inhabitants considered aliens and seditionists with violence and attempts to burn their houses down. Night or day this armed local militia harassed anyone wearing the tricolor cockade of the French, with its red-white-and-blue beribboned topknot. In a letter to her sister, Abigail gloats at the pressure put upon the French cockade: "The publick opinion is changing here very fast...I am told that the French Cockade, so frequent in the streets here, is not now to be seen, and the common People say if J. [Jefferson] had been our President...we should all have been sold to the French" (April 17, 1798).[21] The cockades served as a flash point for theatre audience tempers, as did the songs associated with them. On April 25, 1798, Abigail Adams cheered from her audience seat in Philadelphia's Chestnut Street Theatre the new lyrics to an old song with words that elevated her husband as the scourge of Jacobins and United Irishmen. Federalist newspapers had been lobbying for the playing of the "President's March" in the theatre, and against "*Ça ira.*" The *Gazette* put out a veiled threat of violence against the theatre's fiddlers should they ignore their claque's request for the President's March, and denigrated the French Revolutionary song as painful to the public ear: "As the patriotic enthusiasm increases, such an unwillingness to gratify it may be dangerous to the fiddles and the fiddlers. For the same reason it is to be hoped no more attempts will be made to grate and torture the public ear with those shouts for *Ça Ira*" (April 17, 1798). Reviewing the event, the Jeffersonian *Aurora* followed up with its own demand:

> The following circumstance which took place at the Theatre on Wednesday Evening last may be depended on as a fact…Mr. ****, a member of the Federalist Legislature from New Jersey, accompanied by some other gentlemen, left their seats in the boxes, came into the gallery and began to vociferate for the President's March. The horrid noise…created some alarm in the citizens in every part of the house, who imagined these men had broken out of the Lunatic Hospital…. *These are Federalists, the supporters of Order and Good Government*!! The managers of the Theatre ought to beware how they suffer the theatre to be converted to a political engine. Men of all political creeds resort there…Besides, Mr. Adams was not the choice of the people there, and to aim at thrusting him down their throats will produce something like resistance. (April 21, 1798)

Both press notices give evidence that the theatre company and its audience were not all of the party that had elected John Adams to the presidency.[22] But the First Lady set out to make certain that that would not remain the case.

Abigail had new lyrics written to the music for the President's March. The night of its first performance at the Chestnut Street Theatre on April 25, 1798, Abigail applauded the song not from her customary seat in the President's Box but in another, so as not to be recognized, or so she said—but of course she was. The handbills for the theatre announce that at the conclusion of the evening's performance of *The Italian Monk*, "Gilbert Fox will sing a new patriotic song, 'Hail Columbia,' which young Philadelphian lawyer Joseph Hopkinson [son of John Adams' friend Francis Hopkinson] has written to the tune of the traditional 'President's March.'" (Soon thereafter the young lyricist, lacking experience and knowledge of the subject, received the appointment of head of Indian Affairs from President Adams.) Writing to her sister after the performance, Abigail exults: "The House was very full, and at every Choruss, the most unbounded applause ensued. In short it was enough to stund one….they made him [Fox, the singer] repeat it to the fourth time…at the close, they rose, gave three Huzzas that you might have heard a mile—My Head aches in consequence of it." The new lyrics read in part:

Behold, THE CHIEF WHO NOW COMMANDS,
Once more to serve his country, stands

The rock on which the storm will break,
But arm'd in virtue, firm and true,
His hopes are fix'd on Heav'n and you.
When Hope was sinking in dismay,
When glooms obscur'ed Columbia's day
His steady mind, from changes free,
Resolv'd on Death or Liberty.[23]

Commenting on the same April 25, 1798, performance, Bache's *Aurora* reacted somewhat less "stund" than Abigail:

> When the wished-for song came—which contained, amidst the most ridiculous bombast, the vilest adulation to the Anglo Monarchical Party...they encored, they shouted...And in the fury of their exultation threatened to throw over or otherwise ill treat every person who did not join heartily in the applause. The rapture of the moment was as great as if...John Adams had been proclaimed king of America, and the loyalty was so impressive that even the excellent Lady of his Excellency (who was present) shed tears of sensibility and delight....We are at a loss to determine why the orchestra who had so readily gratified one party, should refuse to play *Ça Ira* when repeatedly called for unless the managers wish to drive from the Theatre every friend to plain republican principles and depend alone upon the Tories for support. (*Aurora*, April 27, 1798)

As for the report she had shed tears at the singing of the new lyrics for the President's March, (the First Lady read the newspapers), she denied having cried, but countered that she would not have been ashamed if she had.[24] In exerting pressure on the theatre's management and orchestra by forcing them to introduce the new lyrics at the end of the performance, Abigail and her husband's party succeeded in banishing *Ça ira* from the repertoire in spite of calls from the audience for it to be played, as Abigail herself reports: "Accordingly there had been for several Evenings at the Theatre something like disorder, one party crying out for the Presidents March and Yankee Doodle, while *Ciera* [*Ça ira*] was vociferated from the other. It was hisst off repeatedly." Abigail as First Lady had come to recognize the theatre's power to affect the body politic—and to further her own agenda. "The theater, you know, has been called the pulse of the people."[25]

In Philadelphia on the same day, April 25, 1798, that the First Lady rallied support for the president and his "Tories" against the "Whigs" in the theatre, the U.S. Senate made its move to introduce the Alien and Sedition legislation. "Today in the U.S. Senate a motion was made by Federalist Hillhouse, from Connecticut, 'That a committee be appointed to consider...removing from the territory of the United States such aliens...as may be dangerous to its peace and safety.'" The following day, both Abigail Adams and Thomas Jefferson state in their correspondences in no uncertain terms who would be the first to be arrested under a charge of sedition. Abigail: "Daringly do the vile incendiaries keep up in Bache's paper the most wicket and base, violent & calumniating abuse.... Nothing will have an Effect until Congress pass a Sedition Bill which I presume they will do before they rise." Thomas Jefferson: "A sedition bill...we shall certainly soon see proposed. The object of that is the suppression of the Whig presses. Bache's had been particularly named...[I]f these papers fail, republicanism will be entirely brow beaten.... All the firmness of the human mind is now in a state of requisition."[26]

John and Abigail Adams and the Federalists staged more theatrics, a street performance and scripted sermons in the churches, to buttress their political standing. As prologue to the president's day of fasting, humility, and prayer on May 9, 1798, the black-cockade brigade paraded through the streets of Philadelphia to the president's house where the militiamen were welcomed by the First Lady and her attendants. They had assembled at noon at Merchants' Coffee House, Cobbett reporting their number as twelve hundred and spectators lining the streets as ten thousand, with "every female in the city, whose face is worth looking at, gladdened the way with her smiles." Abigail observed them marching two by two, "In great order & decorum the Young Men, with each a black cockade, marched through the Multitude and all of them entered the House.... the President received them in his Levee Room drest in his uniform." The president addressed the militia with an odd disclaimer reminiscent of his defense of Mother England against those who would call her Lady Macbeth. "I was called upon to act with your fathers in concerting measures the most disagreeable and dangerous, not from a desire of innovation, not from discontent with the [English] government under which we were born and bred, but to preserve the honor of our country, and vindicate the immemorial liberties of our ancestors."[27] The young men sang new lyrics to "Yankee Doodle," aimed at defaming Benny Bache, a "dirty fellow" who "curse[s] our country day and night/And to the French would sell her." The repeated chorus goes: "Fire and murder, keep it up/Plunder is the dandy;/When some folks get the upper hand/With heads they'll be so handy." Verses attack Benjamin Franklin, "Of every vice which cunning hides/His grandpap gave a sample," and as if in his Franklin's voice, "So deep I played the hypocrite/So simple were my manners/That all admir'd the artless man—/Who bore deception's banners." The concluding verse has "Benny's mind well imbib'd" with Franklin's "education," "'Tis plain he was prepared to be/The curse of any nation."[28] With this and their new lyrics to the President's March, renamed "Hail, Columbia," the black-cockade brigade serenaded Abigail Adams and her husband at the windows of the President's House at midnight. After that, they attacked Bache's house, as reported in his paper: "My doors and windows were battered.... Drunk with wine.... they have hoisted the black cockade...Alas, how many times have we not seen pools of blood spilled for a half a yard of ribbon?"[29] The next day, Tuesday, May 8, 1798, Bache's defenders wearing the red-white-and-blue cockade assembled at the offices of the *Aurora* to defend it against another black cockade attack. That day the U.S. House of Representatives opened debate on a bill "authorizing the President of the United States to raise a provisional army" of ten thousand volunteers, of which the black-cockade brigade would be the foundation. Opponents to the bill spoke out: Congressman and Swiss-born Albert Gallatin of Pennsylvania "looked upon all that was said of an invasion by France as a mere *bug-bear*."[30] A writer from Poland observed that "There is nothing more proper than to be on guard against troublesome and dangerous foreigners, but indiscriminately to place under suspicion all foreigners comes from a desire more to rule than to protect."[31] But from the opposite camp, came Englishman Cobbett's rejoinder, naming a group of foreigners he considered especially dangerous, a "restless rebellious tribe" believed to be in cahoots with the French and conspiring against the country: "A conspiracy formed by the united irishmen, For the Evident Purpose Of Aiding the Views of France In Subverting the Government of the united states of america—."[32] The *Aurora* responded on May 12, 1798, drawing attention to the writer, "William Cobbett, formerly a corporal in the English regiment of foot, still remaining a British subject and a professed royalist," and to his English nationality, "the nationality which attacks the unfortunate and long oppressed Irish."

John Adams called for the nation to observe a day of fasting, humility and prayer for May 9. Skeptical of the president's motives, Bache's newspaper opposed the May 9 Day of Prayer and Thanksgiving, and printed letters of like sentiment. "Mr. Bache, I have been much edified by reading the Proclamation of the President, appointing the 9th of May as a day of general fast throughout the United States... [T]he dangers which threaten have principally arisen from our Administration and...it is it that ought to *fast, reform, and repent*...The good American people are only guilty of one fault.... *It is that of having elected Mr. Adams their President*" (March 30, 1798). "I find most good men look on the President's Proclamation for Fasting, Humiliation and Prayer throughout the States as one of those apparently humble, hypocritical and delusive methods [of] Tyrants...for oppressing the people..." (April 21, 1798). On the eve of Adams' day of prayer and fasting, Cobbett's paper called on the militia to always wear the black cockade on their hats, and "a musket against their shoulder," and for the government to post guards at its arsenal and mint, and cavalry troops to patrol the streets. On the day, in churches around the country, ministers preached sermons espousing the president's anti-French-and-foreigners position, for they had received circulars advising them to do so. With steamy rhetoric the ministers characterized the French as ravishing and licentious monsters, the Jeffersonians as panders. Rev. James Abercrombie singled out French philosophers and playwrights in the sermon he delivered at Christ Church in Philadelphia: "That frantic and licentious spirit of disorder and desolation... originated in the infidelity of Philosophes... a Voltaire... a Diderot, a Helvetius, a Rousseau."[33] In the Adams' home state of Massachusetts, the Rev. David Osgood spoke to his Medford congregation: "Having no other prey at present at hand, the arms of the French Republic are now stretched toward us.... [T]he Aurora of Philadelphia and some other *ignes fatui* are so many decoys to draw us within reach of her fraternal embrace. If you would not be ravished by the monster, drive her panders from among you."[34] That night, the roving black cockades made another attempt to attack and burn Bache's house and offices, but a guard of men stationed there to protect the *Aurora*'s publisher and his family drove them away. So instead they marched toward the State-house, "knocking down lampposts, breaking windows, and smearing mud on the statue of Benjamin Franklin at the Philadelphia Library."[35] The black cockades were met at the State house by thirty or forty Jeffersonians wearing the red-white-and-blue cockade, and "a riot" ensued, resulting in the arrest of some of the wearers of the tricolor cockade, and only them. Abigail Adams concluded that they were part of "a foreign attempt to try their strength & to awe the inhabitants.... Congress are upon an Allien Bill."[36] And regarding Franklin's grandson, Abigail threatens, "Bache is cursing and abusing daily. If that fellow... is not suppressed we shall come to a civil war," and commands the president and Congress, "if they have not a strong Sedition Bill, make one."[37]

But the tricolor cockades were not so easily suppressed. At the Tammany Society's annual festival, held on May 12, 1798, at the Columbia Wigwam on the banks of the River Schuylkill, with Benny Bache, and other leading Jeffersonians, along with recently arrived Irish in attendance, the key note speaker warned them to "be upon their guard not to suffer even the appearance of kingly authority to return amongst us to blast the fair prospects of our revolution."[38] The speakers were followed by cheers, gun salutes, and toasts to honor Thomas Jefferson and the memory of Benjamin Franklin. Two weeks later across the sea, the Irish Rebellion broke out under the leadership of United Irishmen who had organized themselves in the Ben Franklin Tavern in Belfast, an attempt at revolution that spread from Dublin through the southeast of Ireland and north to Ulster in early June. In France, Wolfe Tone now had the attention and aid of the French government and military, with plans to sail for Ireland in September, too late to help, as it turned out. Looking to the future with resolve, Thomas Jefferson wrote in a letter dated May 31, 1798, "A little patience, and we shall see the reign of witches pass over, their spells dissolved, and the people recovering their true sight, restoring their government to its true principles." But much patience would be required, for in the weeks that followed the country very nearly declared war on France. Congress passed and Adams signed the Act Concerning Aliens on June 1, 1798, vesting the president of the United States with the power to seize, confine or transport persons beyond the territories of the United States. On the Fourth of July, the Sedition Act passed, making it a criminal offence to speak out against the president and his government, and forthwith was used as grounds for arresting several journalists including Bache. *The Aurora* on the Fourth of July: "The United States are largely indebted for their independence to the exertions of the Irish both in Europe and America. The Pennsylvania, Maryland, and Delaware Lines were almost entirely composed of natives of Ireland... and what is the return they have met with? A Naturalization Law, an alien law, a sedition law topped off with the most opprobrious obloquy and abuse that ever disgraced a legislative body." On Bastille Day, the Naturalization bill passed into law, calling for a fourteen-year residency before an immigrant could obtain American citizenship.[39]

As a consequence of these new laws, foreign residents of distinction, especially French and Irish "aliens," were forced to sell their property and flee the country. One such was Jefferson's friend, the French explorer and intellectual Count de Volney, painted by Gilbert Stuart on the eve of his departure from Philadelphia. The reach of law against Aliens tragically affected theatre personnel as well. A Frenchman named Gardie had forfeited his family estates in France to marry a beautiful dancer and emigrate to the United States. Like several other educated and talented immigrants from Europe, Gardie found means of making a meager living as a musician in the Park Theatre's orchestra, his wife performing as the company's principal dancer. Anna Gardie played one of the singing and dancing witches in productions of *Macbeth* that featured Charlotte Melmoth as Lady Macbeth. At the threat of deportation under the Alien Act, Mrs. Gardie decided to return to the Dominican Republic. But on July 20, 1798, the night before her departure, Gardie shot her and then himself in their bedroom, waking their ten-year-old son who stumbled over the dead bodies in his fright. Old Hallam, of the family of actors that founded the American Company, took in the boy, whose whereabouts after that are unknown.[40]

Recent historians who have studied Abigail's involvement in her husband's government, some with admiration if a slight bit of trepidation, such as Adams' biographer, David McCullough, others with serious reservations about the nature of that power, such as Joseph J. Ellis and Garry Wills, all agree that she more than any other advisor, more than cabinet or congressional or judicial colleagues, determined President John Adams' decisions. The one, and perhaps only time that he went against his wife's advice, is the one time that these historians praise as the best action of his administration, his refusal to declare war on France when much of the country—and Abigail—were lobbying for it. Had Abigail been in the capital, Philadelphia, when her husband's party was clamoring for war against France, she might have had more success convincing her husband to make such a declaration. Adams admitted to his son it would not have been possible to refuse his wife's demand had she been there in person to pressure him. As it was, she wrote him and other family members from their farm in Quincy letters full of diatribe against "the Jacobins."

In the estimation of all of these historians, Adams' worst act as president was the signing into law of the Alien and Sedition Acts, an action they blame on Abigail's undue influence. In detailing the Acts, Phyllis Lee Levin's biography of Abigail Adams shows how the First Lady pushed for and applauded the final passage of the draconian laws, fulfilling "her most spleenful wishes for retaliation against Jacobin journalists." John Adams' biographer David McCullough acknowledges that while President Adams must have taken "a measure of satisfaction from the prospect of the tables turned on those who had tormented him for so long," it was his wife who exulted in the passage of these laws. Indeed, McCullough reports that "she could well have been decisive in persuading Adams to support the Sedition Act," a law that imposed as much as a two-year prison term and hefty fine on anyone convicted of writing and publishing slander against the president and his government. "It was not uncommon in Philadelphia—or in Massachusetts—to hear talk of the unrivaled influence Abigail Adams had on her husband and of her political sense overall....That Adams valued and trusted her judgment ahead of that of any of his department heads there is no question."[41] While exposing Abigail's wrath, Ellis apologizes for her, attributing her position as coming from her "love for her husband, and her protective sense as chief guardian of his presidency." He points out that she went so far as to use the Alien Act to remove the leader of the Republicans in the House of Representatives, whom she referred to as "that specious, subtle, spare Cassius, that imported foreigner," again drawing on her favorite Shakespeare play for political parallels.[42] What an historical irony that Henry Adams, Abigail's great grandson, wrote an admiring biography of Albert Gallatin, that very same Congressman.

Henry Adams disliked what he learned about Abigail, his great grandmother, how severe and unbending she was toward his grandmother, Abigail's daughter-in-law, who would in turn became First Lady as the wife of President John Quincy Adams. Abigail wanted her sons to marry good New England girls. She considered her son's wife, Louisa Catherine Johnson, English-born, Catholic-educated, and daughter of an American father more southern than northern, as "anti-American."[43] When John Quincy and his wife went to Europe on assignment, Abigail forced them to leave two of their three sons with her to grow up in New England, giving their mother, Louisa, no choice in the matter and much heartache. Garry Wills follows his sources in holding Abigail, "the relentless improver," responsible for the two boys becoming debtors and alcoholics, just as Abigail's own two sons whom she kept in New England became wastrels. Only one of Abigail's sons, John Quincy, escaped her control by going to Europe with his father.[44] John Quincy Adams, the hard-working, roving-ambassador, congressman, first professor of Rhetoric and Oratory at Harvard, U.S. President, shared many of his mother's xenophobic prejudices, such as a denunciation of the Catholic religion and an arrogance toward the Irish. But Quincy's thoughts and actions as a politician diverged from his parents: he broke with the Massachusetts Federalists to support Jefferson's Louisiana Purchase and then resigned from the U.S. Senate when he refused to do Massachusetts House of Representatives' bidding to vote for repeal of Jefferson's Embargo Bill. Wishing to be a man of letters as well as a public servant, John Quincy Adams wrote poetry. And his longest poem, an epic he wrote in the 1830s, is about Ireland, the twelfth-century conquest of Ireland by England's King Henry II. Unlike his parents' disdain for the Irish, the son's attitude, while conflicted, nevertheless shows sympathy for the Irish. Like his father's essay on feudal law, John Quincy's poem depicts "venal monks and worldly convents." But unlike his father, the son supports Irish sovereignty and independence from England, both for the twelfth century and in his own time, when full emancipation for Catholics in Ireland had yet to be achieved.[45] Regarding women, and his wife in particular, John Quincy was less generous in sentiment. Though Louisa Adams had actively campaigned for her husband when he was running for president in the 1820s, and while she was widely appreciated in Europe and America for her intellect and artistry—she played the harp and wrote plays and poems—nevertheless her husband had her relegated to being a White House housewife, cloistered in her rooms. "His use for Louisa ended with his election. He had once sniped, 'There is something in the very nature of mental abilities which seems to be unbecoming in a female.' "[46] As First Lady, Catherine Adams was no Lady Macbeth in the White House, nothing like Quincy's strong minded and outspoken mother, and one may assume that Quincy was determined that his wife as First Lady be nothing like his mother.

John Adams moved into the not yet finished White House in the newly dedicated federal capital, Washington, D.C., on November 1, 1800. The next day, a Sunday, he wrote a benediction for the house: "I pray Heaven to bestow the best of blessings on this house, and on all that shall hereafter inhabit it. May none but honest and wise men ever rule under this roof!"[47] Abigail, his wife, arrived two weeks later to set up housekeeping in what she called "the castle," bringing as helpers the married couple who had been managing the Adams' house in Massachusetts. The one piece of art they brought from the president's house in Philadelphia to hang in the White House was Gilbert Stuart's portrait of George Washington. Abigail had less than four months in the White House, barely time enough to take her laundry down from the clotheslines set up in one of the official rooms, before she had to move out to make way for the next president, Thomas Jefferson, and surrogate First Lady, Dolley Madison. Abigail, perhaps more than her husband, resented the election of Jefferson, formerly a friend. For, not only did it mean the end of her husband's role as the nation's leader, but the end of hers as its "politiciness."

4. Playing for Revolutionaries ✧

The American, French, and aborted Irish Revolutions in the last quarter of the eighteenth century mark the beginning of the modern era in artistic as well as political terms. Charlotte Melmoth's forty-year career on the stage spans those revolutions, beginning in her native Ireland in 1773 where she became a leading Shakespearean actress and opera singer before emigrating in 1793 and establishing herself as America's principal actress of Lady Macbeth. Significant for her teaching as well as performing a range of dramatic texts and musical roles that extends from Shakespeare to opera and Irish song in the vernacular, Melmoth participated in the aesthetic revolution underway in theatre artistry that Denis Diderot posed as a paradox in his letters and essay on acting. Because so little notice has been given to Melmoth previous to this investigation, her history receives a longer treatment than do those of the better-known players of Lady Macbeth in succeeding chapters.

The year that actress Charlotte Melmoth made plans to emigrate from Ireland and come to the United States, James Hoban won the contest to make the final designs for what was then referred to as the "Presidential Palace," and to build it in the nation's newly designated capital city of Washington, the District of Columbia. Hoban was a youth, training to be a builder and architect in Dublin during the years actress Charlotte Melmoth performed there as Ireland's star tragedian and singing talent. As an Irishman and a Catholic, Hoban could advance no further than draftsman and builder in the Georgian building boom of 1780s Dublin, since only English Protestants were awarded major design projects. So he made his way to America, first to Philadelphia and then to Charleston where he and a partner opened a school to train designers. In addition to several private residences, two principal public buildings in Charleston are attributed to Hoban—the Statehouse and the Theatre. So the man who made the final designs for the White House, and supervised its construction from 1792 when the cornerstone was laid, to 1800 when John Adams and his wife entered the not yet finished house, the man who then rebuilt the White

House after the English burned it to a hollow shell in the War of 1812, is the same architect and builder who designed the theatre where Charlotte Melmoth performed for a profitable season—and where she premiered her original musical with Irish characters and songs. No doubt Hoban had seen Melmoth perform on the Dublin stage, little imagining that one day he would design a theatre for her triumphant season in Charleston, South Carolina. Perhaps through the network of Irish émigrés already established in the United States, such as Mathew Carey in Philadelphia, Hoban chose to test his talents across the Atlantic, where he would succeed in not only designing the Georgian theatre in Charleston to house a famous Lady Macbeth, but a Dublin-inspired neoclassical house for a succession of U.S. presidents and their wives, Abigail Adams being the first.[1]

Charlotte Melmoth, the leading Lady Macbeth on the American stage during the years Abigail Adams attended theatre in New York and Philadelphia, as an actress represented that Shakespearean character that Abigail found "detestable," and as a woman everything Abigail detested about immigrants coming to the newly independent United States. Not only because she was an unmarried and independent woman in a questionable profession, but worse, Melmoth was Irish and Catholic. Of the same generation (Abigail born in 1744, Charlotte purportedly in 1749), both were students of Shakespeare, Abigail as a reader and letter writer fond of quoting the bard and identifying personally with Portia in *Julius Caesar*, Charlotte as an actress and teacher, mistress of several roles on the stage and teacher of more, and known especially for her Lady Macbeth. But Abigail derived little pleasure in society. By contrast, the actress had charm and gaiety and enjoyed a large circle of friends. Abigail felt superior to others, born of "pure" English stock and raised in a minister's household reading scriptures and Shakespeare. Charlotte acknowledged in private to her American theatre manager her Irish birth and Catholic religion but little else is known about her origins or education, other than her telling a story about herself, not her own, that she hoped would silence further inquiry.[2] In her will that Charlotte drew up just before her death in 1823, she states her profession as "teacher," with no mention of her forty-year career as an actress, nor of family or blood relations, unless her sole heir, Julia Butler, were to turn out to be a relation, perhaps a daughter. Clearly the actress did not want her public to search too deeply into her past.

From that past "Mrs." Melmoth brought to the American theatre a school of acting developed by Peg Woffington and Thomas Sheridan, and political sympathies aligned with the United Irishmen, some of whom, failing to achieve a revolution of their own, like Charlotte, sought safe harbor in the United States. A survey of Melmoth's dozen years on stages in Ireland reveals how she engaged her sympathies for the Irish patriots in public performances, on stage and in the streets, which culminated in grand celebrations of the French Revolution in Ireland and later in America. For the Irish audiences, her tragic role of Lady Macbeth reflected mistrust of English authority and oppression, just as one of her comic roles satirized "Mrs. John Bull," an English snob, a performance that delighted the Irish patriots. In America, political partisanship in her audiences intensified, rather than dissipated, setting in play the divisive and dangerous "Season of Witches" that First Lady Abigail Adams fostered. At first the "patriots" in Melmoth's American audiences were suspicious of her immigrant status, whether pro-English, pro-Irish and French, or pro-American, suspicions that died down once she became an American citizen and popular performer. Her Lady Macbeth appealed to her generation of Americans not so much for its representation of an enemy's wife, as for the aesthetics of the performance itself, an appreciation of her rhetorical skills representative of eighteenth-century enlightenment, the eloquence of Shakespeare's verse well spoken, and to a particular segment of her audience, the Irish songs she sang and composed. With this closer examination of Charlotte Melmoth in the role of Lady Macbeth, she may come to be seen as America's Sarah Siddons, but a more lyrical, Irish-American one.

A young, lithe, and beautiful Charlotte Melmoth first played Lady Macbeth in Scotland, Macbeth country, three months before the signing of the Declaration of Independence. Then, on November 25th of that momentous year, Melmoth performed Lady Macbeth in London, at the Drury Lane Theatre, engaged by the new manager, playwright, and politician, Richard Brinsley Sheridan. Across the Atlantic, General George Washington and his ragged troops were retreating from their defeat in New York to Valley Forge, while the advancing British troops settled into the burned-out New York City for a seven-year occupation, Melmoth's future home. Press notices say that Charlotte performed Lady Macbeth, as "a wild untutored child of genius," expressive of "feeling and sensibility," but too "energetic." The word "wild," suspect by eighteenth-century standards of decorum, refers specifically to the Irish.[3] The *Morning Chronicle* critic had been watching Melmoth's development since her first London appearances at Covent Garden two years previous:

> Mrs. Melmoth is improved considerably in her acting since we saw her last; she always struck us as a wild untutored child of genius, with a good figure, which lost its effect from an ungraceful deportment, and an unnatural and awkward use of the arms. These defects are now much amended. In her first scenes last night she carried herself easily, and spoke with feeling and force, but her manner was...too generally energetic.

Figure 4   Charlotte Melmoth, as Roxana in *Rival Queens,* engraved by W. Walker from artwork by D. Dodd, 1770s. Engraving in author's possession.

He further notices how Lady Macbeth's costume for the coronation scene "though rich when nearly viewed, looked but meanly from the front boxes." He ends with a corrective and amusing note on the stage scenery for Macbeth's Castle, "let the Scene Shifters be told, [the castle] did not stand in a street—the side wings should represent rocks, and not houses."[4] A week later the same newspaper published a poem celebrating Melmoth's achievement as "bold Macbeth's ambitious dame." "W.K." finds remarkable Charlotte's "unsophisticated" charm, a natural, "artless" way of performing, yet with passion, as evidenced by seeing a tear in her eye and the swell of her bosom.

> "To MRS. MELMOTH,
>   on seeing her play Lady Macbeth"
> Melmoth, tis thine, whose wood-notes wild
> Proclaim thee Nature's artless child,
> With unsophisticated strain,
> To charm the charmers back again:
> To show the lovers of the scene,
> Retiring with disgust and spleen;
> In bold Macbeth's ambitious dame,
> Nature and Shakespeare's still the same.
> ....
> Tis the glittering tear that tells,
> With passion when the bosom swells
>
>   (*Morning Chronicle* December 3, 1776)

From these observations an image forms of Charlotte's 1776 Lady Macbeth, the first in what would be thirty years of playing the role—a tall, shapely young woman moving more gracefully, at times wildly, speaking with a melodious voice, and acting naturally with passion and feeling.

The young actress first appeared in Dublin, in 1773, mentored by Thomas Sheridan, who was co-managing Dublin's Smock Alley Theatre with Thomas Ryder. "Mrs. Melmoth, then in the bloom of life, a beautiful figure, with a remarkably sweet voice, to public notice in Monimia, a part in which she succeeded so well, as to give every hope she would prove a valuable acquisition to the stage. Nor was the public judgment disappointed. Mrs. Melmoth's abilities are capable of commanding a respectable situation in any theatre."[5] She and her partner, "Courtney Melmoth" (Samuel Jackson Pratt), opened a sizeable theatre in Drogheda. This once-picturesque, medieval, walled town on the coast north of Dublin housed an army garrison and fashionable retreat for Irish parliamentarians and so provided a suitable location and audience for the Melmoths' summer season. There the Melmoths performed Portia and Shylock in Shakespeare's *Merchant of Venice*, Cleopatra and Anthony in Dryden's version, *All for Love*. But Pratt lost his inheritance, and so the Melmoths had to abandon their Drogheda theatre project and return to London.[6] Covent Garden Theatre became Charlotte's stomping ground for the next two seasons during which her star rose while Courtney's flickered. They acted together as Hermione and Leontes in Shakespeare's *Winter's Tale*, and Gertrude and Hamlet in *Hamlet*. Of Charlotte's role in *Winter's Tale* the critic for the *St. James Chronicle* (November 22, 1774) guardedly observed: "Hermione (Mrs. Melmoth) was mightily well when she acted the Statue, but no sooner brought into action, than she became awkward to the last Degree; however, she is not a disagreeable speaker." He has no charity whatsoever for Pratt as Leontes, who "is excessively fond of ranting, and is entirely unacquainted with his own Powers. He was most unfortunately dressed and resembled a person just escaped from prison." Charlotte's engagements and roles increased. Noted for her Queen Elizabeth in Henry Brooke's *Earl of Essex* and Roxana, the wife of Alexander the Great in Nathaniel Lee's *Rival Queens*, powerful women presaging her Lady Macbeth, both appearances are illustrated in play publications of the times.[7]

Charlotte's choice to devote herself to a career in the theatre, and part with her "sham husband" Pratt, she makes clear in a somewhat autobiographical novel, *Charles and Charlotte*, published anonymously in 1776. The [co] author, Pratt, acknowledges his authorship in a letter to R.B. Sheridan, newly appointed manager of Drury Lane Theatre who has engaged Charlotte for the current season and to play Lady Macbeth. In this epistolary novel, Charlotte speaks for herself: "Though you found me a fallen woman I am not constitutionally a wretch of purchase, Sir." He puzzles how she "who forfeited her innocence to the seducer, and [had] been reduced to irreputable refuges" now can feel obliged to follow the rules of the "prudes" and "formidably devout." But Charlotte writes back that she has developed an appreciation of her own strengths and aspirations, expressed in words that seem to have sprung directly from Charlotte Melmoth's own mouth rather than Pratt's pen:

> The days of girlish giddiness were past, and the sedater reflections of the woman succeeded. From a state of rusticity and village ignorance, I was able to think profoundly and compare accurately.... *[A]n aweful admiration for illustrious characters, and a more than enthusiastic ambition to reach them seized upon my senses: proportioned to the augmentation of my intellectual powers.*[8]

Charlotte had become an actress!

The theatre in Edinburgh where Charlotte first performed Lady Macbeth in 1776 (and would again in 1779), was situated in Shakespeare Square between the old city covering a steep hill, and the evenly laid out Georgian "New City" below, positioned to feature old plays in a new age. Edinburgh had become the hub of the Scottish Enlightenment, one of the great literary, intellectual, and artistic centers of Europe. "This was the age of David Hume and Adam Smith, of Allan Ramsay...Robert Adam, Macpherson's *Ossian* and the Celtic Revival, of Robert Burns and Walter Scott."[9] Hugh Blair became famous in Europe for his introduction to Machpherson's *Ossian* (1765), a work seminal to Romanticism, in which Blair combines a scientific approach to the study of Celts, with Romanticism's emphasis on the poetic genius of the Celts. Blair credits his fellow rhetorician, Thomas Sheridan, for distinguishing the speaking of ideas and emotions over reading and writing. At the very end of Blair's lectures, he applies to Shakespeare's plays neoclassical standards based on rational thought and good taste, and at the same time embraces Romanticist celebration of Shakespeare's genius and imagination. "Great he may be justly called, as the extent and force of his natural genius...are altogether unrivalled. But, at the same time, it is genius shooting wild; deficient in just taste." Regarding Shakespeare's "praeternatural" beings, "his witches, ghosts, fairies and spirits of all kinds, are described with such circumstances of awful and mysterious solemnity, and speak a language so peculiar to themselves, as strongly to affect the imagination." Blair concludes that Shakespeare's two masterpieces are *Othello* and *Macbeth*, in which "the strength of his genius chiefly appears." He speaks to live audiences, "The Public should return with pleasure to such warm and genuine representations of human nature."[10] Whether or not Blair had the pleasure of experiencing Charlotte Melmoth's "warm and genuine representation" of Shakespeare's Lady Macbeth, in Edinburgh, she may well have attended Blair's lectures, women did. And it would be no surprise to discover that Charlotte had a hand in promulgating Blair's *Lectures on Rhetoric and Belles Lettres* in America, in her public readings and teaching.[11] Her formation as actress and teacher certainly benefited from Enlightenment's systematic training of the intellect, voice, and body, and Romanticism's freer and more lyrical expression of emotion and passion. As a young actress she embodied the wild and poetic Celt that figures in *Ossian*, a "fiery passion" she sustained and American critics applauded twenty years later.

Of the many new roles Charlotte added in Edinburgh's season, Shakespeare's female characters figure prominently: Queen Catherine in *Henry VIII*, Viola in *Twelfth Night*, Desdemona in *Othello*, Lady Macbeth in *Macbeth* on April 10, 1776.[12] The Wednesday evening performance of *Macbeth* went on much longer than one might expect from Shakespeare's shortest tragedy. For, after the play proper, two shorter pieces were performed, the first, a scene from Samuel Foote's *The Devil Upon Two Sticks*, announced as "The Examination of Dr. Last before the College of Physicians— President Mr. Inchbald—with the celebrated song—'Little Bingo.'" After Bingo's song came the farce, act two of David Garrick's *The New Rehearsal*, described as, "Orpheus descending to the Underworld...with dancing cows, sheep and goats. Influenced merely by the power of his Lyre, they will perform a City Dance." Perhaps these light-hearted and comic after-pieces relieved Edinburgh's audience of whatever tragic emotion they may have experienced earlier in the evening with Melmoth's Lady Macbeth and West Digges' Macbeth.[13]

Charlotte may have been dreaming of going to America[14] when she traveled to Paris to join the coterie surrounding Benjamin Franklin, America's most eminent ambassador abroad during the American Revolution. Or she, like Peg Woffington and other actors before her, may have purposed to study acting in France, considered the best. It was in the 1770s that Denis Diderot began writing about the different approaches to acting, a debate about the actor's spontaneity versus conscious control, as represented by Mesdames Marie François Dumesnil and Clairon (Claire Léris de la Tude), the two leading tragic actresses of the period; a debate that Diderot fully developed in his revolutionary *The Paradox of Acting*. The argument would have spoken directly to Charlotte Melmoth as she learned how to control her wild movements and passions. Diderot cites Lady Macbeth's hand wringing as an example of embodied passion, as noted by Joseph Roach:

> Diderot celebrated Lady Macbeth's silent hand washing as one of those sublime moments of bodily eloquence in which gesture triumphs over discourse. At such a moment spoken language collapses in upon itself, and its meaning can only escape the soul as a gesture: "The great passions," Diderot notes in the *Eléments de physiologie*, "are silent."[15]

But Charlotte was also meeting socially with Ben Franklin on several occasions and became friendly with his grandson. She wrote Franklin a poem, teasing the venerable old savant for overlooking her during a grand soirée when he presented a ceramic medallion bearing his portrait to Laura Izard (wife of one of the American commissioners), who happened to be standing next to Charlotte. "Impromptu, To Doctor Franklin," opens with Charlotte taking offense: "...slighted Women play the duce / When they but fancy an abuse.... Did not the happy Laura bear the Prize? / Did not the insult pass before my Eyes?" She asks, did Franklin pass her over because the American was "more fair," "Or breathes, perhaps, your native Air?" Charlotte protests that she has a fervent passion for the revolution and Franklin's mission, "Tyrants I hate, and Slaves I scorn." To the Melmoths' return address *"Chez Monsieur LeBrun Rue Jacob Fauxbourg St. Germain,"* Dr. Franklin responded on January 28, 1778: "I should have been flatter'd exceedingly by Mrs. Melmoth's showing the least Inclination for one of those Portraits," and promised her another, though the only one he had on hand was already promised to the Empress of Russia.[16]

Did Charlotte seek out Ben Franklin for his support of Ireland's independence from England? Irish nationalists made direct contact with Franklin in Paris in December of 1779 when a secret delegation made up of both Protestants and Catholics visited France and presented to Louis XVI a plan for Ireland's independence. English spies documented their mission:

> They propose that Ireland shall be an Independent Kingdom, that there shall be a sort of Parlt, but no king, that the Protestant religion shall be the established religion...but that the Roman Catholics shall have the fullest Toleration. The Delegates are closely connected with Franklin who, my informer thinks, carries on a correspondence by means of his, Franklin's sister, a Mrs Johnstone now in London who has a small lodging in Fountain Court in the Strand.[17]

Upon leaving France, Charlotte performed a season in Scotland and then an English tour before going back to Ireland in 1780. The Gordon Riots may have added impetus for the move; an upsurge of violence against Catholics that shut down London for over a week and caused disturbances in other towns. "London witnessed widespread rioting in which houses were burned and looted, prisoners liberated and distilleries raided. In particular, prominent Catholics and supporters of religious toleration were singled out." Edward Gibbon exclaimed that "forty thousand Puritans, as they might have been in the time of Cromwell, have started out of their graves." Several other towns were affected by "no popery" demonstrations.[18]

Actors regarded Ireland as "the proverbial 'green spot' in the arid desert of the unfortunate comedian,"[19] where Charlotte shared the stage with established talents and those on the rise. The young John Philip Kemble had just begun his apprenticeship when Melmoth, the more accomplished performer, played several major roles to his in the early 1780s.[20] Like Enlightenment Edinburgh, where Melmoth first performed Lady Macbeth, Dublin was experiencing a building boom that created a stunningly beautiful Georgian city. But the outward beauty of Dublin masked the deep divide in Ireland between its disenfranchised and mostly impoverished rural Catholic majority living beyond the Pale, and the Protestant minority inside the Pale on the east coast.[21] Ireland's Ascendancy government in Dublin Castle maintained its hold over the mostly Catholic population by depending on and submitting to English protection and domination, and by upholding the Protestant Church of Ireland (a replica of the Church of England). Penal laws required Catholics to pay tithes to the Church of Ireland, while barring them from owning property, holding political office, voting, attending university, and entering most professions. The Dissenters, an intermediary group made up of mostly Ulster Scots-Irish who belonged to other Protestant sects (Presbyterian, Unitarian), in seeking reform for themselves and the Catholics alike were becoming increasingly radicalized. With the example of the American Revolution before them at the beginning of the 1780s,[22] and the French Revolution at the end of the decade, the Irish "patriots" made up of both Catholics and Protestants, intensified their demands for reform, while the "loyalists" to English authority grew ever more anxious to retain their privileged position.

Theatre reflected these divisions, putting theatre artists at risk of offending one element in the audience while pleasing another. During her dozen years of performing in Ireland's theatres, first based in Dublin with tours to provincial towns such as Cork, Limerick, and Galway (1780–1789), then Belfast, Derry, and Waterford (1789–1792), Charlotte Melmoth appears to have pleased patriots and loyalists alike. But the nature and notices of her engagements indicate that increasingly and more openly her sympathies aligned with the patriot reformers. Mid-decade she joined with Ireland's first and only National Opera Company,[23] receiving accolades in the press: "When we consider Mrs. Melmoth's powers in tragedy, her excellence in genteel comedy and her consequence even in opera, we may safely pronounce that she has no competitor whatever in this kingdom, and scarce an equal in so general a line of performance in any other."[24] The following year Melmoth made her support of Irish culture clear to the public in partnering with Robert Owenson (who regularly played one of the witches to Melmoth's Lady Macbeth) in the formation of a "national theatre" at the Fishamble Street Music Hall. Its mission to revive the music and poetry of their native Ireland pre-dates by a century the similar project begun by Lady Gregory and William Butler Yeats. The venture on Fishamble Street proved popular, too popular, leading to its demise after only one season. The forces that closed it down, political as well as theatre-based, would later bring about a "Season of Witches" that foreshadows the one in the United States.

Opposition to the Irish national theatre appeared immediately after the opening, with "Sham Squire" Francis Higgins calling it "balderdash,"[25] writing dismissively in his treacherously acquired Dublin newspaper, the *Freeman's Journal*, that he made the voice of the government.[26] Higgins does admit to the popularity of the fare at the new theatre, but not to how it could pose a financial threat to the Smock Alley Theatre's box office and its investment partners, they being Higgins himself and Richard Daly, Smock Alley's manager. At the end of the "national" theatre's season Daly expediently hired back both Owenson and Melmoth, with some added inducements, making Owenson acting manager of the company. That arrangement would last until 1789 when Owenson and Melmoth and several other actors left Daly's company for good.

Charlotte's alliance with the Irish patriots and future United Irishmen may be inferred by public notice of her Catholic faith. It became an issue in *The Thespian Dictionary*, published in England early in the next century, saying that Charlotte had come out a Catholic in order to boost ticket sales for her benefit. "Previous to her Dublin benefit in 1786, Melmoth made known her intention of becoming a Roman Catholic and began to attend chapel every morning; 'but the receipts of the house not corresponding with her expectations, she found it was likely to be of no benefit to her in this world, and therefore did not think proper to change her road to the next.' "[27] Written from an English standpoint twenty years after the purported conversion and retraction, the writer for the *Dictionary* was either ignorant of the dynamics of Dublin theatre audiences of the 1780s, or deliberately distorted his account of them for the sake of a *bon mot*. It would have been Anglican aristocrats and officials of the English-controlled government who took the more expensive seats in the boxes and lower galleries. The Irish patrons in the theatre's upper galleries, Catholics and Dissenters, laborers, trades people, and Volunteers, purchased the cheaper tickets. Melmoth's public identification with the Catholics would have risked financial loss rather than gain.

Charlotte played Lady Macbeth continuously during her dozen years in Ireland. Newspaper notices record performances on May 14, 1781, at Daly's Smock Alley Theatre; December 4, 1781, with Ryder's Crow Street Theatre in Dublin; September 4, 1782, in Limerick with Daly's troupe; and January 13, 1787, back in Dublin's Smock Alley Theatre. The Limerick Playbill notes music by Purcell, "the celebrated incantation of the Witches, assembled over their caldron in the Pit of Acheron and all their Magic Spells." To the theatre's "band" has been added a pianoforte, the new keyboard instrument and predecessor to the modern piano that was beginning to replace the harpsichord.[28] Upon leaving Dublin in 1790 to join Michael Atkins' troupe in Belfast and Derry, it may be assumed that Melmoth played Lady Macbeth in that company's production of *Macbeth* announced for January 31, 1790, as she was celebrated in the Belfast newspapers as the company's leading tragic actress. Over the course of these productions, Melmoth matured into middle age, and added on weight. Her more youthful Shakespearean roles of Cordelia, Desdemona, and Rosalind fell away, just as her Macheath, a breeches role like Rosalind that showed off the actress's figure, gave way to that of Lucy Lockit in John Gay's *The Beggar's Opera*. Concurrently, Melmoth's Lady Macbeth gained in strength and power, changing from the wild and seductive beauty of her twenties and early thirties, to the commanding maternal figure of her later years, never losing the lyricism of her sonorous voice or the passion that critics continued to praise. Considering that theatre buildings were increasing in size, from accommodating hundreds of seats to thousands, and that there was no technology for enhancing sound, a trained voice was essential, not necessarily louder, but one that would carry, even in a stage whisper. Melmoth's Lady Macbeth must have been a powerful figure indeed, with that full and finely inflected voice, matched visibly by a tall and large form, altogether a stage presence emphasizing strength and purpose, ambition and intelligence tempered by emotion and sensitivity.

Something happened in 1789 to bring about the following announcement in John Magee's *Dublin Evening Post*, by coincidence the same day as the fall of the Bastille, marking the beginning of the French Revolution on July 14, 1789.

> We are sorry to learn that Mrs. Melmoth, whom we have long admired as one of the most favoured daughters of Melpomene, has quitted the stage entirely— and purposes devoting her future time to the instruction of Ladies in the present fashionable amusement of Filagree; for which purpose she has taken an elegant House, in this city, and is now in London collecting paper of the most exquisite assortment of Tunbridge wares.

But Charlotte would not stay long if at all in her "elegant" Georgian house in Dublin teaching the art of paper filagree, or quilling, to fine ladies. She did quit entirely the Smock Alley stage, and within six months had quitted the city of Dublin to appear on another stage in Belfast, "the Athens of Ireland." Less fortunate was John Magee, publisher and editor of the *Dublin Evening Post*, the newspaper sympathetic to Catholics and patriots, and admirer of Melmoth's work. For Magee, after barely escaping two attempts on his life, fell into the trap laid for him by Smock Alley Theatre investors, Higgins and Daly, at the start of Dublin's "Season of Witches." The same Bastille-Day issue of Magee's paper that announces Melmoth's retirement reports a "disturbance" in Daly's Theatre, caused by:

> A riotous mob of fellows who rushed into the upper gallery about seven o'clock, and bearing down all opposition forcibly took possession of the front row, driving out those who were in it. Their behavior was a continued series of outrageous violence, and often of shocking indecency: yet they were never molested, nor was any attempt made to curb or punish their daring violence. If such enormities are permitted, or connived at, no person of common decency will venture to go to the Theatre.

This is but one account of the increasing number of fights and riots in Dublin's newly renovated Royal Theatre (now on Crow Street with the Smock Alley Theatre permanently closed down). Magee's paper says they were provoked, "connived at," by Higgins' hired "bludgeoners" who attacked the "patriots" in their accustomed seats in the upper galleries. Higgins' retort in his *Freeman's Journal* accuses Magee of instigating the violence, of rallying his patriots to interrupt the performance by shouting from the galleries.[29] With the help of the English-led government, specifically Ireland's Chief Justice, Lord Clonmell ("Copper-faced Jack Scott"), on whose behalf Higgins was running a spy ring as well as a newspaper and theatre, Higgins and Daly intended to build up a theatre monopoly.[30] Clonmel issued Magee with a fiat for "contempt of court" and put him in prison where the editor languished for over nineteen months. Able to leave detention temporarily on 500 pound bail, Magee used the time to orchestrate a highly theatrical and amusing political protest and bit of revenge on Lord Clonmell—the famous "pig chase."[31] Richard Daly filed his own suit against John Magee that put him right back in jail, with a bail of 30,000 pounds, impossible to meet. Daly charged that a poem Magee had published in the *Evening Post* slandered him to such a degree that it deterred audiences and ruined his box office receipts. Judge Clonmell delayed the case for several months and meanwhile Magee's wife died, his health broke down, and his newspaper business disintegrated. Finally in June of 1790, with Clonmell on the bench and Daly's witnesses drawn from his remaining theatre personnel, his prompter,[32] treasurer, assistant treasurer, a box office attendant, assistant manager, and one actor, Magee's trial went forward. The defense lawyer asked how a satirical poem could reduce theatre attendance, arguing that a more obvious reason was the competition from other theatres, and the declining quality of Daly's own, with the lead actors, including Charlotte, gone. The poem, all that constituted the prosecution's case, alludes to the actors' "mutiny," and satirizes Richard Daly as a self-pitying actor/manager, armed with a tin sword, who bewails how his "days of prosperity" are numbered.[33] The prosecuting lawyers argued that by printing this "slanderous" poem, Magee had threatened "freedom of the press." (The same argument was made by John Adams' administration when it prosecuted journalists under the Sedition Act.) Judge Clonmell could barely contain his eagerness to convict Magee. But while Daly had demanded 4,000 pounds in damages, the jury granted him 200. Clonmell kept Magee in prison on contempt of court charges. Within a month of the trial, fellow Catholic printer and publisher, Pat Byrne, brought out a sixty-eight-page pamphlet of the trial's proceedings; so Clonmell had Higgins put his spies on Byrnes. It would be in the back room of Byrne's bookstore on Grafton Street where the outlawed United Irishmen met in the days leading up to the 1798 revolt, where one of their own, bought by Higgins and Clonmell, betrayed them to the authorities. Released from prison in 1802, Byrne immigrated to Philadelphia where he continued to publish, contemporary with Charlotte Melmoth performing in that city.[34]

In the same issue of Dublin's *Morning Post* (July 24, 1790) that Byrne advertised *The Trial of Mr. John Magee*, President George Washington's address to American Catholics appeared. They thanked the president for lifting the restrictions held over from English rule, and for granting them citizenship. Washington responded, "As mankind becomes more liberal, they will be more apt to allow, that all those who conduct themselves worthy members of the community, are equally entitled to the protection of Civil Government." The July 27 issue reported on Ben Franklin's funeral (April 18), finding it remarkable that in attendance were all the clergy of the city "including Ministers of Hebrew congregation." The Irish paper's editor added that Franklin "in a political view...may be considered as a greater enemy to England than even Philip II or Louis XIV." Such reports must have boosted the spirits of those striving for religious freedom in Ireland, such as Melmoth, Magee, and other nascent United Irishmen and women. The reports also assured them that there would be a country to welcome them should their efforts in Ireland prove futile—that is until the Alien and Sedition Laws.

In Belfast, where Charlotte Melmoth performed for two seasons (1790–1792), the public showed enthusiastic support for the French Revolution in print, on the streets, and in the theatre.[35] Pat Byrne's publication of Thomas Paine's *Rights of Man, Part I* had the largest circulation of any pamphlet in Belfast. "[I]t was Paine's attack on 'the old aristocratical system' and on religious intolerance which most struck home."[36] Paine's books "animated the breasts of women with heroic daring."[37] Edmund Burke countered with expressions of horror at attack on the French monarchs in Versailles, employing references to *Macbeth* to sow "in the readers' minds an association between sleeplessness and regicide.... it is almost as if he [Burke] is comparing the assassination of Duncan to the execution of Louis XVI even before the latter event has taken place."[38] Writer Mary Wollstonecraft took exception to Burke, and along with Tom Paine supported the rights of men and women to revolt against the tyranny of monarchs, whether in France or England. Belfast hosted huge Bastille Day celebrations in 1791 and 1792. The first one began at the town center, led off by Volunteer companies (Light Dragoons and artillery corps) carrying a large portrait of Benjamin Franklin with his words scrolled underneath: "*Where Liberty is—there is my country* " "A green cockade, the national colour of Ireland, was worn by the whole body."[39] The Society of United Irishmen formed the following October at a meeting in Peggy Barclay's Tavern, properly named "Dr Franklin Tavern," with "Benjamin's portrait 'awful and pompous... in a swinging frame over the door.' "[40] Their objective: "to make all Irishmen citizens; all citizens Irishmen." The Society adopted the seal of the Irish harp, topped no longer with the king's crown, but with the cap of liberty adopted from the French revolutionaries. The songs of the French Revolution, *Ça 'ira* and the *La Marseillaise*, became theirs. They recruited openly in the press until England declared war on France (1793) and made membership in the Society of United Irishmen an act of treason, a capital crime, forcing the Society members to go underground. Some of those who escaped the death sentence and found their way to the United States continued to call for *Ça 'ira* and the *La Marseillaise* in the theatres of New York and Philadelphia where Charlotte Melmoth would play for them again.

Working for Michael Atkins in his Belfast and Derry theatres, Melmoth found a liberal and humane manager, unlike the one she left in Dublin. And for a time, however brief historically, the audiences, the public, like the membership of the United Irishmen, included Protestants, Catholics, and Dissenters, who put their differences aside to work for reform. Catholics joined the Masons in spite of the Pope's ban.[41] For Masonic night at Atkins' new Artillery Lane Theatre in Derry, "Sister Melmoth" played her role as an honorary member of the Masons, singing their songs and delivering the epilogue.[42] The audience no doubt included the Americans working in Derry, contracted by the City Corporation to build a wooden bridge over the River Foyle, made with oak piers shipped from New England.[43] Perhaps she made connections here to facilitate her emigration.[44] But before she turned her back to the British Isles for good, Melmoth performed the satirical characterization of an English snob, a kind of coarse and ill-educated Lady Bracknell, named Mrs. Peckham in Thomas Holcroft's play, *School for Arrogance*: "a compleat Mrs. John Bull, who believes there is no place in all the world but England," that "excited laughter throughout the whole performance."[45] The playwright Thomas Holcroft invented the character to add to his adaptation of Destouches' *Le Glorieux*.[46] William Hazlitt regarded the play as Holcroft's best.[47] Thinly disguising his politics in the play, and as a member of the London Corresponding Society (like the Society of United Irishmen), Holcroft was arrested and charged with treason by English officials in 1794. He and William Godwin had written an open letter to R.B. Sheridan in his capacity as a member of the English Parliament as well as director of the Drury Lane Theatre, in which they expressed support for the French Revolution and advocated one in Britain.[48]

Upon leaving Ireland, Charlotte performed for a month in Waterford, where tensions were rising in the theatre. The *Waterford Herald* gave her favorable reviews, but also reported how soldiers posted in the audience hit anyone who "slept" through the obligatory singing of "God Save the King." Those who refused to stand and doff their hats for the song had their hats forcibly removed and thrown into the pit.[49] That December the Irish and English governments began arresting and imprisoning United Irishmen. In January of 1793, the French king was guillotined. In February, England declared war on France. Consequently anyone in Ireland and Britain supportive of the French Revolution was suspected of treason. In July 1793, Irish demonstrating for the release of prisoners who had refused to pay tithes to the Church of England/Ireland were fired upon by British militia; eighty demonstrators were killed outright, and all prisoners hanged. Irish reformers turned into revolutionaries. Some escaped to the United States. Wolfe Tone settled in Princeton, New Jersey, for a short time, but left for France to successfully lobby the French for arms and men, and unsuccessfully lead a revolution in Ireland. He died a martyr to the cause. Hamilton Rowan escaped from prison, joined his radical friends, including Mary Wollstonecraft, in France, and with Mary's help sailed to America. However his revolutionary zeal cooled in the winters of Pennsylvania's Brandywine Valley, and Rowan eventually sought a pardon from the English and returned to his castle in Ireland, an Ireland united with and subsumed by England in 1800 as a result of the 1798 rebellion. Others stayed on in the United States permanently, Irish Protestants and Catholics, lawyers, journalists, publishers, physicians—and actors.

Charlotte's motivations for leaving Ireland in the winter of 1792–1793 can only be surmised. It is not known whether her departure for the United States had anything to do with Higgins and Daly attempting to take over the Belfast theatre,[50] or the first assaults on United Irishmen. But her performances and peregrinations playing for revolutionaries gives some indication as to where her sympathies lay. The actress would find in the United States an enthusiastic audience that would embrace her as their best Lady Macbeth, and for a time at least, an audience united in support of the French, singing *Ça 'ira* and the *La Marseillaise* without any British soldiers knocking them on their heads and demanding "God Save the King."

New York City, *Daily Gazette* (February 28, 1793): "It is with pleasure we announce...the arrival of that excellent and much admired ACTRESS, Mrs. MELMOTH, in our city.—She has for several years past been at the head of the London and Dublin Theatres. We understand her views are not *theatrical*—that her intention is to pursue a COURSE OF READING. It must be a capital treat to the people of these States, as she is acknowledged to be one of the best Speakers on the English Stage." A month later New York's *Daily Advertiser* (March 23, 1793): "Mrs. MELMOTH": "At the particular request of several Ladies and Gentlemen of New York" Mrs. Melmoth will recite "Select Extracts from the Most Eminent Authors." Alternating with musical selections, Melmoth's recitations included scenes from Milton's *Paradise Lost*, and Shakespeare's *Julius Caesar* and *Macbeth*. "Tickets could be purchased at Mrs. Melmoth's, at No. 36 Water Street, or at the City Tavern, or at the Printers. The performance would begin at half past six o'clock."[51] Plaudits of Melmoth's concert and reading performances appeared in the *Diary, Loudon's Register,* praising her for the "infinite delight" she accorded "to every rational mind," and her "judgment blended with taste, and the most refined sensibility." Apparently a woman of some means, Charlotte arrived without a job contract, unlike other actors recruited from Britain and Ireland. Instead, modeling her career after that of her mentor, Thomas Sheridan, she gave readings, lectures, and concerts, and opened a school in her New York City lodgings to teach young Americans rhetoric, oratory, and elocution, a school that Washington Irving remembers as just down the street from where he lived as a youngster. Irving at thirteen read aloud to the esteemed actress his early attempt at writing a play.[52]

Middle-aged and overweight, possibly pregnant,[53] Charlotte Melmoth arrived in New York City, with twenty years of acting behind her and twenty to go. A mere two years later, the name "Charlotte Melmoth" appears on a list of newly inducted American citizens, the only female name in the lot.

Did the granting of citizenship to Melmoth mean that she was already a property owner and head of household? Evidence shows she was both in the years that followed. Was she therefore enfranchised to vote? As precedent, a few unmarried female heads of households and property owners in Britain could vote at that time. Did President Washington's administration follow suit in granting citizenship to qualified female immigrants such as Charlotte Melmoth? Whatever the details were for citizenship and enfranchisement in Melmoth's case, the welcoming two-year residency for American citizenship was abolished when in 1798 Washington's successor, John Adams, signed into law a residency of fourteen years in the United States before an immigrant could become a citizen.

By the autumn of her first year in the States, Melmoth's popularity had reached the notice of the managers and actors at the John Street Theatre in New York City, who induced her to return to the stage. Her first production coincided with New York City's tenth anniversary of "Evacuation Day," a holiday commemorating the departure of the British troops at the end of the American Revolution. It was on November 25, 1783, that the Red Coats solemnly marched down to the harbor to the English warships waiting to take them home. Now, ten years later, French warships friendly to the United States anchored in that same harbor. And New Yorkers, led by Governor George Clinton, welcomed the French shipmen and ambassador to their speeches, processions, dinners, and a performance of Arthur Murphy's *The Grecian Daughter* at the John Street Theatre. Based on the ancient Greek story of Euphrasia, the play features a heroine who rescues her father, the country's leader, from prison, by stabbing his usurper. In the legend, Euphrasia finds her father nearly starving to death in his prison cell, and saves his life by nursing him from her own breast, for she has just had a child and has milk enough, a scene graphically represented in paintings, but offstage in Murphy's play. Forty-four-year-old Melmoth played the part of the young heroine. On a previous November 25, in 1776, then as a beautiful, slim young actress, Melmoth performed Lady Macbeth in London before a rather blasé Drury Lane Theatre audience that considered her a bit too "wild" in the part. Now on this November 25, 1793, during her first theatre engagement in America, the large and powerful Melmoth finds herself playing a young heroine before quite a different audience. French officers in their brilliant uniforms sit in the boxes on one side of the house, American officers on the other, and uniformed New-York militia, artillery, infantry, and dragoons mix with the civilians crowded in the pit. This audience, a more eye-catching spectacle than the stage scenery, responded as one voice, united in its enthusiasm, as recalled by William Dunlap, the theatre's awe-struck manager. "The house was early filled. As soon as the musicians appeared in the orchestra, there was a general call for '*Ça ira.*' The band struck up. The French in the pit joined first, and then the whole audience." For this revolutionary song, and the *La Marseillaise* that followed, the audience stood up. "The French took off their hats and sung in a full and solemn chorus." The Americans applauded. Dunlap remembered "the figure and voice of one Frenchman, who, standing on a bench in the pit, sung this solemn patriot's song with a clear, loud voice, while his fine manly frame seemed to swell with the enthusiasm of the moment." "The hymn ended, shouts of *Vivent les François! Vivent les Americains!* reiterated until the curtain drew up, and all was silent." Writing this forty years after the event, Dunlap concludes, "Before or since we have never witnessed or felt such enthusiasm." "Surely the theatre is a powerful engine—for evil or for good."[54] When Euphrasia, armed with her dagger, "strikes the tyrant to the earth," audience shouts drowned applause. Never mind the inappropriate laughter that greeted the actress five evenings previous on opening night. An anecdote that chroniclers enjoy repeating tells how Melmoth's girth undermined the seriousness of the moment. Euphrasia tells the tyrant to strike her instead of her emaciated father, "Strike here, here's blood enough!" With that line and Melmoth's gesture towards her ample bosom such laughter broke out that the performance had to stop for several minutes. But being the professional she was, Melmoth recovered the moment and the audience's appreciation. However, she never again spoke that line when performing the part.[55] So it was not there to disrupt the grand occasion of Evacuation Day.

America's growing political partisanship in the young republic, and Charlotte's need for caution as she made her way through the new landscape, became apparent that winter, two weeks after premiering her Lady Macbeth in America. Melmoth either refused or simply failed to deliver the epilogue to a new piece, called *Tammany, or, the Indian Chief.* This provoked the following outburst in the press: "Mrs. M——th refused to speak the Epilogue in the opera of Tammany, because of the patriotic sentiments contained in it!!! She is to appear on the stage this night. I hope she will be convinced, by the absence of republicans when she appears that the people resent her impertinence. I think she ought not to be suffered to go on the New York stage again."[56] What those "patriotic sentiments" were remains a mystery since the text has disappeared. But the production of *Tammany* clearly served certain interest groups who wanted to create a disturbance in the audience. The "disturbance" started during the pre-show music, when James Hewitt, the music director and composer, did not know the song called for by the rowdy audience. He quickly improvised, but not before the audience set up a racket hissing and yelling at him. A "calm observer" at the performance reported in the *Daily Advertiser* (March 7, 1794), that the crowd quarreled with poor Hewitt because he was a "foreigner."[57] "After much altercation...the play...was permitted to make its appearance"—but not with Melmoth delivering the epilogue. Dunlap observed, "the poorer class made up the bulk of the audience that evening."[58] Evidently they had been "collected" by a "ruse," a notice circulated to the "patriots" that there would be an opposing claque planted in the audience to hiss the play off the stage.[59] (This same practice would lead to deadly violence half a century later in the "Macbeth" Astor Place Riot.) This had the effect of assembling an angry audience of Tammany Society members and supporters.[60] At this time the Tammany Society was made up of Presbyterians, Ulster Scots-Irish who performed solemn street processions to the Presbyterian Church in New York City to hear long speeches and sermons. If the play's epilogue, that Melmoth failed to deliver, voiced any of the early Tammany Society's anti-Catholic sentiments, consistent with the play's Spanish Catholic villains, Melmoth might well have balked at voicing defamation of her Catholic faith in the epilogue, spoken in her own person, not as a character. Or, to discourage a popular newcomer to the company, other actors, jealous of Melmoth, may have organized the claque.

The theatre's manager regarded the script, written by Ann Julia Kemble Hatton, a sister of Siddons and considered the parasitic "bad apple" by her siblings, as "a tissue of bombast," "seasoned high with spices hot from Paris." Only the lyrics to *Tammany*'s songs have been found, not the dialogue or music by Hewitt. Music historian O.G. Sonneck doesn't regret the loss of "that wretched thing." In acknowledging its political stripes, Sonneck shows his own, "This serious opera was taken seriously only by the Anti-Federalists."[61] Opera historian Elise Kirk takes a different view, quoting from the *Daily Advertiser*, that "its language was 'sublimely beautiful, nervous and pathetic.'" She celebrates the piece as America's first serious opera written by a woman on a national subject.[62] The doggerel sung by the Indians tends to support Sonneck's estimation: "Now the battle din is o'er;/Fury swells our souls no more;/Now we laugh and dance and play;/ Happy Indians! Come away." But the sentiments expressed in sympathy with the Indians give credence to Kirk's estimation. For after the Sachem Tammany rescues Manana from the Spanish would-be rapist, the Native American lovers die happy that no white men will be able to enchain them: "You white men deceivers your smiles are in vain/....Together we die for our spirits disdain/Ye white children of Europe your rankling chain," after which a chorus of Indians sing and dance around the graves of the dead couple and deliver the last lines of the piece: "Yet, let humanity still fervid glow/Shewing soft mercy to the vanquished foe."[63] For the theatre audiences of 1794, *Tammany*'s stage scenery and costumes were especially appealing, as designed by Charles C. Ciceri, the American Company's principal scenic artist. It was Ciceri who executed the "elaborate new design" for the *Macbeth* production on February 17, 1794, "the old stock [having] become black with age."[64]

Melmoth's American "patriotism" seems never to have come into question after this episode. By April of her first season, she was hailed as "the delight and glory of the American stage." A review in the *American Minerva* admonishes the other players to "be more perfect" to compensate Mrs. Melmoth for her estimable performance that "contributed not a little to the display of those talents which place her before every other female Tragedian which has yet appeared on these boards and which make her the delight and glory of the American stage" (April 26, 1794). The critics and audiences for her first American season had ample evidence upon which to make their estimation of the actress's worth. In the 1793–1794 season alone Melmoth is featured in over twenty principal roles, some she had played in Ireland and Britain, and others for the first time, in old and new plays.[65] And she continued giving concerts. A favorite intermezzo or afterpiece with the audiences was Mrs. Melmoth's recitation of "Shelah's Voyage to America, with Her Lamentation for the Loss of Drimmindoo, Her Cow," often followed by the company dancing in *The Highland Reel*. The Lamentation for Drimmindoo, a song ostensibly about a brown cow, served Ireland's disenfranchised "Jacobites" as code for lamenting the defeat of the Catholic King James II, and was considered treasonous by the English. Melmoth's rendition, from her days performing it with Robert Owenson in their "national theatre" of Ireland, must have appealed to the growing population of Irish immigrants in New York and Philadelphia.[66]

Melmoth's "American" Lady Macbeth first appeared on February 17, 1794. The orchestra for this "elaborate" production of *Macbeth* played Locke's music, "with alterations by Dr. Arne."[67] The American Company reprised this production for the Philadelphia audience on October 15 of that year. Back in New York City for the January 14, 1795 *Macbeth*, Ciceri backed Charlotte's Lady Macbeth with new scenery. And Benjamin Carr added Scottish music between the acts. With over thirteen singers listed in the cast, and the popular "Witches Dance" around the cauldron, this American production clearly retained some of Davenant's revision, and points forward to Verdi's opera. A critic took exception to the comic mugging of one of the witches: "Mr. Nelson added grimaces and gestures so ridiculous and disgustful, that the audience would have acted with proper dignity, had they driven him with hisses from the stage."[68] As no Lady Macduff appears on the cast list, presumably the part was cut, a common practice until the twentieth century. Charlotte Melmoth's later appearances as Lady Macbeth on the John Street stage include April 20, and December 16, 1796; December 22, 1797, with one of the Witches played by a woman, the other two by men.

Melmoth's Lady Macbeth took command of the big new Park Theatre on April 25, 1798, the same day that First Lady Abigail Adams cheered the new president's song in Philadelphia's Chestnut Street Theatre, and the day that the U.S. Senate introduced the Alien and Sedition legislation. The American Company abandoned the old John Street Theatre for the new Park Theatre, that its manager, William Dunlap, mortgaged his family's property to build. Arranging the audience in a semi-circle without any obstructing columns, with seating for 3,000, the Park's architects followed the fashion of bigger theatres in Europe, imposing broader movement and bigger voices on the actors, suited to the craze for new plays known as melodramas—the dramas with music fashioned on a grand scale of adventure and action as originated by the German playwright August Kotzebue. In accord with Hamlet's warning to Polonius that he should use the players well, "for they are the abstract and brief chronicles of the time," the Park's *Macbeth* seems to have presaged the "Season of Witches," as termed by Thomas Jefferson. For scornful Abigail Adams, now First Lady of the land, Melmoth's performance of Lady Macbeth held, "as t'were," a mirror up "to show scorn her own image, and the very age and body of the time his form and pressure."[69]

The black cockade worn by President John Adams' and his First Lady's supporters in the nation's capital of Philadelphia was cast down by actor Thomas A. Cooper during a performance at the Park Theatre in New York, provoking a protest that nearly touched off a riot. Dunlap's play *André* dramatizes the true story of the popular young British adjutant general, captured in 1780 while carrying a message from Benedict Arnold to the British, who was hanged under General George Washington's command. Cooper played Mr. Bland, an American soldier who befriends André and pleads with the General for his pardon. Charlotte Melmoth, over twice Cooper's age, played Mrs. Bland. During the performance, when Washington sends word that the prisoner would not be pardoned or exchanged, but hanged like a common criminal (because he was not wearing his uniform when captured), instead of by firing squad as befitted an officer, Cooper as Bland, with an unscripted gesture, tore the black cockade from his hat, threw it down, and stomped on it, causing some in the audience to hiss vociferously. Cooper wanted nothing more to do with the play or the cockade, but a compromise was reached with Dunlap: Cooper would take up the cockade from the stage floor and put it back on his head in repentance in the final act. Dunlap, a Federalist, and his family pro-British during the Revolution, put the young actor straight. "This [gesture] was not, perhaps could not be, understood by a mixed assembly; they thought the country and its defenders insulted,...the author made an alteration in the incident, and subsequently all went on to the end with applause."[70] Recalling how Philadelphia audiences were divided at this time between the pro-English black-cockade party, and the pro-French-and-Irish red-white-and-blue-cockade, it seems that Cooper impulsively improvised an anti-Federalist, anti-English protest, offending that element in the New York audience (including Dunlap, the manager). The gesture conforms to Cooper's upbringing in England under the guidance of William Godwin and Thomas Holcroft, Unitarians, supporters of revolution, and members of the London Corresponding Society. Offered a job in America with the Philadelphia players in 1796, nineteen-year-old Cooper went out of Godwin's household as Mary Wollstonecraft came in. Before her early death in September 1797, after giving birth to the future author of *Frankenstein*, Godwin's wife served as a liaison connecting Cooper with her brother, James Wollstonecraft, and other Irish émigrés in the United States.

Young Cooper played opposite the much older Melmoth in numerous and various roles, as lover, husband, and son, most significantly as Macbeth. In the spring of 1798, he played Hamlet to Melmoth's Gertrude (February), King John to Melmoth's Constance (March), and Macduff, not Macbeth yet, to Melmoth's Lady Macbeth (April). The next season Cooper finally got to play Macbeth with Melmoth's Lady Macbeth. No longer a young Lady Macbeth playing opposite older, more experienced Macbeths, Melmoth now found herself in a position to coach a new generation of younger Macbeths, setting a pattern of older Lady Macbeths playing to young Macbeths in America. The refurbished interior of the Park Theatre gave a lustrous setting for the production of *Macbeth* on February 1, 1799. The double columns on each side of the stage were painted to "exhibit a vivid resemblance of variegated marble." The dome above the upper tier was painted azure, "with floating clouds, between which celestial forms [were] visible." From the dome hung a chandelier "containing sixteen lights...with fifteen lustres disposed around it. The number of lights, exclusive of those on the stage and in the orchestra, amount[ed] to seventy-six." The curtain was "of blue mohair fringed with gold, in the centre the lyre of the muses surrounded with the usual symbols" with a ribbon on the bottom that read "To hold the Mirror up to Nature." Over the stage and each range of boxes, sixteen in the bottom tier and twelve above, was a canopy of green and gold. Advertisements in the newspapers celebrate the production's "new Dresses and Decorations...Scenery never before Exhibited," "Gothic Hall and Stair Case," "Apparitions by Shades in the Cave of the Witches," "numerous audience attended...and left the house with but one sentiment, *that they had never seen the play truly exhibited before....* The other parts of the play in the hands of Mrs. Melmoth, Mrs. Hallam, Mr. Tyler, and Mr. Martin did honor to each performer, and the superb dresses and magnificent scenery and decorations formed a *tout ensemble* of unrival'd excellence."[71] Did Melmoth's Lady Macbeth, lit by a single candle carried in her hand, descend that gothic staircase in the sleepwalking scene?

A review of Melmoth and Cooper playing in *Macbeth* the following fall, November 27, received an intelligent, if equivocal appraisal in the *Commercial Advertiser*. "Cooper assumed the character and appearance of a murderer too early; he should remember that to introduce Macbeth as a villain is to destroy the moral of the piece." Mrs. Melmoth in Lady Macbeth "was excellent, particularly in her sleep-walking." But due to the poor performance of secondary actors in the banquet scene she could not prevail: "she was unequal to the difficulty of trying to entertain her guests," with the actors playing the guests "at the supper table quietly and unconcernedly going on with their repast, munching their apples and smirking and drinking healths to the ladies, and the ladies to them. We hope never again to be obliged to witness such a shocking incongruity." And as for the comic singing and dancing witches, "'twas pitiful, 'twas wondrous pitiful.' The sublime bard never dreampt of bringing forward his supernatural personages to excite laughter."[72]

The fifty-two-year-old actress had a falling out with the Park Theatre's manager, Dunlap, over roles, salary, and scheduling her benefit.[73] Provoked by his mistreatment of her, she left the American Company and the City of New York for Charleston, South Carolina. There she was greeted as a star attraction in the theatre that Hoban designed. Critical praise for Melmoth placed her in the company of great actors whose eloquence served to instruct political leaders: "Roscius tutored Cicero, Garrick Camden, and Burke, Quin George III, Thomas Sheridan Queen Charlotte" The critic, identified only as "Benevolus," adds Melmoth to his list of eloquent actors whose performances are so instructive:

[I]n correct, forcible and dignified delivery, Mrs. Melmoth has few competitors. The most eloquent oratory might profit by an attentive study of her declamation; and the young will employ their time well in attending her performances, "*And with a greedy ear, devouring her discourse.*" (*Charleston Courier* March 28, 1803)

For her Charleston benefit, the Irish-American actress premiered an afterpiece announced as, "A Dramatic Pastoral, written by Mrs. Melmoth, called THE GENEROUS FARMER; Or, *A Chead Meelch Faultha.*" The play went on to be performed in New York and Philadelphia, but as yet no script has turned up. The night her piece opened, Melmoth had already played the lead in a full-length play; then, after playing and singing her own piece, she recited "the character of a PORTRAIT PAINTER, wherein she...delineate[d] a couple of Beauxs, a Young Miss, a fine Lady, a Miser, a Glutton, two Georgia Land Speculators, a ruined Gamester, an honest Sailor, and Herself." She concluded the evening's entertainment "*with a PANTOMIME INTERLUDE, called La Bonne Fille; Or, The Banditti*" (*Charleston City Gazette* March 26, 1803). The paper carried a story of her success eleven days later: "The house on the night of her benefit was crowded with the most brilliant audience ever witnessed at Charleston—and every circumstance connected with Mrs. Melmoth's performance...was of the most pleasing nature. The profits of her benefit exceeded one thousand dollars." Charlotte made more money in Charleston than ever, over a thousand dollars from her benefit alone, while her New York manager had begrudged raising her salary to $25, albeit the highest Dunlap paid to a single and independent actress. But New York audiences were calling her back, and she returned after one season in Charleston.

While she was away, Dunlap hired another actress to play Lady Macbeth, Charlotte Melmoth's only major competition during her almost two decades of performing the role on the American stage. Even larger in stature than her sister, Sarah Siddons, Elizabeth Whitlock lacked her sister's stately carriage and dignity, and was coarser in features and more masculine in bearing and voice. Recruited by Thomas Wignell for the Philadelphia Company in 1793, Mrs. Whitlock performed in Philadelphia's new Chestnut Street Theatre for three seasons. Deprived of Melmoth, New York audiences greeted Whitlock for the 1802–1803 season with great anticipation, eager to compare her Lady Macbeth to Melmoth's. When she first appeared as Lady Randolph in *Douglas*, the *Morning Chronicle* apologized for her lackluster performance: "The character is not adapted to the most favorable display of her talents, which, if we may credit report, will be brought into full operation in Lady Macbeth."[74] That "display" when Mrs. Whitlock assayed Lady Macbeth on October 18, 1802, to John Hodgkinson's Macbeth and Cooper's Macduff, received a tepidly favorable review in the *Morning Chronicle* on

October 21, signed "L."; who finds that "in critical situations," ones of "trepidation and irresolution" Mrs. Whitlock is "less unamiable... [I]n that way was she also represented by Mrs. Melmoth—who performed her excellent well." "L" goes on to detail differences in the way the two actresses read Macbeth's letter in Lady Macbeth's first scene of the play at the end of Act One: "Mrs. Melmoth and Mrs. Whitlock differ in their modes of reading the letter. Mrs. M. appears to be giving it a second perusal; Mrs. W. reads it for the first time. The latter mode furnishes the finest opportunity of displaying her emotions." "L" judges Whitlock's sleepwalking scene overdone and too wrapped up, no doubt in imitation of her sister's costume, designed by Reynolds to enshroud Lady Macbeth's head. "The scene in which Lady Macbeth walks in her sleep was well performed—though the ablutions were a little over done; and we think the countenance need not be so wrapped up, as to give that extreme ghastly appearance." By drawing attention to this costume detail it may be assumed that Charlotte Melmoth did not enwrap her head, nun-like, for the scene. Special effects for Hecate no doubt delighted the audience, for the production featured "a grand 'aerial' car" for her to descend and ascend."[75] More of an essayist than simply a reviewer, "L" postulates what he imagines the perfect performance of Lady Macbeth would entail:

> Ambition is the ruling passion of Lady Macbeth. Her characteristic marks are—manly daring which no situation can appall—perseverance which no difficulties can shake—a capacious understanding that comprehends at one glance every person and every circumstance, with all their relations—a nice and accurate discrimination; quick in forming resolutions; rapid and determined in action. She has also a ferocious cruelty, that hesitates not at *any* means for the attainment of her purpose. Even in her dreams her imagination recalls past transactions, but without any of those remorseful agonies which distract the waking moments of her husband.

The critic admits he has never seen such a Lady Macbeth, "with that undaunted firmness which we consider essential to a perfect personation."[76] Had he seen Hannah Pritchard's cruel Lady Macbeth, he might have been satisfied by her "undaunted firmness" and absence of "remorseful agonies." Clearly Charlotte Melmoth's Lady Macbeth remained more vulnerable, "amiable," yet passionate in the fiery spirit of Peg Woffington's Lady Macbeth.

By December of 1802 New Yorkers had definitely decided against Whitlock as worthy of replacing Melmoth. "The public have now had sufficient opportunities to judge of her [Whitlock's] full merit... [she] falls far short of what might be expected in the performer. In those scenes in which the finer passions are to be exhibited, there is an evident lack of sensibility and feeling; indeed, the attempt to express them is attended with such distortions of countenance as rather move us to laughter than win us to sympathy." That was the *Morning Chronicle* on December 10. The paper's review on December 18 is even more severe: "We certainly have a right to expect that an Actress of her experience...should exhibit some traits of power to justify her pretensions. This expectation was entirely disappointed...her countenance, voice, and manner are ill-suited to the soft and pathetic. By Mrs. Melmoth we have seen this character [Belvidera] exhibited with satisfaction; by Mrs. Merry with delight."[77] Even as late as December of 1809 a critic comparing Whitlock to Melmoth finds Siddons' sister lacking in skills Melmoth performed ably. "There is no fault in a good actress, that is not more readily pardoned by a New-York audience than a superabundance of tears. Mrs. Melmoth was remarkable for this, but she possessed a skill in the management, that enabled her to resist the popular disapprobation: Mrs. Whitlock is another and less fortunate instance; she absolutely cried herself to death, and was near drowning the whole dramatis personae by the copiousness of her inundations. At all events, they floated her away at the end of one season, never to return."[78]

The New York newspapers tracked Melmoth's return from South Carolina, a trip made aboard the schooner "Little Edward," "carrying cotton rice and tobacco, fifteen days from Madeira, passengers Mrs. Melmoth, Messrs. McBride [the ship's owner], Kellogg, Avery, and three Spanish gentlemen" (*Morning Chronicle*'s "Shipping News," May 23, 1803). She would play two more seasons at the Park Theatre, reprising her Lady Macbeth to a welcoming audience on November 30, 1803, with James Fennell as Macbeth, and then again at the end of the season on May 11, 1804. James Fennell, a larger than life stage presence at a height of six feet six inches, was certainly a match for the tall and notably large presence of Melmoth. Like Melmoth, Fennell was an actor of cultivation who taught elocution. He also lectured at the University of Pennsylvania. An unappreciative critic in Philadelphia's *Port Folio* felt that if Fennell "were less a scholar he could be a greater actor. He would have shown more at the bar or in the pulpit than on the stage."[79] Fennell enters a curious item in his autobiography that suggests that landlady was another of Charlotte Melmoth's occupations, to add to actor and teacher. "I took a house belonging to Mrs. Melmoth on the Jersey side of the East River and there made a considerable quantity of basket-salt, and the meanwhile engaged at the theatre with Mr. Dunlap at 30 dollars per night." He later started salt works in New London, Connecticut, traveling there with Gilbert Stuart's son, providing a further glimpse into Melmoth's business affairs and friendship with Gilbert Stuart, famous painter of the first presidents and first ladies, a friendship that dates back to the 1780s in Ireland, and perhaps to London before that.[80]

The twentieth anniversary of Evacuation Day in New York on November 25, 1803, featured Melmoth again, reprising Mrs. Bland in the *Glory of Columbia*, a rewrite of Dunlap's play about André. The spectacular production displayed "transparencies, machines, battle scenes with artificial figures and boys to fit into the perspective, ships pulling into harbor and disappearing over the horizon." The patriotic extravaganza was repeated on the following Fourth of July. "During the finale, a transparency descends, and an eagle is seen suspending a Crown of Laurel over the Head of General Washington with the motto 'Immortality to Washington.'"[81] Other of Melmoth's performances during that New York season of 1803–1804 include Elvira in R.B. Sheridan's musical adaptation of Kotzebue's *Pizarro*, Queen Elizabeth to Fennell's Essex in *Earl of Essex*, and Emilia with Fennell as Othello and Mrs. Johnson as Desdemona. In the next season's *Macbeth* at the Park Theatre on October 29, 1804, with Macbeth being played very badly by a Mr. Huntingdon, Charlotte Melmoth brought the house down when she delivered the line from the Banquet Scene, "The king grows worse and worse." The audience let out "a killing shout...and little more of the play was heard."[82] But when Cooper returned to play Macbeth to Melmoth's Lady Macbeth on November 19, the tragic mood was restored, and repeated on December 12.

All was not well for the Park Theatre. The onset of a national economic depression meant fewer audience members could afford tickets to the theatre, and lower receipts for the manager of the Park. Dunlap had mortgaged his and his family's properties to pay for the building and renovation of the Park, and was now unable to pay actors their salaries. "Salaries have been diminished or withheld, and prospects for the residue of the season are extremely gloomy" (*Morning Chronicle* February 25, 1805). Dunlap went bankrupt. So Cooper leased the Park from its new owners and took over its management (hiring Dunlap to manage a few years later). Under Cooper's management, Mr. and Mrs. Hallam were not rehired, and "seemed to slip away" after fifty-four years in the American theatre, the last of the family of actors who had been the first to establish professional theatre in America. And at the end of that 1804–1805 season, fifty-six-year-old Melmoth left New York for Philadelphia. Aging, but indomitable, she continued to act and give recitals in Philadelphia from 1805 to 1812, joining an ensemble of actors that included long-time colleagues such as Anne Brunton who played

Hermione to Melmoth's Andromache in *The Distressed Mother* in 1807, just months before the younger woman died in child birth. They had acted together in Ireland in the late 1780s. There in the Quaker city, "the beautiful but towering Mrs. Melmoth appeared appropriately as the dominating Lady Macbeth and as Queen Catherine...in Henry VIII."[83] Melmoth continued in other Shakespearean roles such as Gertrude in *Hamlet* and Emilia in *Othello*, and revived her comic standard of Mrs. Racket in *The Belle's Stratagem*.[84] And Melmoth's original piece *The Generous Farmer* opened at the Chestnut St. Theatre as afterpiece to the performance of Shakespeare's *Coriolanus* on March 16, 1807. The Irish tenor Webster as Paudeen O'Rougherty sang "Kate Karney" and Mrs. Melmoth sang "Drimindoo." The evening ended with an Irish jig. In that same season, Melmoth performed R.B. Sheridan's musical *The Duenna*, another import from her work in Ireland, which included a song of her own composition. And while eventually some of Melmoth's major roles were taken over by a younger actress, Melmoth continued singing her "Drimindoo" and other favorites of the Irish Americans in such pieces as the "Anniversary of Shelah" until her departure in 1812. Newspapers reported her death that year from injuries suffered in a carriage accident. But while she suffered some broken bones when the carriage overturned that was taking her from Philadelphia to New York to play Mrs. Malaprop in R.B. Sheridan's *The Rivals*, she revived, and played Fiametta in Holcroft's gothic play, *A Tale of Mystery*, for which New York's *Columbian* newspaper entreated its readers to attend "with a liberality worthy of the sympathy of a generous public for an old, respectable and faithful servant." Final retirement came on August 24, 1812, when Melmoth played Mrs. Milfort in *The School for Soldiers*, somehow appropriate on the eve of the War of 1812.

Charlotte Melmoth continued to teach at her school in Brooklyn. The July 22, 1819, *New York Post* calls attention to "Mrs. Melmoth's concern for the faulty pronunciation of English heard in our city," and to "her desire to take children very young and bring their vocal organs upon the way they should go" by teaching them "grammar." Melmoth did die on September 29, 1823, with many newspapers marking the event. One used Macbeth's grief at the news of Lady Macbeth's death to honor the actress who during the formative years of the republic had indelibly planted her portrayal of Lady Macbeth in Americans' imagination, "She should have died hereafter. Tomorrow, and tomorrow..." She was buried in the churchyard of New York City's "Old" St. Patrick's Cathedral on Mott Street. Half a century later, one of her former students, Robert McCloskey, son of poor Irish immigrants from Derry, who grew up to become America's first Catholic cardinal, recalls in his memoirs how the famous actress taught him rhetoric and oratory that served him well in his calling. Attesting to Melmoth's gaiety, spontaneity, and love of music, some years after her death a story appeared in a newspaper, told as if in Melmoth's voice to a friend, that relates how Melmoth as a guest to meet her best friend's new husband, on hearing his voice, falls in love with him—or thinks she did. But the next morning when he appears at her friend's breakfast table Melmoth realizes that she was swept away by his singing alone.[85] That side of Charlotte must have resembled the character Mrs. Racket in Hannah Cowley's comedy *The Belle's Stratagem* that she performed so often, who speaks up for "a fine lady":

> a creature for whom nature has done much, and education more; she has taste, elegance, spirit, understanding. In her manner she is free, in her morals nice. . . . In a word, a fine lady is the life of conversation, the spirit of society, the joy of the public! Pleasure follows wherever she appears, and the kindest wishes attend her slumbers.[86]

"The joy of the public," Charlotte Melmoth was of a generation of actors that referred to themselves as "public servants." In that spirit she brought to the American stage eighteenth-century enlightenment and romanticist passion quite different from the actresses who succeed her as the most prominent Lady Macbeth on the American stage, the future chroniclers of their times.

5. Yankee ✑

With the threat of war with Britain turning to certainty, and the economy geared to military preparations, theatre operations dwindled. The British invaded the young republic, captured the new capital and burned the White House to a hollow shell. At that time the spirited and hospitable First Lady Dolley Madison famously rescued the Gilbert Stuart portrait of George Washington.[1] Dolley's acquisition of the title "Lady Presidentress" contrasts with Abigail Adams' "politicianess." Her influence over her husband was just as strong, but more open minded and open hearted. Politicians welcomed her conversation, sense of humor, sense of style, and love of people of all walks of life. Rather than the stern and secretive wife of Brutus that Abigail identified with in *Julius Caesar*, Dolley Madison shared with her sisters a title drawn from another of Shakespeare's plays—*The Merry Wives of Windsor*.[2] The contrast in the two First Ladies can be detected in their portraits as painted by Gilbert Stuart, the artist who painted all of the first First Ladies—Martha Washington, Abigail Adams, Dolley Madison, on up to and including Louisa Adams—as well as their husbands. Stuart had returned to America from Ireland expressly to paint President George Washington and thereby make a fortune. He succeeded in making the now famous portraits of Washington, but failed to hold onto any fortune. Longtime friend of Charlotte Melmoth's, Stuart arrived back in his native land in the spring of 1793, within a couple of months of Charlotte's arrival. Stuart's seven years in Ireland overlap with Melmoth's last years there. Their friendship continued in the United States right up until Melmoth's death in 1823, as documented in a nineteenth-century history of Brooklyn that describes the location of Charlotte Melmoth's country house, a former inn, located in what is now Carrol Gardens in Brooklyn. There she ran a boarding school, a seminary for the children of Long Island's most prominent families, listed as the Pierreponts, Cornells, and Luquers. Brooklyn historian, Henry Stiles, recounts in his 1869 history of Brooklyn, how Stuart would leave his paintings hanging on her parlor walls in return for his enjoying room and board at her house "on beautiful Red Hook Lane."[3] Where all the paintings have gone that Stuart gave to Melmoth over the years remains as much a mystery as the inventory of Melmoth's entire estate. Melmoth's will, made not long before her death in September 1823, states only that she leaves everything to the friend who has taken care of her during her years of poor health, whom she identifies as Julia Butler. Perhaps one or more of the unidentified portraits of women made by Stuart will turn out to be of Charlotte Melmoth. One can imagine his liking to paint her as America's leading Lady Macbeth, just as he painted John Philip Kemble as Macbeth, the artist's favorite painting and one that disappeared when, prey to debtors prison, he had to make a hasty departure from London.

Having graciously and wittily served as First Lady in the White House for two presidents, as hostess for the widower Jefferson and then as wife of James Madison, the older but ever obliging Dolley Madison was called upon to give help and advice to a new First Lady, and former actress. Thomas A. Cooper's daughter, Priscilla, in her late teens, had performed most of the principal female roles opposite her father—with the exception of Lady Macbeth. After marrying the aristocratic Virginian, Robert Tyler, her acting career ended, as no wife could be respected if she continued working as an actress. Then, unexpectedly, she became First Lady when her husband's father, John Tyler, elected vice president on the ticket with William Henry Harrison for president, after only one month in office found himself president following the sudden death of Harrison. With his wife invalided at home in Williamsburg and his own two daughters unavailable, President Tyler asked his daughter-in-law, Priscilla, to serve as First Lady, who, with her looks, charm, and acting ability, and with Dolley Madison's help, did very well as hostess of the White House. In her diary, Priscilla recounts with pride how at one White House gathering the president of the Senate spoke to her of his admiration for her father's depiction of Macbeth. "When he and John Quincy Adams had seen Cooper play Macbeth, they had agreed that his performance of the role surpassed those of Kemble, Talma, Cooke, Kean, or Macready—all of whom both Southard and Adams had seen."[4] Washington Irving's prediction had come true. Comparing the young Cooper, whose performances he witnessed in New York, with the mature John Philip Kemble, whom he saw in London, Irving mused that Cooper's "warmth and richness would perhaps make up for the want of Kemble's correctness and precision."[5] How striking to recall that Charlotte Melmoth worked with both Kemble and Cooper when the two men were young and just beginning to play Macbeth, Kemble in Ireland in the early 1780s, and Cooper in New York City in the late 1790s. By the time Cooper's daughter had become First Lady, Melmoth and Kemble were long dead, and Cooper had passed into retirement, his prominence in the featured role of Macbeth taken over by younger rivals, esteemed British actor, William Charles Macready, and American star, Edwin Forrest. Old gentleman-actor Cooper would be spared the horrific outcome of those two rival actors performing Macbeth in New York City in a trumped-up competition that led to the deadly Astor Place Riot. Just three weeks before, in April of 1849, Cooper died.

In that White House conversation with the First Lady, apparently no one spoke of actors playing Lady Macbeths. Their generation had yet to produce an actress who could command public attention equal to what actors playing Macbeth could—with one exception—Fanny Kemble (a niece of Siddons, Kemble, Hatton, and Whitlock), barely twenty, who made a sensational sweep through American theatres that, after only two years, ended abruptly in 1834 when she married.[6] But in the wings an unlikely actress had begun a career that would eventually achieve that stature of being the leading Lady Macbeth of nineteenth-century America, and would prove a match for the likes of Forrest and Macready. First Lady Tyler and her White House guests could not have known then, in the early 1840s, that a young, big-boned actress was currently forging her command of Lady Macbeth in Albany, New York, and Philadelphia, soon to become the most famous and admired Lady Macbeth for the next half century. Neither did Priscilla and her father know that when they acted together in New Orleans in 1836, they shared the boards of the St. Charles Theatre with this actress, nineteen years old like Priscilla, but without the confidence or beauty of Priscilla, who had just failed disastrously in her debut as an opera singer. In early March of 1836 in the comedy *Rule a Wife and Have a Wife*, Thomas A. Cooper played together with Charlotte Cushman.

Following their 1836 New Orleans engagement, the Coopers returned home to Pennsylvania, to the sad news from London that Cooper's uncle and guardian, the only father he ever had known, the novelist and Unitarian radical, William Godwin, had died. Cooper never lost touch with him, sometimes through correspondence with Mary Shelley, Godwin's daughter by Mary Wollstonecraft. And there was a moment when the connections between Cooper's European friends and his American ones might have become even closer, when Mary, well after Shelley's death, briefly entertained the idea of marrying Washington Irving had the American writer shown similar signs of interest. But he didn't. Now Godwin, one of only a few remaining of that generation of radical "revolutionaries," was dead. Cooper in his youth, inflamed with the same revolutionary spirit, had wanted to join the French Revolution, but was persuaded by his guardians, Godwin and Holcroft, to try acting instead. Ironically, these four decades later, the venerable old American actor and his offspring were becoming part of that conservative plantation aristocracy of an American South that would in the space of another generation choose to vacate their positions of power in Washington, D.C. to set up a separate government and another White House in Richmond, Virginia, at the start of America's punishing Civil War.

Another southern aristocrat, the same age as Priscilla Cooper and Charlotte Cushman, who would become the North's First Lady during the Civil War, had finished in 1836 her fourth and last year of education at Lexington, Kentucky's leading boarding school for young ladies. There Mary Todd followed a rigorous European academic program taught by a refugee of the French Revolution who came to America in 1792. Mary's demanding but beloved teacher, Charlotte Victorie Leclere Mentelle, liked to tell her students that she had been "the only child of a wealthy Paris merchant who raised her as a son, denying her any girlish frivolities. Her father taught her to ride in infancy and required her to row across the Seine before breakfast." Mentelle and her husband, an aristocratic Parisian (who for his entire life wore the wig and breeches in the style of his youth of the 1790s), and their six children, occupied one wing of their large Rose Hill, Lexington house, and the handful of girls boarding with them occupied another. Mrs. Mentelle's pupils studied literature, learned French, and performed in plays. A proponent of intelligent conversation and vigorous physical exercise, Mentelle contrasted sharply with Kentucky's upper-class women who fancied leisure and beautiful dresses as their proper preoccupations.[7] So Mary Todd, one of Mentelle's star pupils, developed a strong appreciation for French culture and the kind of active and spirited women Mentelle represented. Mary became fluent in French, played lead roles in plays by Molière, and had a command of many passages from Shakespeare's plays. She was also keenly interested in politics, having grown up in a university town and Whig household that welcomed as dinner guests the likes of Henry Clay. Like Priscilla Cooper, Mary Todd would become First Lady by dint of her marriage, but to a husband very unlike Robert Tyler. Priscilla the actress married "up" into a Southern plantation family. Mary Todd married "down" to a backwoodsman, small town lawyer, in debt and living in a boarding house in Springfield, Illinois. And quite the opposite of Priscilla Cooper Tyler, Mary Todd Lincoln became an active abolitionist and supporter of the Union, First Lady precisely at the time when the country split over the issue of slavery and launched into Civil War.

The Coopers left New Orleans after a short three-week star engagement, apparently unaware that they had just shared the boards with America's nascent nineteenth-century Lady Macbeth. They left. But the struggling actress stayed on, holed up in her boarding house room, poring over Lady Macbeth's part, coached by a sympathetic British actor who had seen and worked with several of the Lady Macbeths of the previous generation. Having ruined her voice while singing opera in her first performances before the New Orleans audience, and smarting from the scathingly hostile reviews that greeted those performances, Cushman nevertheless gained from them the insight that she should abandon singing and take up acting. The St. Charles theatre manager, James Caldwell, was of the same opinion, seeing something in her that he thought had the makings of a good, intelligent actress. And so, in a matter of four months, no doubt with great fear but equal courage, the raw Charlotte Cushman went from singing badly the role of Countess Almaviva in Mozart's *Marriage of Figaro*, to sounding pretty good as Lady Macbeth in Shakespeare's *Macbeth*. There might be a future on the stage after all.

The disastrous opera performances took place in the mammoth New Orleans St. Charles Theatre (the stage alone was 95 feet x 90 feet), on December 1, 1835, before a seasoned and critical audience. The nineteen-year-old Bostonian strained in that cavernous house to reach the high notes of Mozart's Countess Almaviva. No bravas, only stony silence greeted her arias, and after a second performance of the opera, when the theatre critic in the New Orleans *Bee* declared "Miss Cushman the worst countess we have had the honor of seeing for some time," the theatre manager pulled the show. The other singing roles she was given in fulfillment of her contract received even worse comment: "we would as soon hear a peacock attempt the carols of a nightingale as to listen to her squalling caricature of singing." The *Bee* gave its final denunciation in April when Cushman attempted to sing the role of one of Cinderella's wicked stepsisters: "Miss Cushman can sing nothing." But the critic made an additional comment that she should stick to acting, a suggestion that was not lost on the theatre manager. He decided to give the teenager a chance to work and train with the company's leading tragedienne, British actor James Barton. The first role Barton gave her to play opposite him on April 23, 1836, the day celebrated as Shakespeare's birthday, was Lady Macbeth.

In his fine biography of Cushman, Joseph Leach recreates the ardor of Cushman's training with Barton, and the thrilling reception of her first performance of Lady Macbeth. As he instructed Cushman, Barton had before his eyes the performances of Kemble and Cooper who had trained with

Melmoth, and of Siddons, who in turn had trained with Thomas Sheridan, Melmoth's mentor. But he urged his young protégée to explore her inner and unique resources, the passion and temper and domineering strength that Cushman had, and Siddons lacked. "This Lady Macbeth embodied a virile determination to cower her weakling husband into total obedience.... the goading force in an essentially masculine play, hands clutching a pair of daggers, eyes blazing an obsessed ambition, chin set firm to the task ahead.... a monumental compound of fierce intensity and organ-like tones." With the result that "an electrified audience saw 'a pantheress let loose.'"[8] Bearing little resemblance to her predecessors, the tall, muscular, square-jawed, Boston-born Yankee of histrionic Irish parentage on her mother's side (Grandma Babbitt was a great mimic of animal sounds), had launched her imposing and overpowering Lady Macbeth, a stage presence that would impress upon future audiences—and especially the actors who played her Macbeth—fear of such a partner, eliciting the phrase, "She made me do it!"

Six months later Cushman played Lady Macbeth opposite the celebrated English-born actor Junius Brutus Booth, on October 11, 1836, at the Pearl Street Theatre in Albany, New York. Booth, twenty years Cushman's senior, at the height of his fame, thereafter remained a valued advisor and friend to Cushman. When she made plans to launch her career in London, he advised her to hold off playing her two big roles that had made her name in America, Lady Macbeth and Meg Merrilies, until the English audiences had acquired a taste for her in other parts. This advice Cushman wisely followed, making her London debut as the smart and witty Beatrice in *Much Ado About Nothing*. Junius Booth, Sr., lived long enough to hear of Cushman's reputation as the most famous and representative Lady Macbeth in the English-speaking world, but not long enough to witness his actor sons playing opposite her in *Macbeth*—all three of them, Edwin, Junius, Jr., and John Wilkes.

Another mentor to Cushman, like Booth, a generation older than the actress, William Charles Macready first played *Macbeth* together with Cushman at Philadelphia's Walnut Street Theatre in 1843. Cushman studied carefully Macready's intelligent and technically precise acting, so closely as to copy his vocal patterns and body movements. Physically the same size, they even looked alike, with the same large and high forehead, diminished nose, and forceful chin. And they sounded alike, sharing the same deep tones and quivering r's. And they moved alike, walking on the toes of their feet. London audiences, who were as eager as American ones to claim Cushman as the leading tragedian of the age, quipped that Cushman and

Macready were so much alike they were interchangeable in the roles of Lady
Macbeth and Macbeth. A British wag put the resemblance in verse:

What figure is that which appears on the scene?
Tis Madame Macready—Miss Cushman, I mean,
What a wondrous resemblance! The walk on the toes,
The eloquent, short, intellectual nose;
The bend of the knees, the slight sneer of the lip,
The frown on the forehead, the hand on the hip.
In the chin, in the voice, 'tis the same to a tittle,
Miss Cushman is Mister Macready in little;
The lady before us might very well pass
For the gentleman viewed the wrong way of the glass.
No fault with the striking resemblance we find,
'Tis not in the person alone, but the mind.[9]

Known for his arrogance and scornful superiority over all other actors,
Macready did manage mild praise for Cushman—perhaps because of her
resemblance to him: "The Miss Cushman who acted Lady Macbeth interested me much....she showed mind and sympathy with me; a novelty so
refreshing to me on stage."[10] Of the two, Cushman was better liked in
America, as Macready projected an attitude of superiority that rankled
coworkers and audiences alike. American "patriots" were especially sensitive to this British foreigner's arrogance, as New York's Astor Place Riot
would bear out, notwithstanding the American literati (such as Irving,
Melville, and Longfellow) who welcomed the scholarly Shakespearean
actor to the American stage.[11]

Those apprenticeship years in Philadelphia in the early 1840s gave
Charlotte Cushman her sense of self, off the stage as well as on. Her infatua-
tion with Fanny Kemble Butler lasted two years (1842–1844), before Fanny
banished her. (They would renew a friendly correspondence over twenty
years later.) Charlotte had sought Fanny's affections; but the older actress,
"Mrs. Butler," beset with worries about her failing marriage and the custody
of her two children that depended partly on her not resuming her theatrical
career, valued Cushman as a professional colleague and friend, not an intimate one. Evidently Cushman, who was managing Philadelphia's Walnut
Street Theatre for the 1843–1844 season, was more interested in Fanny personally than professionally, and she may have been too much interference in
the Butlers' stormy marriage. In any case, Fanny refused her company. With
characteristic resilience, Charlotte turned her attentions elsewhere, and fell
in love with Rosalie Sully, daughter of artist Thomas Sully, who painted

a pleasing portrait of the twenty-six-year-old Cushman during her frequent visits to the Sully household. A passionate correspondence between the two young women that began when Charlotte moved to Britain ended before they could see one another again when young Rosalie died.

Between the age of nineteen, when Cushman first played Lady Macbeth in New Orleans, and the age of twenty-eight when she left America for Europe, Cushman achieved recognition in America as a leading actress of tragedy and character roles. But with success in London's theatre world still considered the pinnacle of achievement for Shakespearean actors, Charlotte Cushman decided to follow after William Charles Macready, "her idol," who had returned to London from his American tour. "It was on Macready's advice that she had come to England to practice her craft, and the Englishman had furnished her with letters of introduction from the London literati." Her success was immediate: "From her first night, she was hailed as the finest actress in the English-speaking world: the papers leaped over themselves to panegyrize her as the possessor of a godlike gift, a dizzying admixture of earnestness, intensity, sensitivity, and passion." Considering her above any living actresses, London's critics compared Cushman to Siddons. Such praise fell hard on Cushman's fellow native-born actor, Edwin Forrest, who costarred for her London debut of Lady Macbeth. "Forrest was outraged that a minor American actor had stolen his crown." He accused her of "Macreadyism, which to him meant mannered, mechanical acting," and "labeled her 'Macready in petticoats.'"[12]

While she preferred performing her Lady Macbeth with Macready's Macbeth, Charlotte Cushman appreciated how Forrest filled the part of a "Bowery B'hoy Macbeth," a hard-drinking tough guy. For she attributed much of the behavior of both Macbeth and Lady Macbeth to drunkenness, and thought Macbeth should be the "grandfather of all the Bowery villains...shaped by the toughs and rowdies and sharp operators who circulated through places like the Bowery." Macbeth should have the "air of reckless intoxication" that Lady Macbeth had, with Shakespeare giving the direction on the line: "That which hath made them drunk, hath made me bold:/What hath quench'd them, hath given me fire" (II, ii, 3–4). That is what Cushman said. In practice, her all-time favorite Macbeth was Macready, who "grasped its [Macbeth's] heart and executed it with a splendor."[13] In practice, Cushman did not associate her style of acting with the Bowery B'hoys. "She never professed to the proletarian appeal of Forrest" and his American school of acting, even though the two Americans were regarded as peers, both of the same generation (he was ten years older), and the two leading native-born American actors whom critics such as Walt Whitman

most admired and celebrated. Cushman was "far more interested in culti-
vating the favor of the 'upper crust' of society and the arts."[14]

For four years Cushman worked the British Isles, finishing with a command performance before Queen Victoria for William Charles Macready's
benefit in 1848. The residency included extensive tours in England,
Scotland, and Ireland, the route forged by previous generations of strolling
players. Dubliners held on to Cushman for several months. And in her tour
of Scotland, she, like other famous stage Lady Macbeths before and after,
paid homage to the historical Gruoch Macbeth's origins. Europe became
Cushman's home for many more years to come. The handsome fortune she
had accumulated by 1850 permitted her to maintain an elegant townhouse
in London where she spent summers, and a villa in Rome where she chose
to live the rest of the time. She made frequent visits to her dressmaker
in Paris, and infrequent but extensive and profitable performance tours to
the United States. Cushman shared some of her semi-retirement in Rome
"married" to the American sculptor, Emma Stebbins (whose most famous
sculpture is now the "Angel in America," in New York City's Central Park),
and supporting a large coterie of female artist friends in her large villa. The
absence of male lovers in her life gave her the reputation of "virgin queen"
of the stage, and she was widely publicized and praised for her upstanding
and virtuous character in a profession decried for its loose (heterosexual)
women. The admiring public was either unaware or chose to be discreetly
unobservant of her lesbian affairs and Boston marriages. Indeed, Cushman's
masculinity added to her acclaim, her role of Romeo was said to have swept
women in the audience off their feet because as a woman Cushman knew
what a woman wanted from someone making love to them. The London
production ran for eighty nights, Charlotte's "shrewish" sister, Susan, playing Juliet. An observer found Charlotte's fencing remarkable, how with one
sword thrust, "as lightening strikes the pine," she struck down Tybalt.[15]

Cushman returned to the United States for a triumphal tour to several major cities in August of 1849, only a few months after her mentor,
Macready finished his last American tour, escaping with his life the may-
hem of the Astor Place Riot in May. Not directly involved, Cushman had
indirectly participated as a third party in the rivalry and hostility that had
developed and intensified between Macready and Forrest during the years
she performed with both of them in London. Cushman and Forrest played
Macbeth together only once, for her London debut in the role in 1845, when
her costar attributed her popularity with London audiences to Macready's
influence, and his own lackluster reception to British anti-Americanism.
Forrest's resentment and jealousy of Macready boiled over while watching

him play Hamlet. Just when Macready put on an "antic disposition" Forrest let out a single, long and loud hiss that momentarily stunned the performer and Edinburgh audience into stony silence. Macready and his supporters were aghast at Forrest's rude and unprofessional behavior toward a fellow theatre artist. Forrest proceeded to defend himself at length in newspapers and pamphlets on the grounds that Macready's performance was flawed and he had the right to show his displeasure as an audience member (adding "falsehoods" such as that he wasn't the only one hissing, when in fact he was).

The Astor Place Riot that resulted from Macready and Forrest performing in competing productions of *Macbeth* in New York City in May of 1849 had as much to do with the one being a British actor and the other an American one, as with their personal feelings and behavior toward one another, and their different approaches to acting Shakespeare. To the British, Forrest represented the impudence and coarseness of a Yankee bully. To the American fans of Forrest, Macready represented the elitism and arrogance of an English snob. Onstage, "Macready was the scholar attempting to inject some taste and decorum into the theatre.... Forrest was the crowd pleaser who thrust his own rugged personality on the stage.... Macready was the greater actor, but Forrest was the greater star."[16] A culture war between Britain and America underlay these differences, and for a time in the 1840s, there was even a possibility of an outright, third war with Britain over America's expansion into the Oregon Territory that extended into British-held Canada. (Instead the United States waged war against Mexico for Texas.) While military war between the two nations was averted, the culture war was not.[17] The competing appearances of the two reigning Macbeth actors brought that culture war into focus in the newspapers, theatres, and streets of New York City, where Forrest played at the Broadway Theatre and Macready at the Astor Place Opera House. Anti-English sentiment was strong in New York, home to a large Irish immigrant population, augmented at this time by those able to survive and flee the great potato famine in Ireland, a working class that considered Forrest one of its own, averse to "high culture" as represented by Macready.[18] The deadly riot that ensued demonstrates how much of a rallying cry the play *Macbeth* has been at times when Americans feel threatened or insulted. Both actresses playing Lady Macbeth, Julia Wallack at the Broadway and Mrs. Coleman-Pope at Astor Place, were British. Macready's Lady Macbeth was observed to have "stood without flinching by the side of Macbeth, displaying undaunted mettle," while in the hurly burly "stones crashed through the windows" of the Astor Opera House, and the "rattle of musketry" could be heard from outside.[19] "Troops of foot and one of horse…passed entirely around the [Astor Opera House] building, partially dispersing the mob." The riot act, permitting firing from the troops, had been read out to the mob, but could not be heard due to all the noise and commotion.[20] Over two dozen died from bullet wounds, rioters and innocent bystanders; and three times as many were wounded. Macready made it through the performance and escaped.

Some of the "rowdies" who stormed the Astor Place Opera House confessed to joining the mob simply for a good "rumble." Others joined as patriots. Forrest's faction put out handbills preceding Macready's fateful performance: "Working men! Shall Americans or English rule in this country? The crew of the British steamers have threatened all Americans who shall dare to appear this night at the English Aristocratic Opera-House. Workingmen! Freemen! Stand up to your Lawful Rights!" Their rallying cry as they marched through the streets was straight from the Witches' mouths in *Macbeth*:

When shall we three meet again
In thunder, lightening, or in rain?
When the hurlyburly's done,
When the battle's lost and won.[21]

These were mid-nineteenth-century democratic, working-class Americans chanting lines written by an early-seventeenth-century monarchist English playwright for the performance of male Jacobean actors dressed as female witches to simulate stalking an eleventh-century battle between a Scottish king and the English forces! But by the mid-nineteenth century *Macbeth* had become as much America's property as it was Britain's, if not more so.

Prologue to the Civil War, the *Macbeth* riot at Astor Place in New York City seemed an invocation to the war gods that "blood will have blood" (Macbeth 3:2:122). With the outbreak of the Civil War, the play *Macbeth* became a mirror held up to the nature of war-torn America, reflecting the horrors of kin killing kin, of assassination. Over half a million Americans lost their lives, more than in all other of America's wars combined. *Macbeth* was constantly before the public throughout the Civil War, in production in both the North and the South. Charlotte Cushman performed Lady Macbeth before the President and First Lady in Washington, D.C. in the fall of the 1863 a few weeks before Abraham Lincoln delivered his

Gettysburg Address. On the other side of the Mason Dixon line, the president and "Mrs. President," for that is what Mrs. Jefferson Davis was called in the South, had many an opportunity to attend *Macbeth* at the Richmond Theatre where it received more performances than any other play during the war. They might have seen Clementina DeBar play Lady Macbeth, Richmond's reigning actress in that role, Irish-born and former wife of Junius Booth, Jr.[22] DeBar's brother ran a theatre in Saint Louis where the youngest of the Booth brothers, John Wilkes, often appeared in the role of Macbeth. A popular matinee idol in both the North and the South, Wilkes performed Macbeth in most major theatres during the Civil War.

Forty-four-year-old Charlotte Cushman played Lady Macbeth in the production that gave twenty-year-old John Wilkes Booth his first performance in the play *Macbeth*. He did not play her husband, Macbeth, in this May 1858 production, but rather the "First Apparition," the first of three ghost-like figures conjured from the witches' cauldron to show Macbeth his future. Booth's apparition on the stage of Philadelphia's Arch Street Theatre would have shown only his helmeted head, mysteriously appearing in the cauldron's vapors to a clap of thunder, intoning the warning: "Macbeth, Macbeth, Macbeth: Beware Macduff, Beware the Thane of Fife: dismiss me. Enough." After which the Apparition "descends." From this eerily prophetic, if not humble beginning, a mere two years later, precisely when the newly elected President Lincoln and his wife were traveling through Albany on their way to the White House, John Wilkes Booth was the featured player in Albany's theatre, performing all lead roles, including that of Macbeth. On the farm in Maryland, alone with his mother and sister and the black farm workers (not slaves), the boy John Wilkes secretly planned to be an actor in spite of his family's objections. He started practicing. And one of his characters was Lady Macbeth. Booth's sister Asia remembers her brother as a youngster posing as Lady Macbeth before a mirror, "He put on my long-trained dress and walked before the long glass, declaring that he would succeed as Lady Macbeth in the sleep-walking scene." He "practiced elocution in the woods every day."

> He secretly "got himself up" after Charlotte Cushman...and terrified me and all the darkies, who shrieked, "Ondress Mars Johnie, ondress him!"....
> Dressed in my skirts, with a little scarf held over his shoulders, he walked the room before the mirror, becoming more and more charmed with himself. He said merrily, "I'll walk across the fields yonder, to see if the darkies can discover me." He put on the tiny bonnet then in fashion, and went out across the fields. The men took off their hats, as they paused in their work to salute him.

He...came back to the house delighted with his success, which he attributed to his "elegant deportment."[23]

He might have attributed bemused courtesy to his black laborers as well.

Begun in youthful jest, Booth conjured up the character of Lady Macbeth in earnest at the end of his short life. After shooting Abraham Lincoln in the back of the head, Wilkes tried to follow his preplanned escape route on a broken leg, a bitter mockery of an actor told to break his leg as a warding off of bad luck. He had never missed that high jump, a feat he had done well over fifty times playing Macbeth and leaping from a precipice down into the Witches den. But his spur had caught in the bunting on the president's box as he jumped down to the stage floor. Dragging his body through woods, wetlands and farms to his own fatal bullet wound in the back of the neck in a burning barn, Wilkes in his last role as a real assassin identified with Macbeth—and Lady Macbeth. He wrote in his diary, "I must fight the course," echoing Macbeth when that character faces a desperate fight to the finish. Booth adds, "Tis all that's left me." Lady Macbeth was on John Wilkes' mind as he wrote a note to the doctor who refused to treat his broken leg but gave him a bite of food before sending him away. To Booth the doctor's qualified help was begrudging, provoking him to write the letter. To underline the doctor's offense, Wilkes uses some lines of Lady Macbeth's in the banquet scene, when she asks for a toast, a ceremony of greeting and kind wishes:

> My Royall Lord,
> You do not give the Cheer, the Feast is sold
> That is not often vouch'd, while 'tis a making:
> 'Tis given, with welcome: to feed were best at home:
> From thence, the sauce to meat is Ceremony,
> Meeting were bare without it. (*Macbeth* III, iv)

Booth enclosed some money with the letter to pay for the food, since it was not given "with welcome" or sincere "ceremony" of hospitality.

"To Dr. Richard H. Stewart, 'Cleydael,' King George County, Virginia, 24 April 1865

> Dear Sir: Forgive me, but I have some little pride. I hate to blame you for your want of hospitality: you know your own affairs. I was sick and tired, with a broken leg, in need of medical advice. I would not have turned a dog from my door in such a condition. However, you were kind enough to give me something to eat, for which I not only thank you, but, on account of

the reluctant manner in which it was bestowed, I feel bound to pay for it. It is not the substance, but the manner in which kindness is extended that makes one happy in the acceptance thereof. *The sauce to meat is ceremony; meeting were bare without it.* Be kind enough to accept the enclosed two dollars and a half (though hard to spare) for what we have received."

Yours respectfully,
Stranger.[24]

Perhaps Shakespeare's word play with "meat" and "meeting" appealed to Booth's sense of irony, for he prided himself on his intellect. The actor compares himself in his diary to Brutus and William Tell, two admired assassins dramatized by Shakespeare and Schiller. But Macbeth and Lady Macbeth are the ones that spring to his mind as he agonizes over the circumstances of his own demise.

Between these "performances" of Lady Macbeth in his youth and at the end, Wilkes conducted a stellar acting career while at the same time running quinine from Canada for the Confederate hospitals in the South. His identity as a member of a famous family of actors, and becoming one in his own right, gave him cover for his spy activities while performing on the stages in the North. He created an athletic Macbeth, the Errol Flynn or Laurence Olivier of his day, making "staggering leaps off precipices and battlements." He put this staging to particularly good effect in the scene where Macbeth seeks out the Wayward Sisters for more prophecies: "When he appeared before the witches in Macbeth ... he had to jump from a high mound of rocks down in to the scene, where lime lights produced effective boiling cauldrons for the witches, illuminated his flying entrances and pinpointed faces in the dark muslin trees of the stage forest."[25] Also, like Laurence Olivier, Booth learned to pace the characterization to build in strength *after* the first act assassination of Duncan, not to climax with the assassination as so many actors did (and do). Playing Macbeth in New York City in 1862, John Wilkes Booth inspired one newspaper critic to give a detailed account of his performance and the actor's fine "points," observing that Booth "finely portrays the irresolution of Macbeth, from the first interview with his wife." However, "the dagger scene was not great; Mr. Booth lacks the delicacy of execution necessary to embody the emotions of supernatural fear." Just before the banquet scene "his reading of 'Duncan is in his grave,' was a fine touch of pathos, made solemn by remorse." And then in the banquet scene, "he was forcible without ranting, a fact greatly in his favor, since so many Macbeths tear themselves in these celebrated speeches." When Banquo's ghost makes its last exit, Booth's "sudden transition from

quivering fear to courteous and even careless ease...was a good point."
From that scene to the end of the play "he was good throughout," "keeping
well in view of the remorse and fear which struggle in Macbeth's troubled
heart." Finally, almost as if it went without saying, the reviewer remarks on
Booth's fight scenes, "Of course the combat was good, though less terrific
than in [his] Richard [III]."[26]

Playing Lady Macbeth to Wilkes' Macbeth, Mrs. Farren (Mary Anne
Russell, or Mrs. George P. Farren[27]), was an established actress twice his age
who played Queen Elizabeth to Wilkes' Richard III, and Queen Gertrude
to his Hamlet. When they played Baltimore, a critic there gave the laurels to
Mrs. Farren as the "best Lady Macbeth upon the stage." How Mrs. Farren
played Lady Macbeth, and what she thought of audience intelligence, the
actress Clara Morris learned straight from the old actress herself. The much
younger actress was intending to play the role as a sensitive, almost sympathetic character, when Mrs. Farren intervened. "The louder, more violent,
more declamatory I was the better the people liked me. They expect to see
Macbeth bullied into action, to speak frankly." When Morris tried to argue,
wondering what the audience would think—and before she could finish her
sentence, Farren interrupted, "The public does not think."[28]

Performances in New York City garnered John Wilkes extensive praise,
and a closer look from a critic who attended Booth's performance of
Richard III at Wallack's Theatre, who didn't like Wilkes' quirks, his more
"cunning expressions," such as the comic mannerism of closing one eye,
and another of half clenching his hand to regard his fingernails. "This is
also a fraternal habit, and we presume is inherited, for those things come
down through the generations as much as...color of eyes or hair." What
must have made Booth proud were the critic's praises of his "intellectual
breadth" and "superior powers of concentration," for John Wilkes considered himself a thinker.

> John Wilkes Booth has great natural gifts for the stage, and an amount of intel-
> lectual breadth in one so young that is most remarkable.... he is not amenable
> to the charge of pompous diction and laboriously unnatural sounds.... [he]
> appears to have mastered especially the rude laconism which Shakespeare puts
> in the tyrant's mouth: for he never drawls, but goes on quickly and conversa-
> tionally always as regards time.... a player who understands the art of making
> talk and action vital.... superior powers of concentration.[29]

The author of this piece, with its close attention to Booth family traits,
might well have been Adam Badeau, drama critic and cultural essayist

bylined as "the Vagabond," and an intimate friend of Wilkes' brother, Edwin. By the time of this review (1862), Badeau had joined the Union Army and become General Ulysses S. Grant's private secretary (later ghost writer for Grant's memoirs). Considering that during the 1863 Draft Riots, Badeau was in Edwin Booth's New York apartment recovering from a battle wound, and witness to John Wilkes' protecting a black worker from the rioters, he may well have been continuing his vagabond journalism as time and circumstances permitted. At the height of his fame as an actor, in 1863, John Wilkes Booth performed in Washington, D.C., billed as "The Youngest 'Star' in the World" in a D.C. paper. After one successful week at Grover's Theatre, he leased the old Washington Theatre and managed his own run of two more weeks, playing Macbeth for his benefit. The engagement was regarded as both brilliant and lucrative. Having seen and admired the actor's performances in Washington, President Abraham Lincoln is said to have made several overtures to meet the popular young star. Lincoln's secretary accompanied his boss to see Wilkes in at least two performances, one the secretary thought "too tame" and another Lincoln thought "rapturous." But John Wilkes would not be wooed. He purportedly said that "he would rather have the applause of a Nigger."[30]

The pivotal year of the Civil War when the North began to win began with Lincoln's Emancipation Proclamation on January 1, 1863. It also marked Shakespeare's three-hundredth birthday in April, celebrated in New York City with the dedication of a statue of Shakespeare in Central Park. To help pay for it, a benefit production of *Julius Caesar* starring the three Booth brothers—John Wilkes as Anthony, Edwin as Brutus, and Junius Jr. as Cassius—was staged in New York City. Just ten days after the Battle of Gettysburg that turned the tide in favor of the Union, on July 13, the New York Draft Riot started at 3rd Avenue and 46th Street where the mob burned down the building that was to have been where the provost marshal would spin the wheel to draw draft numbers. For four days the mob rampaged through the streets, from Union Square to Central Park, targeting and burning abolitionists' houses, tearing up rail tracks, lynching African Americans, even attacking an orphanage of black children. "Only a heavy rainfall prevented general conflagration." The riot subsided after the federal government rescinded the draft for New York City and Brooklyn.[31] In a New York apartment building where lived Cushman's principal Civil War Macbeth actor, Edwin Booth, his brother John Wilkes, there on a visit, hid and guarded a black worker for days until the riots were over. The rioters killed over a thousand innocent people, most of them African Americans.

In 1863, performances of *Macbeth* proliferated and Charlotte Cushman performed Lady Macbeth to help raise money for the Union's hospitals and wounded soldiers. Numerous productions of Shakespeare's *Macbeth* toured. And even a German-speaking company played *Macbeth* in a German translation in New York. Verdi's opera based on Macbeth was the hit of the opera season with Giuseppina Medori singing the cruel Lady Macbeth in New York at the Academy of Music on October 21, 1863, followed the next night by Charlotte Cushman playing Shakespeare's Lady Macbeth in the same theatre. Perhaps the stage sets and costumes and even some of the performers may have been the same for both the opera and the play, since Max Maretzek was the producer/impresario for both events, the same Maretzek who took over the Astor Opera House after the disastrous riots of 1849.[32] And *Macbeth* was the play selected by the Sanitary Commission for a series of performances in five cities to raise money for the Commission's hospital relief fund, with the star performer, Cushman, playing Lady Macbeth in all five. The performance in the Capital took place on October 17, 1863, in Grover's Theatre with the President and First Lady attending in the president's box. Charlotte Cushman was in Rome when she received the invitation from the Sanitary Commission to make the benefit tour. She agreed on the grounds that she would play Lady Macbeth, and then received a letter from her costar, Edwin Booth, requesting that they do a different play. He argued that *Macbeth* would be too expensive to produce and would diminish the Commission's receipts.[33] This was perhaps a little ingenuous on Booth's part, since *Macbeth* was a starring vehicle for Charlotte more than for Edwin, who no doubt would have preferred *Hamlet, his* starring vehicle. Cushman physically towered over the much shorter Edwin Booth, who half joked with his friend Julia Ward Howe that he felt like telling Cushman as Lady Macbeth to kill Duncan herself since she was so much bigger than he was. And he complained that the actress left bruises on his shoulder when she grabbed him, half carrying and half dragging him offstage after the murder of Duncan. She bossed him around in "cello like" tones, and physically attacked him. It was all Edwin Forrest, who was in the audience, could do to keep from laughing at Cushman when she spoke Lady Macbeth's line in the sleepwalking scene: "All the perfumes of Arabia will not sweeten this little hand," when that hand was "as big as a cod fish." Edwin Booth "would have preferred a red-haired little enchantress, very feminine in her ambitions, to Cushman's raven-haired Amazon who bullied her husband, stalked him into a corner and then, as somebody who saw her put it, regularly 'pitched into him' with lifted arm and large, meaty fist." For her part, Cushman had little positive to say about Edwin, either. In the 1863 *Macbeth* rehearsals, she found that Edwin Booth played the warrior Macbeth as if it were Hamlet, an "insipid refined intellectual," and in performance was no more than a "mere willow."[34]

Figure 5 Charlotte Cushman as Lady Macbeth. Engraving in author's possession.

Adam Badeau, Edwin's best friend and culture critic for a New York paper in the 1850s, had already observed that Cushman's acting had taste and intellect, but that she was not much of a woman: "I seldom have been able to detect true tenderness in Miss Cushman; I have seldom noticed real womanly feeling. Those characters in which she excels are masculine." Badeau's articles written for New York's *Sunday Times* under his pen name of "Vagabond," cover a wide variety of subjects with a remarkably modern approach to the arts. Albert Furtwangler describes him as "something of a dandy," and attributes his friendship with Edwin Booth as "evidently" "a homosexual attraction to Booth." Whether or not that was true, Badeau did set out to educate his friend, introducing him to fine arts and urging him "to read critics like Hazlitt, Goethe, and Georges [*sic*] Sand." "He took him to libraries and galleries to teach him about authentic periods and styles. He lectured to him to control his drinking and to learn French. And Badeau's army service as General Grant's secretary drew Edwin into personal sympathy for the Union cause; he and John Wilkes nursed Badeau at Booth's New York house after he was seriously wounded in 1863."[35]

While Cushman had admired and been friends with Edwin's father, she never grew close to Edwin, especially when he wooed and won Mary Devlin, an actress who had played Juliet to Cushman's Romeo. Cushman resented Booth's preventing Devlin from continuing her acting career after they were married, a career that had shown great promise. (Booth and Devlin married in 1860, with Adam Badeau and John Wilkes Booth as witnesses.) And when Devlin died in Boston in 1863, her daughter barely two years old, with Edwin away in New York City on a drinking binge, Cushman felt justified in her assessment that he was not a gentleman. "To my mind he has not more gentlemanly instincts, which would make him hesitate to hurt a woman or give her pain, than Mr. Edwin Forrest." Damning, indeed. Such men were "masters merely for the sake of...showing their power over a weak woman."[36] But however much they complained of one another in 1863, Charlotte and Edwin ended their professional relationship amicably. When Cushman resumed acting in 1870 she played Lady Macbeth again to Edwin Booth's Macbeth. And in 1875 he honored her final retirement at Booth's Theatre in New York with an enormous celebration followed by a parade down the street to her hotel, where a throng of thousands serenaded her beneath her hotel balcony.

Cushman's Civil War Lady Macbeth played to rave notices and sold out performances in her five-city tour of Philadelphia, New York, Boston, Baltimore, and Washington, D.C. Filling these large houses with a voice that could reach the very back even in a whisper, with a throat "like the Arc de Triumphe," she succeeded in raising over $8,000 for the Sanitary Commission. In addition, Cushman performed Lady Macbeth in Brooklyn to benefit the American Dramatic Fund, with some reports that John Wilkes Booth played her Macbeth there. More credibly, it was an actor named Boniface, for according to the *New Haven Register* for October

1863, John Wilkes was scheduled to play Richard III and Hamlet in New Haven during the week that Cushman played Lady Macbeth with Edwin Booth in New York City and with George Boniface in Brooklyn.[37] Clearly, Cushman had other Macbeths besides Edwin Booth on her 1863 tour. J.W. Wallack played Macbeth for the performance that the Lincolns attended in Washington, D.C. To the chagrin of Charlotte's Macbeths, their names disappeared under the banner headline of Charlotte Cushman playing Lady Macbeth. One playbill even bills Hecate in the secondary slot below Cushman's bold-face name, well above the listing for Macbeth.

With such attention, such success and at a time of such anxiety, Cushman's reputation as America's foremost Lady Macbeth was reaffirmed. George Templeton Strong, a civic leader in New York and commissioner for the U.S. Sanitary Commission, records in his diary his impressions of Cushman's performance for the New York City engagement of October 22, 1863, a Thursday.

> Tonight at the Academy of Music. . . . *Macbeth* for the benefit of the Sanitary Commission, with Charlotte Cushman and Booth; a strong cast. Immensely crowded house. The commission would have made ten thousand dollars but for the fact that seats were bought up by speculators instead of being sold at auction as they should have been. They were selling at twenty dollars each in Wall Street today. The performance excellent. The sleep-walking particularly intense; indeed, Miss Charlotte Cushman is the best Lady Macbeth I ever saw—beyond all comparison.

The following Tuesday (October 27) the Strongs had Charlotte Cushman to dinner, along with "Bellows, Van Buren, Agnew, and Dr. Weston," and Strong found Cushman remarkable in person as well as on the stage, if not more so. "The tragedienne is a cultivated woman and made herself most agreeable. She looks far better off the stage than on it."[38]

Nineteenth-century critic William Winter remembers vividly how Cushman performed Lady Macbeth, becoming a legend in her own time, honored and celebrated wherever she went. He was still arguing thirty years after her death in favor of her Lady Macbeth over more recent interpretations. In terms of technique, he observed how Cushman had none of the idiosyncrasies of "modern" actresses. Rather than Sarah Bernhardt's "long pauses" and stares fixed "at nothing," or Eleanor Duse's wandering "to the back drop and whisper[ing] to the scenery," Cushman had "always a distinct purpose, and that purpose she distinctly executed." Winter defends Cushman against the accusation that her performance style was "melodramatic," rather, he says, her style was "strong, definite, bold and free." She did not "refine" "Shakespeare's meaning," as had become so "common of late years"; but "perceived and imparted the obvious meaning." For Winter, Cushman's Lady Macbeth made manifest Shakespeare's play as "the most weird, portentous, sinister, afflicting work of poetic imagination that the brain of man has produced." Images from her performance horrified and haunted him long after the actress's death, with her "personification of evil," "deep, thrilling, pitiless tones," and "wild, roving, inspired glances." His blood still chilled with the memory of her "fiend-driven" invocation of dark forces, those "murdering ministers." "Nothing has been seen since her time to surpass her appalling importment of predestinate evil and sinister force," "the awe-inspiring, preternatural horror which is the spirit of that great tragedy."[39]

Losing a long struggle with breast cancer, Cushman performed Lady Macbeth for the last time at the Academy of Music in her native city of Boston. For her address to the audience, the actress chose to speak Lady Macbeth's lines, with sincerity, not the feigning implied in Shakespeare's play. It was a curious misapplication or misinterpretation of Lady Macbeth's lines welcoming Duncan to Dunsinane, "under her battlements." Cushman used the speech, the language of which resembles that of a dissembling accountant making the figures lie, to thank her audiences for their favor and to say goodbye. But with true courtesy, not the false show of courtesy and hospitality expressed by Lady Macbeth, the aging and ailing actress spoke these lines as she bid farewell:

> All my service
> In every point twice done, and then done double,
> Were poor and single business to contend
> Against these honors, deep and broad, wherewith
> You have ever loaded me. For those of old,
> And the late dignities heaped up to them,
> I rest your debtor.[40]

6. "Hellcat" ❧

The audiences of New York's Academy of Music had the opportunity to compare Shakespeare's Lady Macbeth as performed by Charlotte Cushman, with Verdi's, a queen more evil yet, and sung by Giuseppina Medori the night before. The performance history of Giuseppe Verdi's *Macbeth* in America parallels that of Shakespeare's play, having had its most frequent performances and strongest impact during wartime. But remarkably, the opera, so popular during the Civil War with its several performances on both coasts of the United States, does not reappear on the American stage until 1941 at the beginning of World War II, concurrent with a sensationally long run of Shakespeare's play on Broadway. The large and imperial presence of Cushman, an overpowering Amazon and domineering virago figure, made Shakespeare's character seem indomitable from the outside, but by the sleepwalking scene showed her to be all too human from within. Shakespeare's play provides the language and actions for this transition. Giuseppe Verdi's score does not. Verdi's Lady Macbeth unmasks a treacherous viper within. The opera libretto changes Shakespeare's story to make Lady Macbeth the arch villain of the piece, lusting after power and completely dominating her husband and the plot, musically as well as dramatically. Unlike Shakespeare's Lady Macbeth, Verdi's is no longer ignorant of Macbeth's murderous deeds that follow their shared complicity in the murder of Duncan. It is she who plants the seeds for the murders of Banquo, Lady Macduff, and her children. In some sense (though not plot), Verdi's Lady Macbeth has more in common with Ducis' Fredegonde than Shakespeare's queen, not so coincidental when one considers that Verdi was composing his opera in Paris at the time of the 1848 Revolution. Contrasting what Verdi does with Lady Macbeth in the sleepwalking scene to Shakespeare's treatment, Jonas Barish says, "Lady Macbeth's outpouring consists of entirely new material....an unexplored realm of tormented sensibility....a last gorgeous act of assertion." The beautiful aria makes it hard for Barish "to imagine the Lady Macbeth of this scene as other than beautiful, and hard." Verdi "is not so much interested in making Lady Macbeth psychologically convincing as in making her vivid and terrifying." Throughout the opera "he inserts outbreaks of open triumph and gloating from her, which forbid any hint of the coming collapse that Shakespeare charts so carefully. Verdi never quite allows her the psychological veracity that marks her Shakespearean model. What he provides, in truth, is something closer to the 'fiend-like queen' of Malcolm's final description."[1] And while the physically overpowering Lady Macbeth of Charlotte Cushman did not mirror the appearance of First Lady Mary Todd Lincoln, Medori's Lady Macbeth in the Verdi opera looks quite like Mary. But the opera's vicious character in performance reveals none of the deep suffering shown in Shakespeare's Lady Macbeth, similarly experienced by the Civil War First Lady, Mrs. Lincoln.

Abraham Lincoln could deliver long passages of Shakespeare's plays from memory, especially from *Macbeth*, his favorite. And over the span of his twenty-three years of marriage he often read or recited aloud from them to his family. He acknowledged how he and his wife were ambitious like the Macbeths, she for him, striving for his advancement from their earliest days together, and for herself as his political as well as domestic partner. With his dry sense of humor, Lincoln obliquely compared their partnership to the Macbeths. When he was a lawyer traveling the Illinois circuit with a colleague in 1854, Lincoln spoke of "Molly," his pet name for Mary, and their shared political ambitions using the phrase from Macbeth's letter to Lady Macbeth to refer to his wife as "my dearest partner of greatness." On another occasion, a journalist sharing a train ride with the future president reported how amused Lincoln was at Mary's high expectations for him, "Mary insists that I am going to be Senator and President of the United States too," and then he laughed at such an idea. He mixed ambition with affection, confiding to a fellow onlooker at one of the First Lady's White House receptions, "My wife is as handsome as when she was a girl, and I a poor nobody then, fell in love with her and once more, have never fallen out."[2]

Mary, too, was a close reader of Shakespeare, and quoted from his plays in her letters to friends when Lincoln was courting her—and she him. When their engagement was renewed she wrote, "Richard should be himself again."[3] And *Macbeth* remained in Mary's thoughts, cropping up in her correspondence. She uses a line preceding Macbeth's famous "Tomorrow and tomorrow" speech in an 1864 letter to her friend, Senator Charles Sumner, as a means of indicating her sympathy with him as together they grieved the death of a fellow abolitionist. Macbeth's grief at his wife's death that "she should have died hereafter, there would have been a time for such a word, tomorrow and tomorrow…" rings in Mary Lincoln's mind as she writes to Sumner. Except that she changes the pronoun to "*He* should have died *hereafter* [her emphasis]," regretting Owen Lovejoy's death, an abolitionist congressman from Illinois who had died suddenly. In another letter from Europe written four years after her husband's death, Mary gives an enthusiastic account of her tour of Scotland, her ancestral home, with a reference to Duncan, the king assassinated by Macbeth. She comments hurriedly "*Castles unnumerable*—… visited Glamis castle—saw the room & the bed on which poor king Duncan was murdered."[4]

Mary Todd Lincoln was different from the other Washington wives. They had little relish or preparation for active participation in their husband's affairs, or politics in general. "Wives were generally undereducated, poorly read, and completely ignorant of the public affairs that sustained conversation in wartime Washington." Mary was well educated, well read, and knowledgeable about public affairs, and had been since growing up in a household that welcomed her participation in political discussions. She was also attractive, fashionable, and sociable, "With a natural taste for the spotlight that entertaining brings and a sense of duty that matched her husband's, Mary Lincoln charmed her guests." Biographer Janet Baker draws on a wide variety of contemporary accounts. She quotes historian George Bancroft who wrote glowingly about his visit with the First Lady, how she held her own in conversation with him, conversing one-on-one over a wide range of topics, only the two of them left in the reception room. Regarding the war, he says she "repudiates the idea that her secessionist brothers can have any influence on her." On the press she "spoke of the *Herald* as a paper friendly to Mr. Lincoln" and eloquently discussed its coverage of the president. She spoke of the White House renewal and "her elegant fitting up of Mr. Lincoln's room—her conservatory and love of flowers." On parting, she extended a gracious invitation to Bancroft to come back, and told him she would send him a bouquet of her flowers. The historian went home "entranced"—and subsequently received a bouquet of flowers from Mary's White House green house.[5] Sending flowers from the White House to colleagues and visitors of distinction, as well as hand delivering them to wounded soldiers in Washington's hospitals, became something of a hallmark of Mary Lincoln's management of the White House. But "eloquent," "gracious," "entrancing," Bancroft's adjectives for the First Lady, were not the words that commonly appear in descriptions of her then or now.

"Bad tempered," "deranged," "insane" became the working vocabulary of historians. Here is how a Washingtonian writing in 1941 describes the Civil War First Lady, a description born of Mary Lincoln's detractors.

> The ladies of Washington society persistently jeered at Mrs. Lincoln as an outrageous vulgarian.... [feeding] on an often unconscious perception of the dark tides of her personality. There was a look "very like cunning" in the smiling face under the artificial roses; an almost coarse tone in the affable, company voice. Mary Lincoln had been an attractive girl, plump, blue-eyed and animated. Greed and jealousy and rage leave their marks on the face of a woman of forty-three. When she had her headaches...she lost all control, picked quarrels, railed at servants and screamed like a fishwife.... If Mrs. Lincoln appeared to be acting an unnatural part when she politely received her callers in the Blue Room it was not for the reason the gossips whispered, that she had wanted gentle training, but because her emotional instability was too great to be concealed by the mask of acquired discipline.[6]

Had Mary Lincoln been First Lady at any other time than the Civil War years, her detractors probably would not have been so heated and even vicious in their criticisms. Being First Lady of a country violently divided on regional, economic, and moral issues placed Mrs. Lincoln in an unprecedented position. A tenuous one, for there was another First Lady in another White House just a few miles away in Richmond, a southern White House with close ties to anti-abolitionists and secessionists in the North and West as well as in the South, and allies in England and France, countries more friendly to the South than to the North. No First Lady of the United States before or since Mary Lincoln has had to contend with such a crisis. Initially Mary could have expected to perform her role of First Lady by fulfilling the duties as formulated and practiced by previous First Ladies, to redecorate the White House; to be a gracious and fashionable hostess, welcoming the public and dignitaries; to be a partner to her husband, looking out for his wellbeing and happiness; and to show interest and give suggestions regarding his work when appropriate. All this she did, and sometimes to a fault. Any misstep received public censure in the fractured and factious atmosphere of civil war.

Regionalism played against Mary Lincoln. Southerners and Northerners, Easterners and Westerners, all had their reasons to condemn the First Lady. Because Mary Todd was born into a Southern, aristocratic, slave owning family of Lexington, Kentucky, and because some of her brothers and cousins were fighting and dying for the Confederacy, she was hated by Northerners who accused her of being a Confederate spy, an accusation that was taken seriously enough to be investigated by Congress. Because of her active support for abolitionists and the emancipation of slaves, the First Lady was hated by Southerners—and many Northerners, and there were many—who opposed the emancipation of the slaves and detested abolitionists. When the war began, secessionists made up a majority of the capital's population and at least a third of New York City's. The border state of Maryland harbored such a threatening contingent of secessionists and anti-Lincoln Democrats that the president elect had to arrive at the capital under cover, on a night train, whisked through Maryland with guards posted along the tracks, not exactly a triumphal passage to Washington. Though a little embarrassed by such an indignity, Mr. Lincoln maintained a sense of humor and nonchalance. But Mrs. Lincoln was offended, and remained ever anxious about her husband's safety in a city full of enemies.

The Lincolns faced condescension mixed with hostility from Easterners. After their move into the White House, they were greeted by colleagues, power brokers and their wives, who considered the newcomers vulgar Westerners. (Kentucky and Illinois, the Lincolns' home states, formed part of "the West" at the time.) A group of Washington wives paid a visit to the new First Lady with an offer to help her learn their ways, offending Mary Lincoln who considered herself already an accomplished hostess. Mary's taking offense in turn offended those who had patronized her, creating a lasting wedge of dislike. Condescension toward the Lincolns continued. Some of the most vicious attacks on both Mr. and Mrs. Lincoln came from the *New York World*, a partisan newspaper that spoke for many New Yorkers who had wanted the State to secede at the beginning of the war. Here is a quote from that paper that uses a phrase reminiscent of Lady Macbeth's "infirm of purpose" used to taunt Macbeth in Shakespeare's play, twisted to defame President Lincoln's character. The journalist writing in the *World* claims that "the key to Mr. Lincoln's character" is "a hesitating *infirmity of purpose* which can with difficulty rescue itself from the suspense of conflicting motives, and makes a decision feeble when at last a decision is reached," adding that Lincoln's "personal manners" are "ungentlemanlike" and "vulgar."[7]

Mary was determined to show the Easterners that she was every bit as cultured and refined as they, and she did, earning even more calumny for being a spendthrift on White House improvements and a fashionable wardrobe at a time when the country was at war. Journalist Mary Clemmer Ames, a New Englander writing a society column in Washington, D.C. during and after the war, wrote lengthy diatribes criticizing the First Lady. Carl Sandburg's bleak picture of Mary Lincoln that evokes the sleepwalking Lady Macbeth (examined at the end of the chapter) relies heavily on Ames' opinions, even though he acknowledges in the slim biography of the First Lady that Ames' description of Mary "was partly overstatement, partly and in degree a harsh judgment." He justifies using her on the grounds that she "reported what was in the heart of numbers of women." But by the looks of it, Ames wrote history by hyperbole, based more on her partisan opinions than on any heartfelt consensus among women: "In reviewing the character of Presidents wives, we shall see that there was never one who entered the White House with such a feeling of self-satisfaction, which amounted to personal exultation, as did Mary Lincoln. To her it was the fulfillment of a life-long ambition, and she made her journey to Washington a triumphal passage." With a war going on, Ames describes what good women were doing in contrast to what the president's wife was doing. "While her sister-women scraped lint, sewed bandages, and put on nurses' caps, and gave their all to country and to death, the wife of the President spent her time in rolling to and fro between Washington and New York, intent on extravagant purchases for herself and the White House. Mrs. Lincoln seemed to have nothing to do but to 'shop.'" But what Ames condemns in Mrs. Lincoln's expenditures on refurbishing the White House, she praises in Senator Charles Sumner's sumptuous Washington house with its book and art collection.[8] Ames was mistaken, for the First Lady was active in visiting and caring for the wounded in Washington's hospital. It was little remarked upon because she made no fanfare and show about it, arranged no "photo ops."

> The thousands of wounded languishing in military hospitals throughout Washington benefited from her loving, almost maternal sympathy. She carried them flowers from the White House conservatory, had delicacies sent from the White House kitchens, and distributed among them some of the gifts sent her family. She made her hospital calls alone or with a friend such as Mary Jane Welles [wife of the Secretary of the Navy, Gideon Welles]; the visits were frequently unannounced and were rarely reported in the press, with the result that few were aware of this side of Mrs. Lincoln's character.[9]

At first, Mary was undaunted by all the negative criticism aimed at her— until national and personal tragedy broke her spirit. She went about performing her duties as First Lady, presiding over White House receptions, by all accounts, ever tireless and hospitable. But unlike the first ladies who went before her, with the exception of Abigail Adams, Mary Lincoln continued to have opinions and ideas regarding politics—and to express them, sometimes in opposition to her husband, especially when she mistrusted the men he trusted who held high positions in the government.

The First Lady's political role did not go unnoticed in the press. Not yet a year into her White House residency, the *New York Times* (February 23, 1861) reported that "Mrs. Lincoln is making and unmaking the political fortunes of men and is similar to Queen Elizabeth in her statesmanlike tastes." To parse that loaded statement leads to all manner of implications. Since the unmarried Queen Elizabeth of Shakespeare's day ruled solo, what was the *Times* saying about Abraham Lincoln's effectiveness in leading the nation? And what was the paper implying by saying that Mary Lincoln makes and unmakes men's political fortunes similar to Queen Elizabeth, when everyone knew that the English queen had personal and private reasons for favoring some of her followers and suitors over others? No doubt it was on account of certain of Mary Todd Lincoln's "favorites" that such a comparison could be made.

Some of the company the First Lady kept led to rumors that she was romantically involved with certain White House guests, her escorts to the theatre and opera when her husband was unavailable—one in particular, the "Chevalier" Henry Wikoff. A deep and lasting friendship with Senator Charles Sumner, the distinguished abolitionist and art collector from Massachusetts, withstood the false rumors and he remained a loyal friend to the First Lady well beyond her residency in the White House. Not so with Wikoff, whose reputation varied from cad to valued friend. All agreed he knew everyone who was anyone, including the ruling families of European states. Wikoff was not only on friendly terms with the politically and socially prominent, but as an impresario he promoted artists such as Fanny Essler and Jenny Lind. As a younger man in the 1830s Wikoff and his traveling companion Edwin Forrest made "the grand tour" of Europe, adding Russia, the Crimea, and Turkey. Both of them kept journals of their travels. Wikoff's diary focuses on the sights and important people he met along the way, while Forrest's reports on how each country provided for his appetites, especially the whorehouses that appear to have been his nightly haunt. Wikoff and Forrest made a strange pair of Americans traveling abroad. Unlike the tough Forrest who rose from a dirt-poor family in Philadelphia, Wikoff as described by himself in his own voluminous and highly readable memoirs, was of *haute* Philadelphia family and a man of independent means. A contemporary detractor of Wikoff—and of Mary Todd Lincoln, whom he disdainfully calls "her grace"—speculates on how Wikoff's attractions worked upon the First Lady:

> Among the persons who thus won access to her grace was the so-called "Chevalier" Wikoff, whose name figured as much as any other in the press in

those days...a sort of cosmopolitan knight-errant...but was, in fact, only a salaried spy or informer of the New York *Herald*. . . . Wikoff was of middle age, an accomplished man of the world, a fine linguist, with graceful presence, elegant manners, a conscious, condescending way—altogether, just such a man as would be looked upon as a superior being by a woman accustomed only to Western society. . . . I myself heard him compliment her upon her looks and dress. . . . She accepted Wikoff as always welcome company for visitors in her salon and on her drives.[10]

Wikoff's welcome in the Lincoln White House was short lived, lasting only the first months of the Lincoln administration. It ended when the press leaked an advance copy of the president's inaugural address, a leak attributed to Wikoff and his closeness to the First Lady. The White House gardener took the rap.

Mary Lincoln had no doubt welcomed Wikoff as a witty raconteur to her "salon." Politically she had her reasons, for she was looking over cultured gentlemen as possible candidates to replace Seward as Lincoln's secretary of state. Later in the administration, she would push for Senator Charles Sumner to replace Seward. Mary never liked William Henry Seward, initially wary of his loyalty to her husband when he made it obvious to everyone that he resented being defeated in the presidential race by a backwoodsman from out West. Then when it became apparent that with experience in Lincoln's cabinet, dinners, fireside conversations, and going to the theatre together with the president, Seward had come to appreciate Lincoln's abilities and vigor, and to regard him as a friend, Mary grew jealous of Seward. And as to foreign affairs, Mary sided with those who criticized Seward for being too disagreeable to the English and the French, evidently failing to recognize how Seward, together with Lincoln, had forged a foreign policy that kept England and France at bay and uncertain about the legitimacy of the Confederacy, in spite of both countries having strong economic interests in the South. Formerly governor of New York, U.S. senator, and rival candidate in the 1860 primary that elected Lincoln, Seward was a prominent leader of the Eastern establishment. Known for his erudition, hospitality, and affability in the North, he became "a symbol of everything the South abhorred about the North," regarding abolition of slavery especially. As for how Seward saw himself, he drew upon an unlikely source in Shakespeare: "as gentle a lion as he who played that part before the Duke, in the 'Midsummer Night's Dream.' "[11] The character of Bottom for the cosmopolitan Seward perhaps reveals an inner kindness, and certainly a sense of humor in human affairs, like Lincoln. To the First Lady, Seward seemed more like an Iago. Educated by French immigrants, and enamored of French culture and the fashions set by France's Empress Eugenia as well as by England's Queen Victoria, Mary wished her husband's administration would establish friendlier relations with foreign powers. And from her point of view, Seward was not the man to do it. She called him an enemy from within. And her distrust grew so far as to suspect the secretary of state as having been part of the conspiracy to assassinate Lincoln, even though Seward himself was nearly killed by one of Wilkes Booth's conspirators the same night the president was shot.

A passion for the theatre was one thing Mary Lincoln had in common with Henry Seward, and with her husband. In her youth she had written to one of her friends that any husband of hers would have to like going to the theatre. Lincoln was her man. He even attended the theatre by himself if just for an act, to find relief from the pressures of the war room, or with Seward if Mary was out of town or indisposed. The Lincolns and Sewards supported rival theatres in Washington, befriending the managers and hosting prominent actors and actresses in their private dinners and public benefits. Charlotte Cushman was Seward's celebrity. He had long been a close friend of the actress, ever since the 1830s when he was governor of New York and living in Albany where she played Lady Macbeth with Junius Booth, Sr. Whenever Cushman came to Washington she was his houseguest. On at least one occasion the secretary of state invited the leading lady and her costar Edwin Booth to his house for an after-performance dinner, and once offered advice to Booth on his acting that was not taken amiss by the small and melancholy older brother of John Wilkes. Seward walked the large actress of regal bearing from his palatial house over to the White House to meet with the even taller but not so regal president. Cushman first met Lincoln in July of 1861 and didn't like him at first, not finding his jokes that funny. But she went into his office prejudiced against him; he had beaten her friend Seward for the presidential nomination. And like Seward, she had supported letting the South secede in order to avoid war, and to ensure the abolition of slavery in the North. But as they talked about theatre and the Shakespeare plays that Lincoln had seen, and when he asked that she not retire until he had a chance to see her in the role of Lady Macbeth, Cushman saw "something in his somber manner, his character, and quick wit [that] made her suddenly happier about this new president."[12] When Cushman returned from Rome to perform Lady Macbeth on behalf of the Sanitary Fund in the fall of 1863, she was able to satisfy the president's wish, and play Lady Macbeth for him in Washington's Grover's National Theatre.

Just as Seward had his actor friend and correspondent in Cushman, Lincoln had his in the old actor James H. Hackett, famous for his Falstaff.

Nearing retirement, Hackett nevertheless played several times before Lincoln in Washington and received invitations to the White House for private conversations with the president. In one such conversation, Lincoln suggested that Hackett reinstate a scene he had cut from his performance of Falstaff in Shakespeare's *Henry IV, Part I*, a recommendation that demonstrates the president's close attention to the performance of Shakespeare, and specifically to his study of leadership in Shakespeare's plays. The tavern scene he wished to see Hackett perform (Act 2, scene 4) has Falstaff and the Prince drinking and play-acting: first Falstaff plays the King talking to his errant son, Prince Hal, then they switch roles. Lincoln proved wise in the ways of Shakespeare, for Falstaff in this little play-within-the-play, acting as Hal's father, berates the Prince for the bad company he has been keeping—with one exception, "that virtuous man... Falstaff... I see virtue in his looks... Him keep with, the rest banish." Then when they switch roles, Prince Hal, playing his father the King, refers to Falstaff as "that villainous abominable *misleader* of youth... that old white-bearded Satan." The joking has taken on a darker cast as Falstaff playing Hal tries to defend poor old Falstaff, concluding that if he is banished then "banish all the world!" To which the Prince as himself as King replies, "I do, I will." And he does, but not until the very end of *Henry IV, Part II* (Act 5, scene 5), when this play-acting becomes real action. Hal, having become King Henry V, does indeed banish Falstaff, beginning with "I know thee not, old man. Fall to thy prayers," concluding "I banish thee, on pain of death/As I have done the rest of my *misleaders*." A lover of words, and aside from the joking that he always enjoyed, Lincoln saw the significance of the repetition of that word "misleader" in these two scenes; the latter one, separated by two play lengths from the former, directly answers it. Hackett, however, ever the actor, focusing more on his own performance, disagreed with the president's suggestion to reinstate the scene. For Hackett the scene lacked the big comic effects he liked to perform, and made Falstaff less likeable.

The president and his Falstaff continued to converse and correspond. Significantly, in August of 1863 Lincoln wrote to Hackett about his favorite Shakespeare plays: "Some... I have never read; while others I have gone over perhaps as frequently as any professional reader [performer]. Among the latter are 'Lear,' 'Richard III,' 'Henry VIII,' 'Hamlet,' and especially 'Macbeth.' I think none equals 'Macbeth.' It is wonderful."[13] Hackett "proudly had the letter printed as a broadside" which proved to be an embarrassment when the press used it to make fun of the president. Nevertheless, Lincoln took it in stride and never lost his enthusiasm for Hackett's performances. When the actor returned to Washington in December of 1863, the president is reported to have attended four in a row.[14]

Leading up to the assassination, the First Lady had become extremely agitated and unnerved by her husband's poor health. The war was killing him. And she feared that his enemies would assassinate him. Lincoln, himself, had premonitions. Nevertheless, the president carried on, and recovered his spirits as news of the war coming to an end grew ever more encouraging. But Mary, her nerves frayed, lost her temper in an embarrassing public display of jealousy that seemed to confirm all the bad things that were being said about her. Mary Lincoln's behavior on this one occasion did more harm to her future reputation than almost any other event in her life. At General Grant's invitation the President and First Lady and their son Tad traveled to City Point to review part of the Grand Army as the war's end was coming in sight, in March of 1865. The half-open carriage in which the Missus Lincoln and Grant were riding arrived late, having badly jostled and muddied the women inside, especially upsetting Mary. By contrast, General Ord's beautiful wife had arrived on time, riding sprightly on horseback side by side with the President at the head of the procession, and mistaken by the troops for being the First Lady. Mrs. Ord graciously conceded her place to Mary Lincoln after the muddied and furious First Lady finally caught up with them. But Mary was beyond herself in rage and jealousy. Having insulted both Mrs. Grant and Mrs. Ord, Mary launched an attack on her husband in front of all the gathered officials and troops. Badeau recalls how:

> Mrs. Lincoln repeatedly attacked her husband in the presence of officers.... He bore it as Christ might have done, with an expression of pain and sadness that cut one to the heart, but with supreme calmness and dignity. He called her "Mother," with his old-time plainness; he pleaded...and endeavored to explain...till she turned on him like a tigress; and then he walked away, hiding that noble, ugly face that we might not catch the full expression of its misery.

This story, told and retold over the years, has put the stamp on Mary Lincoln as a "Hellcat" (Hay's term), a "tigress" (Badeau's), who made marriage with Lincoln "a domestic hell" (Herndon's), evocative of Malcolm's description of Lady Macbeth as a "fiend like queen." Ashamed and regretful, Mary made up with her husband in private. And in 1870 when Badeau was U.S. Consul General in London and Mary Lincoln then living there at 9, Woburn Place, he received an invitation from the former First Lady to join her for dinner with the governor of the Colorado

Territory who was in England to place his son in school with her son Tad.[15] This later courtesy from a more subdued Mary Lincoln, Badeau does not mention. He sided with Julia Grant, his boss's wife, and Mary's successor as First Lady. Julia was jealous of Mary, for Lincoln's wife was prettier, better educated, and ran a more refined White House, than the General's wife.

A more positive picture of the First Lady in the days leading up to the end of the war appears in the letters written by a French visitor to the White House to his wife, General LaFayette's granddaughter. The Marquis Adolphe de Chambrun became a welcome guest of the Lincolns. On first meeting Mary he observed that she was wearing a gown very much like one of his wife's, that "she must have been pretty when young." Her White House receptions provided a dignified atmosphere, "unlike those of her predecessors." On first meeting the president, Chambrun observed that he was "exceedingly thin, not so very tall." He saw "immense force of resistance and extreme melancholy" in Lincoln's face, concluding that he had "suffered deeply." "His eyes are superb, large and with a very profound expression when he fixes them on you." Lincoln's "simplicity," his "elevation of mind" and "heroic sentiments" obviated any awkwardness. "He dominates everyone present and maintains his exalted position without the slightest effort.[16] In April, Chambrun expanded on his portrait of the president, noting his sense of humor as well as his sadness.

> After passing some time with Mr. Lincoln you were left with a profound impression of poignant sadness. He was, however, extremely humorous, with a trace of irony always to be found in his wit. His stories bring the point out clearly. He willingly laughed either at what was being said or at what he himself was saying. Then, suddenly, he would retire into himself and close his eyes,...After a few moments...he would shake off this mysterious weight and his generous and open disposition again reasserted itself. I have counted, in one evening, more than twenty of such alternations of mood.

Chambrun was especially impressed by Lincoln's political acuity and judgment.

> No one who heard him express personal ideas, as though thinking aloud, upon some great topic or incidental question, could fail to admire his accuracy of judgment and rectitude of mind. I have heard him give opinions on statesmen and argue political problems with astounding precision. I have heard him describe a beautiful woman...with the sagacity of an artist.

And with regard to literature the French visitor found Lincoln's taste equal to any celebrated critic, the Bible and Shakespeare being his teachers.

> In discussing literature, his judgment showed a delicacy and sureness of taste which would do credit to a celebrated critic. Having formed his mind through the process of lonely meditation during his rough and humble life, he had been impressed by the two books which the Western pioneer always keeps in his log-cabin, the Bible and Shakespeare.... From Shakespeare he learned to study the passions of humanity.

What made Lincoln such a great orator were not only his incisive short and proverb-like sentences, but his knowledge of his listeners, the American people. And Chambrun, writing so soon after the assassination of Lincoln, saw clearly what Lincoln's legacy would be.

> Originality explains Mr. Lincoln's talent as an orator. His incisive speech finds its way to the heart; nay, reaches the very soul of his listeners. His short, clear sentences captivate and his remarks become proverbs. It is he who, more than any other, defined the character of the war in these well-known words: "A house divided against itself cannot stand; this government cannot continue to exist half-slave and half-free."... He knew the exact will of the American people.... Lincoln is now the greatest of all Americans. The tragic prestige which assassination lends its victims has conferred upon him a superiority over Washington himself.[17]

In the days immediately preceding Lincoln's death, Chambrun was present when Lincoln read aloud from *Macbeth*.

The Confederates were in retreat, having just set afire their capital city of Richmond before abandoning it altogether. President Lincoln and some of his top officials journeyed down the Potomac River to visit the Union troops and to see Richmond and Petersburg. Within a couple of days he was joined by his wife who brought along Senator Sumner and Chambrun, who recorded the journey in another of his letters to his wife. Before returning to Washington, docked at City Point aboard the official naval steamer, the *River Queen*, a military band from headquarters came on board and the president asked it to play the *Marseillaise* one time for himself because he liked it, and a second time for Chambrun. Lincoln then asked for *Dixie* "to show the rebels that with us in power, they will be free to hear it again." The next day, as the *River Queen* proceeded up the Potomac: "Mr. Lincoln read aloud to us for several hours. Most of the passages he selected were from Shakespeare, especially *Macbeth*. The lines after the murder of Duncan, when the new king falls a prey to moral torment, were dramatically dwelt on. ['Duncan is in his grave. After Life's fitful fever he sleeps well; Treason has done its worst; not steel nor poison, Malice domestic, foreign levy, nothing Can touch him further.'] Now and then he paused to expatiate on how exact a picture Shakespeare here gives of a murderer's mind when, the dark deed achieved, its perpetrator already envies his victim's calm sleep. He read the scene over twice."[18] Those who heard Lincoln recite this passage came to interpret the moment as a foreboding of death. "Malice domestic" finds an echo in Lincoln's "malice toward none" and points to a close identification with the kindness of Duncan. And with that identification the scene makes Lincoln prophetic: he would be that Duncan assassinated and asleep in his grave. That was the impression that Chambrun took away on Sunday evening, April 9, five days before Lincoln was shot in Ford's Theatre.

It would seem the president had been identifying with Duncan in a premonition of his own death, but the character of Macbeth was the one that held his interest. On the return from Richmond, as the presidential party approached Washington, D.C., Chambrun overheard the President hush the First Lady from saying that the town was filled with "enemies." She was right, but the weary president longed for peace, and for peaceful sleep the way Macbeth does. As Lincoln had identified with Macbeth's ambition, he also understood Macbeth's "moral torment" brought on by war's horrendous death toll. At the end of the war, like Macbeth, he was feeling sick, sleepless, and haunted by the dead of a war he had waged, a toll of over half a million. Lincoln's identification with Macbeth is made more explicit and extreme in a recent article entitled, "Lincoln, Macbeth, and the Moral Imagination," in which the author attempts to show that Lincoln's ambition had been overweening from the beginning to the end of the war, an exaggerated opinion that corresponds with John Wilkes Booth's.[19]

John Wilkes Booth, who identified with Macbeth, would have agreed with Lincoln's identification with Macbeth as well, but not for the same reasons, but rather as how he perceived Lincoln as an unlawful leader and perpetrator of war crimes. Wilkes' sister Asia judged Lincoln's attendance at Ford's Theatre an outrage, calling the theatre a "devil's den," paradoxically, considering how many of her family made their living in the theatre. She thinks that following his return from Richmond, he should have gone to church rather than the theatre. Scornful of Lincoln's "triumphant entry into the fallen city" of Richmond "which was not magnanimous" raised a "moan of the religious people" that Lincoln "had not gone first to a place of worship."

> It desecrated his idea to have his end come in a devil's den—a theater—in fact.... That fatal visit to the theater had no pity in it; it was jubilation over fields of unburied dead, over miles of desolated homes. It was neither the Te Deum of a noble conqueror nor the Miserere of a Christian nation.... It was contemning the Constitution. It meant to him, to this one desperate man who shouted "*Sic semper tyrannis,*" the fall of the Republic, a dynasty of kings.... "He saved his country from a king," but he created for her a martyr.... We regard Boston Corbett as our deliverer, for by his shot he saved our beloved brother from an ignominious death.

And regarding accusations that her brother was insane, she replies, "Wilkes Booth was not insane; he had a powerful and active brain, and was given to weigh his intents and reflect upon his actions." Asia's husband, an actor of comedy and sometime partner in theatre management with Edwin Booth, called all the Booths "Iagos."[20]

But to Lincoln's mourners, the identification of President Lincoln with Duncan became all too evident after the assassination. Before the state legislature, Governor Andrew of Massachusetts used Shakespeare's description of Duncan to eulogize the dead president:

> Besides, this Duncan
> Hath borne his faculties so meek, hath
> Been so clear in his great office, that his virtues
> Will plead like angels, trumpet-tongued, against
> The deep damnation of his taking-off.[21]

This would prove prophetic as well. For Abraham Lincoln's virtues continue to be called forth by historians and educators—Not so for his "partner of greatness," First Lady Mary Todd Lincoln.

There would be few kind words for Lincoln's beleaguered "partner of greatness," and not for another 150 years. Catherine Clinton's biography of Mrs. Lincoln (2009) begins with a sympathetic portrait of the First Lady's exclusion from her dying husband's bedside:

> Edwin Stanton barked, "Take that woman out and do not let her in again."
> The deathbed of a loved one was perhaps the most hallowed of nineteenth-century ritual settings. Mary's ancestors were Irish women who might keen for

hours, if not days, over the body of a departing loved one. In Victorian America, attending a dying husband was a wife's most privileged obligation.... Everyone crowded in the room that night knew a wife's sacred duty. When Lincoln's breathing became halting and labored around 7:00 a.m., however, no one summoned Mary.[22]

The late-twentieth-century biography of Mary Lincoln by Jean Baker does compare the First Lady to Lady Macbeth in recounting Mary's dismay at the disparaging remarks made about her by Lincoln's Illinois law partner, William Herndon, who claimed that her husband had never loved her. Mary swore an oath against him, "like a star-crossed Lady Macbeth," Baker's curiously intuitive admixture of Shakespeare's "star-crossed" lovers Romeo and Juliet with Lady Macbeth.[23] What Mary wrote in a letter regarding Herndon's claim that the Lincolns' marriage was a "domestic hell" does read like one of Lady Macbeth's invocations to dark spirits: "He will be closely watched.... in attempting to disgrace others, the vials of wrath, will be poured upon his own head.... In the future, he may well say, *his prayers—* 'Revenge is sweet' especially to womankind." Like Polonius who attributes Hamlet's madness to his thwarted love for Ophelia, Herndon started the rumor that Lincoln had loved only one woman, Anne Rutledge, early in his youth, and that her death explained Lincoln's melancholia from which he was said to suffer ever after. Herndon claimed that Lincoln felt only a cold, affectionless friendship for his wife. Historians and biographers, including Carl Sandburg, have taken up Herndon's claims as historical fact. And while Herndon stands discredited in the letters of Mary Lincoln as annotated by editors Justin and Linda Turner, and in Jean Baker's careful examination of the evidence in her biography of Mary Todd Lincoln, even more recent treatments of Lincoln have begun to give Herndon credence again. In his book on Lincoln's melancholia, published in 2005, Joshua Wolf Shenk neither disputes nor agrees with Herndon on the former First Lady's standing with her husband. However he does make a case for accepting Herndon's interviews, shorn of commentary. About Mary Lincoln, Shenk has very little to say, but what he does say takes on a dismissive tone as he refers to her having gone to a "fancy" school in Lexington, and as being a bad tempered flirt with her own history of mental illness yet to be written.[24]

The trial of Mary Todd Lincoln for lunacy in an open courtroom, the former First Lady's last public appearance, was taking place at the same time as Charlotte Cushman's final farewell performance of Lady Macbeth, in May of 1875. Mrs. Lincoln was declared insane and sentenced to an asylum. Cushman's last lines could as well have served as a coda to Mary

Lincoln's trial and conviction of insanity; her service to her son Robert could not contend with the [dis] honor deep and broad he loaded upon her. And her immediate response to her public ordeal had the markings of Lady Macbeth's—attempted suicide. But when released after months of confinement by the efforts of America's first female lawyer who proved her to be sane, Mary had one pressing aim—to escape.

The question of whether or not Mary Lincoln was insane and suicidal in her later years is similar to the critical quandary circling Lady Macbeth's sleepwalking scene and offstage death, that is, unresolved. Plunged into debilitating grief by the tragedy of her husband's assassination in 1865, her precariously regained equilibrium received another blow when another of her four sons died in 1871, leaving only one, Robert, and she became frantically fearful for his life. From 1871 to 1875 Mary seemed to wander aimlessly, not unlike her sleepwalking counterpart whose "eyes are open, but their sense is shut"—until the shock of Robert's perfidy woke her up and propelled her forward. If she was insane, when and for how long, remains an open question. But when Mary was fifty-seven the decision was made by an Illinois court of law that she was. And on the night the verdict was handed down and she was sentenced to an asylum, it is said that she did try to commit suicide.

It was Robert Todd Lincoln, the only surviving child of Mary and the late president, who pressed the charges against his mother, having secured doctors' and lawyers' cooperation. She was accused of incompetence due to insanity. Robert's arguments rested principally on Mary's behavior over the previous five years, following the death of his brother, Tad. Mary Lincoln's overindulgence for shopping and hoarding had become manic. Especially alarming to her son was how she obsessively worried about money and hid large amounts of her life's savings in cash and bonds about her person, sewn into her hemline. In addition, Robert blamed his mother for driving a wedge between him and his wife, and accused her of threatening to kidnap their child, her grandchild, Mamie. The court passed down the insanity verdict and put Mary's financial holdings in Robert's care, which to his credit he managed on his mother's behalf down to the penny. Mary was to be confined to an asylum.[25]

The night of the verdict, still free in her Chicago hotel room, Mary attempted suicide by drugs obtained at a pharmacy. But the suspicious pharmacist substituted something harmless rather than what she had requested, so the drugs had no effect. The next morning, with the bonds forcibly removed from the stitching in her dress, she was taken away. Once institutionalized, while seemingly compliant, Mary surreptitiously contacted lawyers, spiritualist friends, and newspaper reporters to press for a retrial. In a matter of a few months, the first professionally practicing female lawyer, Myra Brodie, helped to get the conviction of insanity overturned and to secure Mary Lincoln's release from the asylum. She found a temporary safe haven at her sister's in Springfield, but worried that her son would come after her there. So she escaped to Europe where she lived for four years, mostly in the fashionable retreat of Pau in southwest France, near the Pyrenees and in the therapeutic mountain air.[26]

In France, the ex-patriot kept up an affectionate and lively correspondence, especially with her sister's teenage grandson, Mary's grandnephew. In one of her long letters to him in 1879, Mary reacted to the news that her son Robert was being considered as a presidential nominee. The passage is worth quoting in full as it recaptures Mrs. Lincoln's thoughtful and articulate state of mind that retained some lingering anger, but also some self-mockery.

There is a paper published at Pau, called the "American Register," which is issued once a week, & which I sometimes see. Recently, I had the privilege of seeing a short article in it, mentioning that Robert T. Lincoln and Stephen A. Douglas, [Jr.] were practicing law in Chicago both prominent in their respective political parties, with *quite* the *certainty* of being at no distant day, candidates for the Presidency. You can imagine how elated I felt, in my quiet way, over such a prospect—the triumph of the "*just*" *slightly different* from the great and good father, however who was kind even to *his stepmother*—I began to study over in my own mind, with such a certainty in view, what never once occurred to me to do in my good husband's time notwithstanding articles that often appeared in the papers, that "Mrs. Lincoln was the power behind the throne." I found myself revolving in my own *feeble* mind, of what superior persons the *Cabinet* would consist— Swett of *Maine*—& *Little Mamie* [her granddaughter] with her charming manners & presence, in the event of *success*, will grace the place [the White House]. By the way, dear Lewis, should I again enclose any thing for this dear child again, I will not trouble your good Grandmother—only if you will write R. T. Lincoln—a formal note—remitting what is sent. *The* young man, who makes *no* concessions to the *Mother*, whom he has so cruelly & unmercifully wronged—So that he will be a *temperate* man, is the boon, for which I *daily* kneel. How terrible is the death of young Lewis [sic] Napoleon! The Ex-Empress is alone & desolate, like my own very sorrowful self! Cut to pieces, after receiving the fatal shot, in so unnecessary a cause. Write to me very frequently, my dear Lewis. I write so rapidly, that I fear my letters are not easily read. Please present my best love to all friends. Always, your very affectionate Aunt, Mary Lincoln.[27]

A year after Mary Lincoln returned from Pau, France, to Springfield, Illinois, her son Robert paid her a visit accompanied by her granddaughter and namesake, eleven-year-old Mamie, a visit that put the mother and son on speaking terms. Robert Lincoln had just been appointed secretary of war in President Garfield's cabinet. Later that year, almost blind and partially paralyzed, taking prescribed electric bath treatments in New York City, Mary put up one last fight for Congress to augment her pension. She won, and returned to Springfield to die.[28]

Like Lady Macbeth, the former First Lady spent her last days keeping to herself in a perpetually dark room, lit only by a single candle. This scene captured the imagination of poet Carl Sandburg in his short biographical reverie of Mary Lincoln's life, a scene he describes in images reminiscent of the setting for Lady Macbeth's sleepwalking. Substituting himself for the Doctor and Gentlewoman who watch Lady Macbeth in "slumbry agitation" with only a single candle to pierce her dark distress, Carl Sandburg imagines Mary Lincoln's "tragedy" of "a mind gone wrong," imaginings he has written in prose, that I have excerpted and formatted as verse:

> In the year of 1882 there was a woman in Springfield, Illinois,
> who sat in widow's mourning dress,
> who sat in a room of shadows where a single candle burned....
> Her habit now was day on day to go to this room of shadows
> lighted by a single candle....
> She would stay with her candlelight and the shadows....
> She lived in the candlelight and shadow....
> It was...the end of a woman
> whose life since maturity seldom had a pleasure
> not mixed with pain and fear.
> The headaches, the hot tongue lashings....
> a racked and driven woman....
> She sat in candlelight and shadows,
> and passed out from the light of the living sun.
> They carried a burial casket out
> over the threshold
> her feet touched
> as a bride—
> and that
> was all.[29]

I interpret Sandburg's description to read almost like a paraphrase of Macbeth's "Tomorrow and tomorrow and tomorrow" speech. After being told, "The Queen, my Lord, is dead," Macbeth answers: "She should have died hereafter. There would have been a time for such a word: Tomorrow.... Out, brief candle.... Life's but a walking shadow...signifying nothing." Sandburg's references to Mary Lincoln's "pain and fear," "hot tongue lashings," ending with "that was all," echo Macbeth's last line of grief and bitterness, life being "a tale told by an idiot, full of sound and fury signifying nothing."

Sandburg has configured Mary Lincoln as a bogey of the imagination rather than a human being. Witch-like qualities of Lady Macbeth inform his portrait. Not only does he use "racked and driven" to describe Mary's condition, as in the above description of her dying in darkness, but these same words he uses another time to tell how the youthful Mary Todd "haunted" young Abraham Lincoln during their courtship. "For two years [she] haunted Lincoln, racked him, drove him to despair and philosophy, sent him searching deep into himself as to what manner of man he was." When married, like Lady Macbeth, Mary goads her husband with tongue lashings: "When his melancholy weighed down...Mary Todd with her tongue, arguments, reminders, was a 'whiplash.'" Called a vixen and a shrew, she was like a tigress brooding over her children. "Whiplash" and "tiger" merge Mary Lincoln with performers of Lady Macbeth, such as Sarah Bernhardt and Judith Anderson, who will be seen to have been called exactly the same names. Lincoln's secretary called Mary Lincoln a "Hellcat."[30] And Charlotte Cushman was called a "pantheress."

The saint maker of Abraham Lincoln and devil maker of Mary Lincoln, Sandburg acknowledges that they both were ambitious, "Nearly always between these two there was a moving undertow of their mutual ambitions." But the two ambitions are not the same. Lincoln's ambition is noble, his wife's is not. Lincoln's is a quest, a hoping for achievement: "Though his hope of achievement and performance was sometimes smothered and obliterated in melancholy, it was there, burning and questing, most of the time." His wife's ambition was a desire, an anxiety, a preoccupation with eminence and social approval: "And with Mary Todd Lincoln the deep desire for high place, eminence, distinction, seemed never to leave her." Lincoln's noble ambition was on the grand scale of History, Sandburg's capital "H": Lincoln "cared much for what History would say of him." She cared only for what "the approved social leaders of the upper classes would let her have." Sandburg seems to be saying that Mary's ambition was nothing more than greed and social climbing, "signifying nothing," in direct inverse proportion to her husband's ambition signifying everything.[31]

The way Sandburg makes Mary Lincoln's ambition bad, and Abraham's good, follows a tradition that goes back to Greek and Latin tragedy. Belgian novelist and Classicist, Marguerite Yourcenar, explains in an essay contemporary with Sandburg's *Mary Lincoln*, how the ancient Greek playwrights differentiated tragic heroines from tragic heroes. In Classical Greek tragedy heroines fight like wolves, heroes battle like lions. The heroine is slave to a cause, a crime machine for one crime. The hero is free, pursuing an open path of virtue. The heroine's willful actions bring on suffering and guilt that follow her into old age. The hero acts in acquiescence to a heroic destiny, dying young but fulfilled and honored in his accomplishments. In her own reconfiguring of tragic heroines, such as Clytemnestra and Mary Magdalene, rather than perpetuating traditional representations, Yourcenar disrupts their stories and frees up their voices to expose how their society has alienated them, and made them scapegoats.[32]

Mary Lincoln gets categorized as deranged and suicidal, like Lady Macbeth. Looking down from the heights of his tragic hero, as if standing on the Lincoln Memorial itself, Sandburg casts pity and damnation upon Mary Lincoln in a whirligig of contexts, now Biblical, now post-Freudian. He blames her for committing one of the seven deadly sins, "pride of a depth and consuming intensity that might ally it with the pride which the Puritans named as the first of the seven deadly sins." Shifting to a modern lexicon, he substitutes condescension for blame, damning the former First Lady with it: "We do not kick the physically clumsy for being what they are. Neither can we deal with the mentally thwarted in a vocabulary of blame." In terms more metaphysical than scientific, almost like an exorcism, he casts her down into an inferno like netherworld, "outside the realm of sanity, balance, respectability, serenity, sweetness and light." An inhabitant of Lady Macbeth's "murky hell," Mary Lincoln sends her ghost to haunt the wary poet biographer, to justify her poor performance as a First Lady with "an alibi so perfect that her ghost could answer, 'Did God in His infinite wisdom ever weigh down any White House woman with a devastating curse such as rode in my blood and brain?'" Sandburg achieves Sadean enthusiasm in describing that "curse," Mary's malady "gnawing at her brain": "tongs of fate that clamped tighter and tighter in the lobes of her brain," before calming down to a simpler conclusion that "She was...the victim of a cerebral disease." However understanding Sandburg tries to be, writing in the twentieth, Freudian century about the mental state of nineteenth-century Mary Lincoln, his images of her revert to the gothic.[33]

The scenario for Mary Todd Lincoln, the life of the Civil War's "Lady Macbeth in the White House," does read like the plot for Shakespeare's Lady Macbeth, and biographers have made something of the comparison.

High-born, attractive, and smart, she inspires the love of an ambitious husband. Ambitious herself, she strives for her husband's success. Her goal is achieved when he gains power, which she, his "partner of greatness," shares. She beautifies her house and her wardrobe, and dutifully entertains her husband's associates in official banquets and receptions. Her influence on her husband in state matters makes her increasingly unpopular, even more so than her husband. She is known to consort with spiritualists and to believe in ghosts. And eventually, grief stricken over a series of tragic deaths, trauma weakens her balance. In Lady Macbeth's case the deaths include Banquo, Macbeth's best friend, and the wife and children of Macduff. In Mary's case, the losses cut deep, her husband is assassinated, three of her four sons succumb to illnesses, and brothers and cousins die fighting for the enemy in the war. The effects of overwhelming grief, including suicidal tendencies, seem symptomatic of derangement or insanity. In the case of Lady Macbeth remorse and guilt add to her despair, and suspicions are that she does commit suicide, offstage. For Mary Lincoln, her one living son and doctors accuse her of insanity in a public court that sentences her to a sanitarium. Given these circumstances, Mary Lincoln could well echo Lady Macbeth when Shakespeare's character recognizes that the fruits of her labor have come to nought: "Nought's had, all's spent, /Where our desire is got without content."

But Mary Lincoln resisted giving up, and her desires and efforts as wife of Abraham Lincoln and First Lady of the Land did amount to something. Her husband was the first to acknowledge how she married down to a "nobody" and helped him achieve political advancement. He made a pleasantry of their similarity to the Macbeths as "dearest partner[s] of greatness." Rather than being pained by such comparisons, Lincoln was amused. Had he and their favorite sons lived beyond the Civil War, Mary Lincoln's life would not have been such a tragedy and history might have been kinder to her memory.

7. "Innocent Flower" and "Serpent Within" ❧

On board a cross-Atlantic steamship, a glamorous French actress who would play a sensuous new Lady Macbeth in the theatre collided with an aging American First Lady, who had played out her version of "Lady Macbeth in the White House." The ship *l'Amérique* had sailed four days out from Le Havre, when, on an October day in 1880, at seven in the morning, the actress taking the air on deck noticed a sorrowful looking woman dressed all in black. Suddenly an enormous wave welled up from a placid sea and crashed over the railing, knocking the actress down and propelling the woman in black toward the hold, where she was about to be thrown head first "down to a most certain death." But instantly the actress bounded to her feet and grabbed the old woman by her voluminous black skirts, rescuing her just in time, with the assistance of two attendants. Distracted and confused, the older woman thanked the actress in a soft, faraway voice. The actress said, "Madame, you could have been killed down that horrible stairwell." "Yes," came the response with a sigh full of regret, "But God didn't grant it." Then looking at her rescuer, she asked, "Are you Madame Hessler?" "No, Madame, my name is Sarah Bernhardt." The woman recoiled stiffly, her face turning white and implacable, and with a sorrowful voice, "a voice of the dead," she exhaled, "I am Lincoln's widow." It was Bernhardt's turn to recoil, filled with sorrow and regret that in rendering a service to the unhappy woman she had prevented the one service she longed for, to be saved by death. Her husband, President Lincoln, had been assassinated by an actor and now it was an actress "that prevented his widow from rejoining her cherished dead."[1]

Later in the voyage, in a sequel to this incident, following another of Sarah Bernhardt's rescues on board *l'Amérique*, Mary Lincoln appeared a little less dolorous and self-absorbed. Bernhardt coaxed back from the brink a young pregnant and abandoned Portuguese immigrant who intended jumping overboard. Then the actress descended into the suffocating hold packed with immigrants and assisted with the baby's delivery, wrapping him in her own expensive robes. Returning to the fresh air of the first-class deck, Bernhardt met again with the former First Lady. Mrs. Lincoln touched her gently on the shoulder and kindly addressed her, "Madame Sarah Bernhardt, you are going to be loved in America."[2] The prophecy received immediate confirmation when the boat docked in New York, and all the passengers were pushed aside, including the hardly noticed Mrs. Lincoln, to make way for the Divine Sarah. Apparently, the former First Lady did not mind, "she had long since come to terms with anonymity."[3] The former First Lady, now in decline at sixty-two and no longer in the public eye, after four years living in Europe, had decided to return to her sister's home in Springfield, Illinois, to die in the same house where she had married Abraham Lincoln. Enfeebled by a recent back injury, nearly blind, and obsessively worried about money, Mary Todd Lincoln lived only two more years.

Sarah Bernhardt at age thirty-six was on the rise, launched toward unparalleled fame and fortune. She opened on November 8, 1880, at [Edwin] Booth's Theatre in New York City with *Adrienne Lecouvreur*, marking twenty-five years since the idolized French actress Rachel had played the same role in New York. Bernhardt went around the country playing (in French) such crowd pleasers as Marguerite Gautier in *La Dame aux Camélias*, a great favorite since the 1850s when Laura Keene introduced the role to the American public, after Dumas *fils* premiered his play in Paris in 1852. This performance of *Camille* in America was Bernhardt's debut in the role; she would play it 65 times out of 156 performances on this first American tour.[4] Having earned a fortune, Sarah Bernhardt returned to France and invested her earnings in new roles, new writers, eventually her own theatre—and the lifestyle of a movie star. In her subsequent eight tours to America she would repeat this pattern of recouping her wealth in America and returning to Europe to spend it.

Gifted with a "golden" voice with "silver tones," a sinuously expressive body, and enormous energy, in addition to intelligence, talent, and an indomitable will, Bernhardt set out to conquer the most challenging dramatic roles, male as well as female, Hamlet as well as Medea. She played Hamlet, the E. Morand and Marcel Schwab translation, in 1898, the same year she played Catulle Mendes' *Medea*, both in her own theatre that still bears her name, Sarah Bernhardt Théâtre, located in the center of Paris on the right bank.[5]

Figure 6 Sarah Bernhardt as Lady Macbeth, photo by Paul Nadar. Courtesy Laurence Senelick Collection.

But before that she appears as Lady Macbeth—in a startlingly new interpretation, in 1884, the year the actress turned forty. A *New York Times* reporter followed Sarah Bernhardt through rehearsals to *Macbeth*'s opening night, observing how the actress took command of all aspects of the production at the Porte-Saint-Martin Théâtre. Bernhardt designed her costumes to be form fitting, emphasizing her sensuality, costumes the reporter thought "splendid," describing them in some detail: "A white jersey embroidered in black flowers, with sleeves of blue and gold and white draperies at the shoulders, over a skirt of plaited white cashmere, which was changed for the banquet scene for another of corn color and dark blue, with, in both, an embroidered girdle and a gold circlet over her hair. It was not a bit Scottish, but it was very becoming" (June 7, 1884). The colors of blue and gold suggest a Viking queen, Germanic rather than Celt, "a heroine of the Niebelung" is what Bernhardt's translator/writer intended. This ethnic, or to use the nineteenth-century term, "racial" distinction may have had its origins in the earlier French play by Ducis, a completely different version from Shakespeare's, that models Lady Macbeth after an especially vicious Frankish medieval queen. Ducis' *Macbeth* fulfilled Lady Macbeth's threats of infanticide by killing her own son and then herself at the end of the play.

To make a fresh, new, and more faithful translation of Shakespeare's text, Bernhardt went after the rising young "Bohemian" poet, Jean Richepin. The two had recently established a working—and personal—relationship, when Bernhardt acted in two of Richepin's plays. Five years Bernhardt's junior, the poet looked the role of the longhaired rebel-advocate of the working class, and had put in his time at being a sailor, docker, boxer, and circus acrobat. Actually from an upper-middle-class background, Richepin was the son of an army doctor stationed in Medea, Algeria. And he completed his higher education at the elite École Normale Supérieure in Paris. His disturbing and not at all sentimental play *Pierrot Assassin* that premiered at the Trocadero Théâtre in April of 1883—with Bernhardt playing Pierrot—presages his adaptation of *Macbeth*. Pierrot murders Madame Cassandre, runs off with Madame's money and the servant Colombine (played by Réjane), and ends in madness and attempted suicide.

Under a time pressure ("*dans le plus brèf delai*"), probably translating as the actors rehearsed, Richepin condensed Shakespeare's twenty-five scenes to nine, retrieved the character of Lady Macduff, all but lost in nineteenth-century English and American productions, and put it all into fast-paced French prose, resulting in the most literal, "lively," and bareboned French translation of the play to date.[6] Richepin gave an extensive and edgy interview about his adaptation thirty years later, on the eve of World War I, when his *Macbeth* was revived on the stage of the Comédie Française. He thought of Macbeth as a "visionary Celt" who is reduced to being Lady Macbeth's "housewife." Of the pair, it is Lady Macbeth, "a perverse Saxon," "a little red headed viper," who makes herself "head of the household."[7] The phrase "red headed viper" seems to be an expression of personal vituperation against his former lover, Bernhardt, rather than a description necessary to the characterization of Lady Macbeth, Saxons not having been known for their red hair. Richepin's lengthy interview makes other idiosyncratic comments about the Macbeths: "She's a very pretty woman...[with] the air of a monster. But so many pretty women are monsters." "Macbeth is a warrior, and like so many warriors, gives in to his wife's demands." Julia Bartet, the actress playing Lady Macbeth in the World War I revival of Richepin's adaptation, had like Bernhardt become the writer's lover at the same time she became his Lady Macbeth. Unlike Bernhardt she had a soft look and "womanly" persona, more like Ellen Terry's Lady Macbeth.

Sarah Bernhardt premiered her Lady Macbeth on May 21, 1884, in a performance hailed as "marvelous" by "discerning" critics. She "perfectly expressed all the duplicity and ferocity of the astute Lady Macbeth." In her sleepwalking scene Bernhardt reenacted the murder night with "swift movements" and "flashing countenance," with such passion, screams, and groans, that she terrified her audience. Making the assumption that Lady Macbeth was "infamous and sensual" before Bernhardt played her, the critic for *Le Figaro* was pleased to report that the actress performed "with an energetic and wild grandeur the...infamous and sensual Lady Macbeth."[8] On his honeymoon in Paris, Oscar Wilde attended the production—several times—finding Bernhardt's Lady Macbeth irresistible:

> There is absolutely no one like Sarah Bernhardt....Her influence over Macbeth's mind is just as much influence of womanly charm as of will. She holds him under a spell: he sins because he loves her: his ambition is quite a secondary motive. How can he help loving her? She binds him by every tie, even by the tie of coquetry. Look at her dress—the tight-fitting tunic, and the statuesque folds of the robe below.[9]

Over the following decade Wilde became a close friend and professional colleague of Bernhardt's. In 1893, the Anglo Irish playwright wrote in French a symbolist tragedy about the Biblical enchantress Salomé and cast Bernhardt in the principal role. It was already in rehearsal in London when the English censors banned it. Soon afterward, Wilde himself became a public scandal, and his trial, imprisonment, and early death precluded his ever seeing *Salomé* publicly performed. Aubrey Beardsley, the artist closely aligned with Wilde's vision of the French actress, depicts Sarah Bernhardt as Salomé in his illustrations published with Wilde's play.

The tight fitting tunic costume, adorned with Scottish thistles suggestive of French fleur de lis that Wilde found so seductive, appears in Paul Nadar's photographs of Sarah Bernhardt. Nadar took several shots of Bernhardt's Lady Macbeth, especially of her sleepwalking scene in which the actress wears a simple white gown, nothing else, and noticeably barefoot. These photographs show a remarkable artistic synergy between Nadar and Bernhardt, and demonstrate how the actress played with the new medium of the camera's eye as seductively as she must have with a live audience, a sensibility matched in the following century by Greta Garbo and Marilyn Monroe.

Londoners responded with mixed feelings to Sarah Bernhardt's Lady Macbeth when she toured England and Scotland. The Scots proved more receptive, acknowledging her modernity, her dangerous siren-like quality: "She depicts for the present generation the kind of woman in whom it is strongly interested, the dangerous, siren-like creature by whose fascinations men are enslaved....A Cleopatra-like seductress, with a queenliness and grace of bearing that would also befit the mistress of Anthony." But English audiences grew alarmed at Lady Macbeth's tight-fitting costumes that revealed Bernhardt's "lithe and undulating form." And they found her costume, or lack of, in the sleepwalking scene downright shocking, the actress in a night gown, and nothing else, letting her red hair fly loose and wild, and—even more vulgar—showing bare feet. The *World*'s critic emphasized Bernhardt's "otherness," seeing her Lady Macbeth as "oriental, feline, caressing, nervous...the most subtly fiendish one could wish to see."[10]

What really rankled with the English—the effrontery of this Parisian actress of dubious reputation performing Lady Macbeth in French in Shakespeare's homeland! This was not Shakespeare's Lady Macbeth: "She [Bernhardt] had to play a famous part which she did not, and could not, understand as her audience understands it, and which, even if she did understand, would suit her very little." This particular London observer found Bernhardt "sadly lacking in dignity," the sleepwalking scene having "none of the weird *solemnity* and *quiet* horror for which we look *here* at the hands of a *great* tragedienne."[11] But recognized for her energy, eroticism, and silver-toned voice, how could the Divine Sarah have met the English standards for solemnity and silence in the role of Lady Macbeth, an English tradition based, rightly or wrongly, on Siddons' more dignified interpretation.

Disappointed with the English outrage at her "insidious erotic influence," Bernhardt returned home. She revived her Lady Macbeth for two more weeks in Paris, and then shelved the role for the rest of her very long career. It had not proved to be lucky for her, neither personally (Richepin had deserted her) nor professionally at the box office, the more determining factor in her abandonment of the role. But all was not lost. Though her Lady Macbeth had only a brief run in Europe, it made a lasting impression, inspiring Oscar Wilde's *Salomé*, and benefiting her later dangerous seductress roles in French versions of Cleopatra and Medea. Americans, who did not see Bernhardt as Lady Macbeth, would appreciate in her other roles the same intensely sensual and Delilah-like power over men that characterized her Lady Macbeth. Lady Macbeth, Cleopatra, and Medea, all passionate, dangerous, and seductive wives in Bernhardt's repertoire, frightened and fascinated late Victorian sensibilities, challenging standards that demanded quiet devotion and dignified submission from the role of wife. Sarah Bernhardt provokingly played noisy and ostentatiously erotic roles, a performance style thought to be more appropriate for the role of mistress or whore than wife or queen, more like Antony's "strumpet" Cleopatra than Macbeth's wife.

Bernhardt's young friend Ellen Terry, who had seen Sarah's Lady Macbeth in London, played the wifely Lady Macbeth, not the strumpet. While Terry admired her French friend's performance, for her own she followed the directions given her by her acting partner, Henry Irving, whose Macbeth appeared as the dominant partner, instigator, and controller of the play's action throughout. Premiering their *Macbeth* in London in 1888, Terry and Irving subsequently performed the play several times on tours in America, beginning in 1895, when Terry turned fifty.[12] Ellen Terry last appeared as Lady Macbeth in the United States at the beginning of World War I in a performance of excerpts, or lectures of Shakespeare's women, that included scenes of Lady Macbeth. From the start Terry made her Lady Macbeth a loving and submissive helpmate to Macbeth—"the innocent flower"—naïve and devoted, the Victorian ideal of womanhood and wifehood. Sarah Bernhardt played the fiendish queen as a sexual powerhouse, sinuous and seductive, rendering the role of her husband an attendant to her will and desire. The actors who played Bernhardt's Macbeth disappeared into the scenery. A *London Times* critic who had witnessed firsthand both actresses performing Lady Macbeth contrasts Bernhardt's "animal passion" with Terry's "sweet winning womanliness." "Madame Sarah Bernhardt's sketch of the character is the only one with which [Terry's] can be compared; and there is a wide difference between the sensuality of the French

Lady Macbeth seeking to work upon her lord's nature by means of animal passion and [Terry's] sweet winning womanliness."[13] Bernhardt terrified Terry. Reflecting on the performance she had seen when the French actress toured Britain as Lady Macbeth, Terry, in awe of Bernhardt's sleepwalking scene, wondered at its strangeness, wishing she could capture something like it in her own performance. "Sarah Bernhardt I saw in just this one scene, and there was something strange, something aloof, something terrifying about her. It was as if she had come back from the dead. Oh, that I could remember how she got that effect!"[14] But she didn't, and her Lady Macbeth did not terrify.

Henry Irving believed that the thinking and planning to become king stemmed entirely from Macbeth's ambition, making Lady Macbeth a helping accomplice, but not an instigator. So Terry's "dove-like" Lady Macbeth, the Victorian ideal of an "angel in the house," devoted herself entirely to Macbeth and his ambition, even in crime. Together, Irving and Terry scoured Scotland for clues to their parts in *Macbeth*, and researched historical and critical texts, finding particularly useful a mid-nineteenth-century essay that distinguishes a feminine from a masculine Lady Macbeth, the necessary "moral energy" deriving from a more "delicately feminine" Lady Macbeth. "Such sentiments [as Lady Macbeth's] from the lips of what is called a masculine looking or speaking woman, have little moral energy compared with what they derive from the ardent utterance of a delicately feminine voice and nature."[15]

Terry acknowledged and rejected the kind of masculine Lady Macbeth that had been so highly regarded earlier in the nineteenth century, as she recites in her "Lecture" performance. "It seems strange to me that anyone can think of Lady Macbeth as a sort of monster, abnormally hard, abnormally cruel, or visualize her as a woman of powerful physique, with the muscles of a prize fighter! But it is clear from records of some performances of the part, and from portraits of the actresses who gave them, that it can be done!"[16] It would seem Terry is describing one of her predecessors, the native-born American actress Charlotte Cushman who had become an international celebrity in the previous generation. Rather than physical energy, Irving and Terry chose the delicately feminine "moral energy" for their Lady Macbeth, as demonstrated by Terry in her opening letter-reading scene: "more than once," she stopped reading long enough "to kiss the miniature of Macbeth on her neck chain." She "covered the letter itself with kisses," becoming "lost in a dreaming of a splendor to come," not realizing "the measure of her crime."[17]

The notes to herself that Ellen Terry made in the margins of her *Macbeth* script trace her performance choices moment to moment through the play, revealing what she thought of the character. Ellen Terry's *"Macbeth* Book" preserved in her Smallhythe Cottage in Kent, England, contains a script with Terry's marginal notes and drawings, the Lyceum program for her December 29, 1888, *Macbeth* premier, a copy of an essay by J. Comyns Carr, clippings of articles, and a lock of Irving's hair. Some of the marginal notes on the script were made after the premier, for she says of the Castle scenery for the sleepwalking scene, represented by "C.C.," Comyns Carr, "Absurd Scenery==and my acting in it was all wrong somehow=." Presumably the music for the 1888 production proved more satisfactory than the scenery. Arthur Sullivan, of Gilbert & Sullivan, composed the music for full orchestra, including an overture, preludes between the acts, and chorus for the witches. He conducted the orchestra on opening night, and the music rehearsals leading up to it. Unfortunately, only the overture has been published. Worth noting as well, Bram Stoker, the Irish author of *Dracula* (1897), managed the Lyceum Theatre where Terry and Irving premiered *Macbeth*, and accompanied them on their several tours to the United States.

A striking feature of Terry's script is how she instructs herself to perform the very same instructions that in the play's dialogue Lady Macbeth gives to Macbeth. One instance is to "be the innocent flower," and another later in the play when Lady Macbeth observes "you lack sleep." Consistent throughout her notes Terry insists that Lady Macbeth be a woman in love, a woman whose motivation is her love for a man, adding, as if she needed to explain, "women love *men*!" The actress takes for herself Lady Macbeth's advice to Macbeth, to "play the innocent flower," as she writes in the margin of her script next to act two, scene one, when Macduff demands to know the business. Terry writes, "Play here not the loud voiced commanding Queen but the frightened 'innocent flower.'" But that "innocence" can get to be too much, even for Terry, who suspects her loving Lady Macbeth of having "half dulled knowledge," even of being "rather stupid." Terry notes these opinions in the margin of Lady Macbeth's own little epiphany of disenchantment in the middle of the play, the scene after the Macbeths are crowned and as Macbeth becomes increasingly obsessed with his murderous schemes and ignores his wife. At this moment Shakespeare gives Lady Macbeth a four-line soliloquy:

> Nought's had, all's spent,
> Where our desire is got without content:

'Tis safer, to be that which we destroy,
Then by destruction dwell in doubtful joy. (III, ii)

Terry writes in her script on the page opposite this speech:

> Express here (when *alone*) a "rooted sorrow"—a half dulled knowledge of the fact of her husband
>
> having been all the while deceived in him.
>
> She sees clearer now!!!
>
> Knows she has missed what she had hoped to gain == I sometimes think she is rather stupid!!—

The actress is not stupid. In the space at the top of this same page of her script, Terry notes, "His trouble affected her==for she loved him." This, then, is the motive and cue for all her actions, "for she loved him." She verifies this with notes further along in the script, such as, "Cheer up *for him*." In a final note on the end papers of her script Terry repeats the motivation for Lady Macbeth, "she loved him," developed into a curious love theorem with unexpected emphases:

> Lady M—is capable of affection—
>
> she loves her husband—Ergo—she is a *woman* [underlined three times]
>
> == and she knows it., and is half the time afraid [while] urging M. not to be afraid, as she loves a man == women love *men* [underlined three times]—

Why such emphasis, and whether or not she is arguing with someone else or with herself, Terry does not make clear.

At the end of the banquet scene, when all the guests—and the ghost— have gone, and the Macbeths are alone on stage, Terry tries to help once more, "How about trying to ease his heart by taking off his crown—which he the more firmly now plants on his head =[on his line] 'Now I'm bent to know.'" She encourages him to get some sleep, though Terry notes that she, Lady Macbeth lacks sleep just as direly as Macbeth does. Terry writes the marginal instruction about her Lady Macbeth, "She is near dead from lack of sleep" next to Lady Macbeth's line to Macbeth, "You lack the season of all natures, sleep." Terry made notes as to how Lady Macbeth progresses from being "anxious, uncertain and rather ill," before the banquet scene, to being "frightened" immediately afterward. The fear is brought on by Macbeth's ominous: "We're yet but young indeed." "A flash of awareness hits Lady Macbeth, "she knows him==*now* Lady Macbeth shall sleep no more—for she is at last—<u>frightened</u>."[18] Terry's loving Lady Macbeth becomes too aware of her husband's perfidy at this moment, and it frightens her, and evidently breaks her, for the next and last time the audience sees her she is unconscious in the sleepwalking scene and then dies.

Irving exits the banquet scene, leaving Terry's frightened Lady Macbeth alone on stage with no more lines to speak. Terry takes this unscripted opportunity "to show the futility and indignity of the reward for which she sold her soul.... Snatching the crown from her head, she takes it in her hands. She walks slowly behind the empty throne, then sits in desolation."[19] Here is a hint of the grandeur of Ellen Terry's performance, her creation of a female Faust figure in Lady Macbeth, whose pact with evil forces leads to nought—"a tale...signifying nothing." This moment is Lady Macbeth's penultimate scene in the play, before she loses consciousness and perhaps her sanity as seen in her last, the sleepwalking scene.

Ellen Terry's stage work with the crown at the end of the banquet scene may have been the inspiration for J.S. Sargent's famous painting of Ellen Terry as Lady Macbeth that the artist made during Terry's opening run in London over the winter of 1888–1889. It now hangs in the Tate Gallery in London. Sargent depicts a regal figure proudly holding the crown high over her head, not at all the same interpretation as Terry's performance of snatching the crown off her head and sitting on the throne with the crown in her hands in "desolation." Sargent did not immediately settle on this image, but tried out different ideas, making Terry run about his London studio in a variety of poses. The ubiquitous Oscar Wilde watched from his London townhouse as Miss Terry rode by in a four wheeler, dressed in her Lady Macbeth robes, on her way to Sargent's studio: "The street that on a wet and dreary morning has vouchsafed the vision of Lady Macbeth in full regalia...can never again be as other streets."[20] In Sargent's finished portrait of Ellen Terry as Lady Macbeth she wears that "full regalia," her stage costume for the opening scenes, a blue-green gown bespangled with iridescent beetle wings, the sleeves draping down to the knee, to the same length as her long red braids. The Smallhythe Cottage collection displays several of the stage costumes worn by Terry, including the extraordinary Lady Macbeth gown with beetle wings. Its size is a reminder of how petite Ellen Terry was when she played the role, unlike the impression Sargent gives of her as tall and commanding. Sargent has painted her standing alone, her body erect, back slightly arched. She holds a crown in both hands up above and a little forward of her body, her head tilting back slightly, giving her an angle to gaze up at it, though he shows her eyes directed inward at some inner thought or dream, perhaps that "dreaming of splendour to come," Ellen had noted for her letter-reading scene. Her arms make a wide circle with the crown at the circle's apex, and she looks as if she is about to move her head forward to receive it. She balances the "golden round" in her hands, fingers faced to the back, palms front, as if someone else were placing the crown on her head. This gesture, together with the train of her mantle draped like a proscenium curtain around her feet—all together give the impression of a stately, though solitary, coronation ceremony. Sargent's picture suggests that Lady Macbeth is ambitious for a crown for herself, for her own advancement. But Terry's interpretation of Lady Macbeth does not fit this image. The artist had a reputation for reading his own "beastly" interpretations into a portrait.[21] Sargent's portrait of Ellen Terry as Lady Macbeth does bring out "beastly" ambition for the crown, but that Terry and her audiences did not see in her performance of the role. Sargent's visual interpretation of Ellen Terry as Lady Macbeth, one clearly not based on Terry's performance of the role, has nevertheless served observers as an accurate representation of Terry's acting the part. For example, the art historian Stuart Sillars (who erroneously attributes the painting to Whistler) observes: " Voluptuously serpentine in clinging green and gold...she holds the crown above her head in an insistent revelation of the ambition that is, in Bradleian terms, her tragic flaw. She is revealed in full sexual power, and the image conveys a true sense of performance."[22]

While Terry praised Sargent's portrait and the artist, she had her misgivings about it. In a letter to an American friend, Terry proffers effusive, if imprecise, praise: "the wonderful drawing—colour—the *meaning* [her emphasis] behind it all—can't be explained." She dotes on the artist: "I think it's the best [of Sargent's work]—his simplicity, and his devotion to his art, is most loveable." At the end of the letter she adds a postscript: "Of course Mr. Sargent has idealized me (and of course I am delighted he has done so.)"[23] But according to Margaret Weir, the curator of Ellen Terry's Smallhythe Cottage and archives, Terry expressed disappointment with the painting for the very reason that it did not represent her interpretation of the role. She preferred instead, one of Sargent's unfinished studies of her Lady Macbeth, the one showing her greeting Duncan to the castle at Inverness. In this sketch Sargent shows Terry's Lady Macbeth striding forward, the plentiful fabric of her robes in full sail with the thrust of her movement. On either side of her are ladies in waiting and courtiers, stationary as they bow in greeting and reverence directed more at Lady Macbeth passing through them, than forward to align with her focus slightly off center toward the arrival of her guests, the king, Duncan, and his followers, who are not depicted. The courtiers make way for Lady Macbeth's grand

Figure 7   Ellen Terry as Lady Macbeth, by John Singer Sargent for Terry's Jubilee program. Courtesy of Don Wilmeth who owns the program.

entrance, rather than for Duncan's arrival. It is this picture of Lady Macbeth surrounded by her household, performing the ceremony of hostess, welcoming her guests to her castle, a group picture of greeting that Terry chose to appear in her jubilee program.[24] She wanted to be remembered as a pleasing and lovable woman adored by all. Sargent generously insisted on making for her a new copy of the sketch, in black and white, so that it would reproduce well in the printing of the program.

Initially, the idea of Ellen Terry playing "the fiendish queen" Lady Macbeth seemed too incongruous, casting against type. Having seen her create pleasing and lovable interpretations of Portia in *Merchant of Venice* and Beatrice in *Much Ado about Nothing* in the 1870s and 1880s, an American critic could not imagine the actress doing Lady Macbeth. For him, Terry was too much a "ravishing dream of youth, beauty, and sweetness…exquisite images of womanhood." Furthermore, she lacked the "broad intellectual power and fervid passion" demanded by the part. Some reviews bear this out, such as the *Standard's* "ironical note" that Ellen Terry's performance showed how "Lady Macbeth can be metamorphosed into a model of womanly sweetness and charm."[25] Terry bristled at the term "dove-like." But in arguing that her Lady Macbeth was not a "gently lovable woman," she undercuts her argument by using the phrase "That's all pickles," an expression that makes her appear all the more gentle and lovable. "I by no means make her a gently lovable woman, as some of them say. That's all pickles; she was nothing of the sort, although she was not a fiend and did love her husband."[26] But Terry's Lady Macbeth did prevail precisely for the reason that it did conform to the ideal of womanhood of the prewar age.

Bernard Shaw, Ellen Terry's devoted correspondent, admirer, and critic, observed that Terry had become a legend in her own time, this in spite of—or possibly because of—"the holes left in her mind by the curious patchiness of theatrical culture and the ladylike ignorance of her day." To Shaw, Ellen Terry had been too pliant on stage, too eager to please her audience. She had failed to plumb the depths of her power. "Her value was so promptly and easily admitted that she did not realize it herself at all fully.…She literally did not think enough of herself." Shaw wished Terry had not been so devoted to supporting her acting partner of thirty years, Henry Irving, which Shaw says was "her greatest self-squandering of all." "Privately she showed more pluck and independence." Shaw wanted Terry to play in Ibsen's plays, and *his* plays, and concern herself more with modern issues and less with Shakespeare.[27] Shaw, after all, is the wag who penned the word bardolatry for fans of Shakespeare.

Terry's innocent flower and Bernhardt's serpent under it together prefigure the public and private traits of Edith Wilson as a Lady Macbeth in the White House. President Woodrow Wilson had become a fan of Terry's performances in America, as early as 1884 when he was a twenty-eight-year-old doctoral student of history at Johns Hopkins University. He raved about Ellen Terry in an exchange of love letters with his fiancée, Ellen Axson, who at the time was an artist studying at the Art Students' League in New York City. Miss Axson wrote to say that she would be going to see Henry Irving and Ellen Terry perform. Wilson wrote back from Baltimore that Ellen Terry was the best actress he had ever seen, "beyond comparison." "I am sure that you will think, as I do, that Miss Terry is infinitely better than Irving—at least if you see them in parts anything like those in which I saw them—namely Hamlet and Ophelia. His strut is almost as execrable as his pronunciation. She is beyond comparison the finest actress I ever saw. Ah, Eileen, what would I not give to see her *with you!*" Months later when Ellen saw Terry and Irving again, she wrote to Wilson, wondering "Why do you suppose Shakespeare made his men such poor creatures as a rule and his women such paragons!" To the Wilson generation Terry's stage roles constituted a paragon of womankind.

Wilson's own expectations for a loving and submissive wife made him as demanding of Ellen Axson as Henry Irving was of Ellen Terry. In another letter to his fiancée, Wilson insists, with regret, that she must give up her aspirations to become an artist if she is to be his wife. "I hate selfishness; it hurts me more than I can tell you to think that I am asking you to give up what has formed so much of your life and constituted so much of your delight. And yet that is what is involved in becoming a wife.... I am asking you to give your life to me—for me, to be merged into mine."[28] Wilson admitted to the selfishness of his demands, but he made them nevertheless, believing "that is what is involved in becoming a wife." They were married in 1885 and she did give up her art for her husband's sake, and she raised a family and lent moral support to Woodrow in his career, a rise from a college professor to president of Princeton University to governor of New Jersey to the president in the White House where Ellen Axson Wilson died of cancer in the first years of Wilson's administration.

On her last tour to America, the sixty-six-year-old Ellen Terry performed a recital of Shakespeare's women, "Lectures" she called the performance, with a reading of Lady Macbeth in her category of "Pathetic Women." American audiences gave her a warm welcome, as they had been doing since the 1870s. As a strong supporter of the controversial pacifist views of her close friend and colleague, Bernard Shaw, Terry was in sympathy with President Woodrow Wilson's peace position and his determination to keep the United States out of the war. Criticized in Britain and later in the United States for objecting to the war, Terry held to her convictions. She cries out in her diary, "What madness! Thousands of lives lost today to gain ten yards in a little field."[29]

On a dark autumnal night in 1919, in the master bedroom of the White House, President Woodrow Wilson lay half conscious and partially paralyzed, laid low by a massive stroke. By his side, his second wife, married since 1915, has put the president's business into her dispatch. She acts as his messenger, allowing no one in to see him but the doctors complicit with her commands. He has only to nod his approval. All the rest is left to her. For so it appeared that Edith Wilson was in charge of the executive functions of the U.S. government for several months following Woodrow Wilson's stroke, until he had recovered enough to be moved from his bedroom to the oval office and receive attendants other than his wife and doctor. His true condition was kept a secret. The public was told he had collapsed from exhaustion. By this ruse, and Edith's ostensible role as courier, the White House gave the appearance it was functioning without the need of the vice president. But few were fooled, and that period of eighteen months from President Wilson's stroke to the end of his second term in office has been dubbed the "petticoat government" and "Mrs. Wilson Regency," with Mrs. Wilson called simply "Mrs. President."[30]

Edith Bolling Galt, a stylish and well provided for widow living in her luxurious apartment in Washington, D.C., met President Woodrow Wilson in April of 1915. He had been mourning the death of his wife Ellen for eight months. Edith was forty-three and Woodrow fifty-eight. The new First Lady, a tall and full bosomed figure in the fashion of an Impressionist painting, was to all appearances demure and charming in a Southern manner. She was born and raised in Virginia in a large family of limited means. Edith's first husband, a successful businessman, left his business and secure stream of income to Edith upon his premature death. Edith charmed President Wilson from the moment they met—he proposed one month later. Letters between them show how early on in their love affair Edith wished to be a "dearest partner of greatness," and to share in Woodrow's plans and ambitions, like Lady Macbeth: "Much as I love your delicious love-letters, that would make any woman proud and happy, I believe I enjoy even more the ones in which you tell me (as you did this morning) of what you are working on—the things that fill your thoughts and demand your best effort, for then I feel I am sharing your work—and being taken in to partnership as it were."[31] As for the president, Edith's charms initially had more to do with the bedroom than the executive office. As pointed out in the entertaining book *Wild Women in the White House*, "when the *Washington Post* asserted that 'The President spent much of the evening *entering* Mrs. Galt,' many maintained that the typo was more credible than the correction." In fact, the reporter only observed the head of state "entertaining" his lady friend.[32]

Chic and social, Edith Galt charmed the American public. Approving notices appeared in the press following the couple's outings to baseball games and stage plays. The day after they announced their engagement on October 8, 1915, Edith accompanied Woodrow to Philadelphia where she watched him throw out the first pitch of the World Series (Philadelphia versus Boston), the beginning of a tradition that succeeding presidents would follow. Later that month, they were seen at the Belasco Theatre attending the double hitter of Bernard Shaw's *Androcles and the Lion* paired with the comically and coincidentally titled one-act play by Anatole France, *The Man Who Married a Dumb Wife*.[33] What a convergence of theatrical talent (and love affairs) in America mid-World War I! The designer for the 1915 double bill at the Belasco was a young American making his debut, Robert Edmond Jones, who designed the geometric and pre-art deco sets for *Man Who Married a Dumb Wife* that launched him on a long and successful career as America's first "modern" designer. Jones' work was indebted to the innovative designs of Gordon Craig, Ellen Terry's brilliant and peripatetic son. The director of the two one-acts seen by the Wilsons was Harley Granville-Barker who that same year, 1915, fell in love with an American, a married woman living in New York, who would later get a divorce and marry the influential British director. Thereafter Granville-Barker, once Shaw's premier interpreter, lived in the United States, teaching at Yale University and writing his *Prefaces to Shakespeare*, reflections partly based on his experience directing Shakespeare's plays in England that foreshadowed the revolution in twentieth-century approaches to Shakespeare. Rather than "straining towards a psychological and pictorial realism for Shakespeare," Granville-Barker's work foreshadowed the revival of Elizabethan nonillusory, presentational staging of Shakespeare's plays, opening "new worlds for discovery and conquest" directly leading to Peter Brook.[34] Granville-Barker died in New York at the end of World War II.

Both Woodrow and Edith Wilson enjoyed attending the theatre. Edith relates excitedly how in 1912, three years before she was introduced to Woodrow, when the president elect and the first Mrs. Wilson attended Billie Burke's show at the National Theatre, Edith and her cousin felt privileged indeed to have seats right under the presidential box. As the cares of wartime beset him, the president found attending the theatre relaxing and distracting, just as Abraham Lincoln had during the Civil War. Edith describes her husband's preference for vaudeville fare: "Mr. Wilson enjoyed vaudeville and was a regular patron of Keith's Theatre. No matter how foolish the skit, he said it rested him because it took his mind off responsibilities and refreshed his spirit to see light-hearted people who 'took on no more at their hearts than they could kick off at their heels.' Particularly he enjoyed the tap dancing, and [George] Primrose always pleased him. The manager of the theatre, Mr. Roland S. Robbins, and his assistant Mr. Chevalier, always met us at the entrance and escorted us to our box."[35] This custom of the manager escorting the President and First Lady to their special box is a tradition that goes back to Abraham Lincoln and even before, to President George Washington, a custom derived from English protocol when the monarch visited the theatre.

With theatre outings, baseball games, his courtship and second marriage all aside, Woodrow Wilson had to focus his presidential duties in 1915 on the war in Europe and his efforts to keep America out of it. A peace president and future Nobel Peace Prize winner, Woodrow Wilson devised a plan for the nations of the world to join an international organization that could mediate and negotiate conflicts between nations, what would become the League of Nations, predecessor to the United Nations. German imperialism pushed Europeans into World War I in the summer of 1914 when President Wilson was half way through his first term of office, and his first wife, Ellen, lay dying. As the war advanced it became clear that this one was not like any before it; that Germany, with its new weaponry and highly trained nationally conscripted army was threatening the very survival of other nations and their civilian populations. In one of the darkest hours for British civilians the German blockade on imports reduced their food supply to six weeks' provision. The British and their allies successfully appealed to the United States for supplies and finally for war assistance. On April 6, 1917, the United States officially entered the war, most immediately in response to the Germans having launched submarine attacks on the as yet neutral America's ships. The submarine assaults all but ended early in 1918 when the United States laid a barrage of mines across the 250-mile-wide passage between Norway and Scotland. In April 1918, American troops began arriving on the battle front in time to support the allies in pushing the Germans back and forcing their surrender on November 11, 1918.

Traveling with the President and First Lady to Paris for the peace treaty negotiations in December of 1918, the coterie of American officials and their wives included the young assistant secretary of the Navy, Franklin Roosevelt and his wife Eleanor. They all received an enthusiastic welcome from the international community and press, a warm reception that extended to the official treaty talks. Wilson's proposal for a League of Nations was entered as a term of the treaty that led to its eventual approval by the participating foreign governments. It was rumored that the First Lady hid behind a set of heavy curtains in order to hear how her husband's negotiations were going. But when the president returned home to the United States, his League faced stiff opposition from Republican Congressmen led by the president's nemesis, Henry Cabot Lodge, who succeeded in blocking the U.S. government from becoming a member of the League, thus undermining its viability and shortening its life. It was on his long and arduous campaign crisscrossing the country by train to drum up support for the League that on September 26, 1919, the president collapsed in Kansas, and was rushed back to Washington.

Determined to see that her husband's plans would be carried out, and evidently assuming that she alone was the one to do so, First Lady Edith Wilson put this great business at her dispatch. She prevailed upon the president's private physician to announce to the public that the president was suffering from nervous exhaustion, and could perform his duties from his sickbed. In actuality the doctors were treating a stroke victim suffering both physical and mental impairment. For several ensuing months, all access to Wilson's bedroom in the White House was controlled by Edith Wilson. She monitored every communication to and from the president. She wrote out and sent presidential directives in her own handwriting beginning them with the phrase, "The President says." Objections came from every quarter, from the president's time-honored opponents: from the Republicans, for Wilson was a Democrat; from big businesses, for Wilson was a scholar and intellectual not beholding to business lobbies; from industry in the North, for Wilson was a Virginian. In due course, the First Lady's secretive control of the President also alienated loyal supporters and White House insiders. Consequently Edith's popularity declined. She was no longer regarded as the sweet and loving wife. Now she was suspected of duplicitous interference and overweening ambition for power over the president and his office. She appeared to be like another Lady Macbeth, playing the "innocent flower" kind of wife on the surface, but in her actions the "serpent" beneath.

A historian reading Edith's personal papers detects "something beyond rapt commitment to Wilson," rather "overtones of curiosity and ambition and possessiveness," like a Lady Macbeth, "sinister," "willfully betraying the public interest," and "distorting history." Edith's secretiveness regarding her husband's illness is called a Machiavellian ploy to stay in power. Edith lied in order to circumvent what would have happened if the true nature of the president's illness had become known. The vice president would have stepped in for the incapacitated president in a legitimate line of succession. In this study, Edith is characterized as vain, superficial, narrow-minded, poorly educated, misguided, ignorant, determined, and manipulative.[36]

More damning than most of Edith Wilson's critics, the author finds justification in the 1990 disclosure of Woodrow Wilson's medical reports written by his physicians at the time of the president's collapse in 1919, which attest to a stroke and paralysis not the "nervous exhaustion" reported to the public. This author's characterization of the First Lady, affixed to her book's narration like a postage stamp, flattens out the character analysis. A more balanced interpretation of Edith Wilson as the president's wife would take into account her naivety, sensuality, and willful devotion to her husband. In her short tenure in the White House, this First Lady performed her public role very much like Ellen Terry's Lady Macbeth who did all for love of her husband, and in private enthralled the president with her sensuality, a la Sarah Bernhardt's Lady Macbeth.

During World War I, Sarah Bernhardt devoted what would be her last tour to the United States and Canada to rally support for the war effort on behalf of her homeland. At the beginning of the war, she had been determined to remain in besieged Paris for the duration, just as she had during the Prussian War of 1870. But her old friend Georges Clemenceau, who would become prime minister of France in 1917, persuaded her to go south, having secret intelligence that she was on the Germans' list of French notables to be taken hostage to Berlin.[37] In 1915, soon after the amputation of her right leg, the seventy-year-old-actress left Bordeaux to tour France's front lines, entertaining and visiting with the soldiers. Afterward, ever indomitable, she decided to go to America, partly to make money to support her lavish lifestyle and that of her son's family, as she had done on her previous eight tours, but more pressing to help persuade the United States to enter the war. With her company of twelve actors and fifty trunks of costumes and stage properties, Sarah Bernhardt set out to perform short scenes "designed to win sympathy for her ravaged country"[38] in over one hundred different towns, many of them more than once, for a tour that lasted almost two years. Accompanying the "Great," as her son's family called her, her granddaughter, Lysiane, recorded many of the details of their tour. Old Great, on one leg, was no longer able to move about the stage and sustain a full-length play performance. (Injuring herself on a fall from the stage, she had suffered the pain of the bad leg for several years before finally asking her surgeon to cut it off.) So she performed single scenes or acts from her major roles, as well as shorter pieces written specifically for this tour. She played Hecuba, Cleopatra, Camille's death scene, Portia from *The Merchant of Venice*, Prince Napoleon from *l'Aiglon*, and Joan of Arc's trial scene. The role Bernhardt chose especially to rally support for the war was George Courteline's short piece called *Du Théâtre au champ d'honneur*, the story of a dying French infantryman being cared for by a wounded British officer. Famous for her death scenes, in this one, Bernhardt's little French soldier dies "with a French flag clasped to his breast and the name of his beloved France upon his lips." Bernhardt transformed the French soldier into "the tragic symbol of a wounded France, his voice a clarion of war, and his last utterances the very soul of France crying for vengeance." The prayer uttered by the dying soldier changes Christ's plea from the cross from "Father, forgive them, for they know not what they do," to a cry for vengeance, "Father, forgive them not; they know well what they do." Bernhardt made this "the most magnificent of curses against the barbarians," with all the "old flaming" and "overwhelming passion in her voice."[39]

When she was not performing in theatres across the United States and Canada, Bernhardt appeared at rallies for the Red Cross, and in parades to promote the sale of government bonds, as well as for other charities on behalf of the wounded and fallen soldiers and their survivors. "The Bernhardt" continued promoting the war effort in the United States even after the United States formally declared war. She and her granddaughter donned white gowns to appear as featured guests in a "Liberty Bond" parade in Los Angeles, riding in an open carriage covered with white flowers, drawn by white horses conducted by two coachmen all in white. To honor Bernhardt whose husband had been a Greek, the parade officials organized an escort for her made up of Greeks in native costumes. But due to some error, the costumes looked Turkish rather than Greek—the beginnings of Hollywood. "We were at war with Turkey.... would [Bernhardt] laugh or get angry? Neither one nor the other. She made a point of saying nothing."[40]

The war won, mission accomplished, loaded with purchases from a final shopping spree in flu-infested New York City—where the unknown actress and future Lady Macbeth, Judith Anderson and her mother were recovering from the flu in their boarding house room—Bernhardt returned home to Paris in time for the armistice. Allied government leaders gathered in the French capital to negotiate the peace treaty, principally President Woodrow Wilson and France's Prime Minister Clemenceau, Bernhardt's old friend and advisor. To celebrate their victory and welcome the dignitaries, and to benefit a French charity, Sarah Bernhardt performed her short pieces for an audience of special guests that included First Lady Edith Wilson. With this performance before the First Lady, Bernhardt, who had enjoyed and profited by a warm welcome in the United States, now was in a position to return that hospitality to the Americans in Paris. Edith Wilson recalls in her memoirs the particulars of this occasion, and tells an especially amusing tale with regard to American ignorance of French literary figures:

> Madame Sarah Bernhardt recited a poem by Fernaud Gregh. This was after she had lost her leg; so she was borne in on a sort of float with white draperies so arranged that she seemed to be emerging from clouds. Her voice was exquisite and as musical as that of Madame Tetrazzini who sang later on in the performance. The Queen of Rumania was there in a box, and I had as my guests Madame Poincaré (wife of France's President) and Madame Deschane; also the wives of our Peace Commissioners. The performance was a sort of revue, and one scene represented the great literary men of France—Balzac, Dumas, and so on. When Dumas entered one of my French guests exclaimed: "Voila, Dumas," at which a U.S.A. lady was instantaneously transformed from a languid, disinterested listener to a lion hunter keen on the scent. "Oh," she exclaimed, "I didn't know he was in Paris; we must have him to dinner![41]

This triumphal celebration in Paris marks a glorious finish to the Great Sarah Bernhardt's career. And it also marks the apex of Edith Wilson's "reign" as First lady. The press in Paris and abroad reported favorably on every aspect of the First Lady's public appearances and dress. All this ended months later when Congress refused to ratify Wilson's League of Nations, the president suffered a stroke, and the First Lady took over the functions of the Executive office. Edith's management of the "Washington Court" during her husband's collapse and recovery resembles Lady Macbeth's efforts to control Macbeth's strange behavior, his "sickness" at the sight of Banquo's Ghost, and to explain it to the courtiers.

The Wilsons' generation, bridging the nineteenth and twentieth centuries, held on to the Victorian ideal of marriage and the good wife, honoring Ellen Terry's loving and supportive Lady Macbeth as a performance of that ideal. But that generation was equally fascinated and terrified by the kind of wife Sarah Bernhardt played in her role as Lady Macbeth, her "animal passion" and enthralling eroticism. When First Lady Edith Wilson assumed the powers of her husband, as well as powers over him, finally dispatching his business herself, she became suspect, giving the public, and historians, evidence of a serpent under the appearance of an innocent flower.

8. Vampira ᘓᕽ

Touring her native Australia in the 1930s in her Broadway hit vamp role of "Cobra," Judith Anderson provoked a Sydney critic to rhapsodize, "She is made of that spiritual material that lives forever. She is Superstition itself, emerged from the fissures of the human soul...the Lady Vampire of the Ages."[1] Alfred Hitchcock cast and directed Judith Anderson (with Laurence Olivier) as the sinister and terrifying housekeeper Mrs. Danvers in the 1940 film *Rebecca*, a role that fueled the collective memory of Anderson as a fiendish female. To this "Lady Vampire of the Ages" could be added "Lady Macbeth of Twentieth-Century America," for Anderson commandeered the role in America, on stage, screen, television, and recordings. Her acting career spanned seventy-five years "in a country not my own," she would say. For she never became an American citizen, remaining ever proud to be a British subject to the very end of her long life, living and working in the United States.

Nineteen-year-old Frances Anderson, later Judith, left Australia for America in 1917. Arriving in New York City almost broke, she and her mother shared a room in a boarding house, and while her mother took in sewing, Judith auditioned for acting jobs. Anderson would not be deterred from her goal of becoming a famous actress. With Sarah Bernhardt her idol, the young Aussie prided herself that she looked like Bernhardt: small, lithe, alluring, with a large nose in a handsome and expressive face. Over the span of her first twenty years of acting in New York, Anderson succeeded in working her way up to starring roles in artistic triumphs by Eugene O'Neill and Luigi Pirandello for the Theatre Guild, and in several commercial successes for producer/playwright David Belasco. By the late 1930s she had achieved the fame and fortune she had sought, living on her own in an elegant New York apartment with Italian furnishings, and wearing an expensive designer wardrobe. She bought properties overlooking Santa Barbara, California, that would become her home for the next fifty-five years. Her ambition and persistence combined with talent had paid off.

Approaching forty, Anderson told a reporter in Boston that she felt ready to take on the role of her dreams and ambition—Lady Macbeth. The first opportunity came in 1937 at the Old Vic in London, giving the actress her first Lady Macbeth and Laurence Olivier his first Macbeth. Neither of them liked the results. The clunky costumes were said to have resembled Kubla Khan. The brown and black set had muddy lighting that made Anderson's descent down the staircase in the sleepwalking scene truly treacherous. Once offstage, she found herself tripping over pieces of Birnam wood in the darkness. One critic said that Anderson's sleepwalking scene was "deliberately grotesque" and "horrible but unsatisfying."[2] Olivier was equally unenthusiastic about the bizarre costumes and a stage set that delayed the opening because it was too big to fit through the theatre's loading gate and had to be cut down to size. But Olivier must have retained a vivid impression of Anderson's Lady Macbeth, observations he may have passed on to his future Lady Macbeth, Vivien Leigh. A writer for the *Los Angeles Times* experienced the sensation of déjà vu when in 1955 he reviewed the production of *Macbeth* that featured Leigh as Lady Macbeth and Olivier as Macbeth. "Things had not gone very far with this Lady Macbeth before it all began to have a familiar ring. Before long it dawned on us what was happening: nearly every nuance and inflection of the voice, even to the unearthly keening in the sleepwalking scene, were those of Judith Anderson. To one who has lived long and lovingly with the Anderson/Evans recording it was simply unmistakable. Maybe this is all tradition and did not originate with Miss Anderson, but there it was."[3]

The Anderson and Olivier *Macbeth* production had its share of bad luck traditionally associated with the play. Managing director of the Old Vic Theatre, Lilian Bayliss, suddenly died before the opening, throwing the company and opening-night audience into a state of mourning. Anderson and Olivier however did enjoy visiting with the Queen of England, the late Queen Mother, when they were summoned to the royal box at the play's intermission after the banquet scene. The Queen spoke to them of her royal Scottish ancestors including the Macbeths, and her birth place in Glamis Castle, and taught them how to pronounce it correctly—"Glawms" rather than "Glam-is." Anderson complained to Her Majesty that the director, Michel St. Denis, would not permit her to put the candlestick down during the sleepwalking scene, insisting that she follow tradition and carry it throughout all the hand wringing. The Queen responded that if Anderson knew the dark terrors of Glamis Castle she wouldn't want to put the candle down, "Oh, I think that if you'd ever lived in *Glam's*, you'd want to keep the candle in your hand every minute!"[4]

Returning to the United States, Anderson played Hamlet's mother to John Gielgud's Hamlet in an especially Oedipal interpretation fashionable in the glory days of Freudian analysis. This production occasioned Judith Anderson's first invitation to the White House and lunch with First Lady Eleanor Roosevelt when Anderson and Gielgud were performing *Hamlet* on tour in Washington, D.C. In a letter to her first husband, English professor at the University of California Berkeley, Benjamin Harrison Lehman, the actress writes how in awe she was of the First Lady. But admitting to being maniacally neat herself, she found the First Lady's quarters in the White House a bit too untidy. "Had lunch with Mrs. Roosevelt at the White House, and I am completely captivated. I could talk for hours about her charm and humor and graphic description [*sic*] genius.... I wasn't nervous till halfway through lunch when I realized I was in the presence of a great woman, and sitting on her left, if you please.... I went all over the house, in her bedroom and study which is much more untidy than any room I could live in, but all so warm and simple and with such great dignity. Lincoln's room is sad and ghost-filled with its enormous bed and massive furniture."[5]

Eleanor Roosevelt lent her support to the theatre, especially during the 1930s and in particular the WPA Federal Theatre Project, which the First Lady tried to help keep afloat against stiff and ultimately victorious right-wing opposition. The First Lady often attended the theatre when staying in her apartment in New York City, and she wrote in one of her weekly newspaper columns how she admired Judith Anderson's performance in *Family Portrait* (1938), in which Anderson appeared as Mary, Mother of Jesus. Mrs. Roosevelt writes: "To play as she does must mean there is something within her which can soar above most ordinary mortals. I wonder if the part itself does not leave something indelibly written on the soul of the person who plays it."[6] Eleanor Roosevelt's speculation as to whether an actor playing a particular role, especially one as divine as the Virgin Mary, might have something of that character imprinted on the actor's soul, suggests an innocence on her part with regard to the actor's craft. As Anderson's future work would bear out, there is no evidence that she as a person acquired depth and understanding from her roles. Margaret Webster, who cast against type and directed the "glamorous" Miss Anderson as a "soft-spoken, mousy woman in peasant dress" in *Family Portrait* (and herself played the role of Mary Magdalene),[7] directed her again playing Lady Macbeth, and observed how little depth of intelligence, feeling, and mystery is needed for an enormously talented, ambitious, and vain actress to succeed with the public.

A month before Pearl Harbor, Judith Anderson began her long run of playing Lady Macbeth on Broadway. Unlike her London experience, this

New York production that opened at the National Theatre on November 11, 1941, thrilled her. It played for over a year, the longest continuous run of *Macbeth* on record. Anderson became absolutely ebullient about her American debut as Lady Macbeth, regarding the happy triumvirate of herself, her Macbeth played by Maurice Evans, and their director Margaret Webster, as an antidote or talisman to the bad luck usually associated with a *Macbeth* production. "Puff" quotes from drama critics' reviews of the play's opening, clipped from the New York papers and printed in the production's glossy touring program, give enthusiastic endorsement to Judith's performance. John Mason Brown of the *World Telegram* applauds Anderson's projection of "sulphurous villainy and an imagination unequalled by any of the Lady Macbeths of our time."[8]

The director, Webster, and the actor/producer playing Macbeth, Maurice Evans, agreed on changes in the script. Among them: "They cut the Hecate scene.... Seeing no modern equivalents for the witches, they played them as instruments of darkness. Webster also exercised diplomacy to dissuade Judith Anderson from her determination to be seen in bed with Macbeth." Evans based his interpretation on the aphorism, "'Power corrupts, and absolute power corrupts absolutely,' to remind audiences that the mood and lessons of Shakespeare's tragedy were suited to the times."[9] The response to Anderson's interpretation of the sleepwalking scene fully vindicated her objection to how she was obliged to play it in 1937. Under Webster's direction she could put the candle down, and proceed to rub both of her hands together, vigorously. Brooks Atkinson felt that her "nervous washing of the hands is almost too frightful to be watched." Richard Lockridge expands on the moment: "Its broken words and stiff unnatural gestures were incredibly poignant. As she rasped her hands together and swayed uncertainly, she showed us all we could need to know about the human mind in torment, about a spirit breaking slowly under a burden of remorse too heavy for the mortal spirit and because of terrors too horrible to be spoken."[10]

The actress had found a way to make her sleepwalking more realistic. A psychiatrist friend arranged for her to observe a patient moving and speaking under hypnosis, as a close approximation of a sleepwalker. Anderson, Webster, and several psychiatrists watched as the young patient removed her shoes and went under hypnosis. Like Bernhardt, Anderson went barefoot in the sleepwalking scene. (Fuseli's 1784 picture shows Lady Macbeth with one slipper on and one off.) Anderson watched closely how the girl walked. "I was fascinated to see that she did not move with the assurance and security of someone walking when wide awake: she felt for the floor, she held to it with the soles of her feet, she tested what was under them until she

Figure 8 Judith Anderson as Lady Macbeth, photo by Vandamm, 1940s program for Broadway run and touring production. Program in author's possession.

finally trusted her weight to them." To hear her voice, the patient was asked to speak about a childhood trauma, which she did "in a terrified little girl's voice, muffled by sleepiness." Anderson requested to see what she would do to try to remove something unpleasant from her hands, something she couldn't get off, and saw:

> not the languorous and graceful hand-stroking that I had been told was characteristic of some previous Lady Macbeths... but the concentrated, obsessive,

almost savage scrubbing that I later tried to imitate. Here was Mrs. Siddons' "vehemence" to the life. Shakespeare's words demanded it. Duncan's blood had clung to Lady Macbeth's hand. She could not remove it, it was in her nostrils, in her pores, in her bones, in her very bloodstream. It was her own corroding guilt and it drove her, quite literally, mad. On this depended the whole horror of the moment.[11]

The director anchored the sleepwalking scene by directing Anderson to haunt the same landscape and echo the same movement exactly as done in the earlier scene before and immediately after the murder of Duncan, "so that you can repeat, move for move, exactly what you did in the earlier sequence.... I shall even give you a lamp which you can park in the same place that you will later use for the sleepwalking lamp."[12] To this a jubilant Anderson replied, "At last, a production in which I would be able to put the lamp down!" As Webster watched the actress put this new sleepwalking scene into performance, she noted, rather bemusedly, that:

> The lessons of all this were not lost on Judith; but they began to acquire a slightly theatrical dimension. The scene is, Heaven knows, difficult at the best of times, but especially on Saturday matinees when the theatre is crowded with schoolchildren. In America, for some reason known perhaps only to high school teachers, the line "Out damned spot" is the second funniest in all dramatic literature, beaten only by "something is rotten in the state of Denmark." Judith, infuriated by a laugh at this point, would become more and more dramatic, which, bless their dear little hearts, they thought funnier than ever. (In fact, the only way is to wait—whisper as quietly as you dare—and cheat the rhythm so that the line is gone before they recognize it "Out.... damned spot out! I say...").[13]

Webster would know how to deliver that line, for she had played Lady Macbeth herself at the Old Vic a few years before, and Lady Macduff before that, and had begun her career acting in *Macbeth* in the 1920s by playing the Gentlewoman who watches Lady Macbeth sleepwalking.[14] The *London Times* critic who reviewed the Old Vic production, found Webster's Lady Macbeth "extremely acute in its perception, and she does not make the mistake of playing the many-sided woman in one key."[15] Clearly Webster's Lady Macbeth did have that depth of understanding and intelligence, and "acute perception" that allowed for the character to be more a human and less a monster, though perhaps less exciting than Anderson's Lady Macbeth. When Anderson got sick on tour, Webster filled in for her.

After its long Broadway run, *Macbeth* toured extensively in 1942 and 1943. In Philadelphia, the critic Robert Sensenderfer praised the production's modernity in a long and thoughtful essay. Drawing on pertinent theatre history, he shows how Anderson's Lady Macbeth was a new and modern conception.[16] Tracking Anderson's Lady Macbeth scene by scene, the essayist watches her hold back until the climactic sleepwalking scene. Because she "has neither the vocal endowment nor the heroic mold to play Lady Macbeth in the classic tradition," she "makes no attempt to give her in the grand manner." "Yet the woman she does draw is complete, logical, understandable and deeply moving—fit to stand beside the great impersonations of the past. It is an interpretation almost wholly in the modern manner." The critic contrasts Anderson's interpretation with famous actresses of the nineteenth century: "There is little of that formal regalness one might expect. Her first appearance is not impressive. She reads Macbeth's letter almost casually, with pauses. The announcement of Duncan's coming is not received with an exultant shriek that startled the hearers of Cushman and Modjeska." Anderson's Lady Macbeth is "brooding" and "sinister" from the very start, "insinuating rather than domineering," a conception that takes a while to grow on him, but which he finds totally convincing by the time of Duncan's murder. And by the sleepwalking scene:

> This mounting terror reaches a fearful climax when she totters out in her sleep, with open, staring eyes that do not see, and blood-haunted hands that will not whiten. Here Miss Anderson, haggard and groping, makes known her secrets in thick, broken mumblings, gasping out the horrid revelations, at times barely audible. The effect is terrific.

Webster's directing is wholly modern as well: "Margaret Webster has a talent for presenting Shakespeare in terms of contemporary drama. Without sacrificing the poetry or juggling the scenes too much, she manages to create an impression that this is a modern play." Sensenderfer describes how Webster gets over the hurdle of handling the Witches scenes for a contemporary audience. She eliminates Hecate entirely and the Witches appear "as distorted shades with writhing arms and taloned fingers weaving their spells in silhouette." When Macbeth approaches them, "they take material shape as, beneath a gaunt and spectral bough, they conjure up the 'horrid image' in Macbeth's receptive mind," and vanish in a blinding flash. Webster says she was just presenting the Witches as Shakespeare describes them, without any fancy tricks, "Evil in this play, is invisible, twisting and echoing through all its patterns, not a series of conjuring tricks like a souped-up séance. It is best to keep things simple." The Witches are introduced for the last time in a dream: "Macbeth is asleep at the side of the stage as the Sisters enumerate the dreadful ingredients of their hellish brew. Then Macbeth appears hovering over the glowing cauldron to hear his final fate." Sensenderfer's thoughtful account ends with a proclamation and a prophecy that, "This is a 'Macbeth' to see, and discuss and ponder over. Its like will probably not be here again for many years."[17] He was right that there would not be another like it for years to come, but could not have anticipated that this duo of Anderson and Evans would continue doing their *Macbeth* for over twenty years—but with another director.

When Margaret Webster later reflected on this World War II production of *Macbeth* she was less sanguine than Anderson and the critics. Webster found Anderson's acting too "manic," it didn't delve deep enough. She felt that Anderson and Evans together fell into the easy trap of playing the Macbeths as melodrama, "as a splendid thriller with two actors of star quality and a trio of 'witches' thrown in as a necessary device to get the play going." She, the director, wanted "darkness and black magic in it." While acknowledging their production's "pace, drive, excitement, clarity of pattern" and its "great favor" with the public and the press, Webster was "not very happy with the results": "The verse made sense. Too much sense, perhaps. There was little mystery... I would still approach it rather as if I were defusing a bomb."[18] Webster's evaluation of Anderson's performance of Lady Macbeth applies equally to Anderson's politics and her refusal to acknowledge, much less engage, in her colleagues' battles with McCarthyism. Anderson concentrated on career opportunities all her seventy plus years in the United States. By contrast, Margaret Webster's approach to *Macbeth* as if "defusing a bomb" could be said to characterize her efforts to defuse and dispel the evils of the black listing under McCarthyism for which she and her career would suffer.

After the production went on tour to other cities, it played to thousands of troops at Fort Mead where, in spite of the officers' doubts that the enlisted men would cotton to Shakespeare, the troops applauded wildly. Hailed as the "GI Lady Macbeth," Anderson rejoined her Macbeth, Maurice Evans, in Honolulu to play for the troops there. Evans, a British subject, became an American citizen, enlisted in the U.S. Army, and took up his post in Hawaii as captain and head of the Entertainment Section of the Department of Special Services. He arranged for a young private, George Schaeffer, to step in for Margaret Webster as the director of production. This is the same George Schaeffer who directed all of Anderson's future Lady Macbeths, on television and film as well as on stage, and whose name became synonymous with television's series of plays called the Hallmark Hall of Fame, two of them *Macbeth* with Judith Anderson, a live broadcast from a studio in Brooklyn (1954), and the second, a film shot in Scotland (1960). He also directed Anderson's Hallmark Hall of Fame star appearances as *Medea* (1957), and *Queen Elizabeth the First* (1967) with Charlton Heston as Essex, about the same time Heston played Macbeth to Vanessa Redgrave's Lady Macbeth at the Ahmanson Theatre in Los Angeles during the Vietnam War.

Back with Judith Anderson in her "GI Macbeth" on tour in 1943, as she prepared to leave Hawaii for the Pacific battlefront, she received another luncheon invitation from Eleanor Roosevelt. The First Lady was stopping over in Hawaii on her return from a scouting trip in the war zone, preparing reports for her husband and writing her weekly news columns for the public. Anderson was heading out to cover much of the same territory, and so perhaps the First Lady was able to give the actress a briefing as they lunched, advice on conditions at the war front, as well as poignant accounts of her visits to the wounded in base hospitals. Like the First Lady, and like her idol Sarah Bernhardt in World War I, Anderson wanted to get close to the frontlines to visit the troops. With her small company of two young women entertainers and a military escort, Anderson toured bases as far as New Guinea. In addition to performing scenes as Lady Macbeth, she recited Psalms and sang patriotic songs, with her more youthful cohorts providing sexier fare. Much of her time she spent visiting the military hospitals, singing, talking, and praying with the wounded and dying. Years later Anderson remembered that tour in the middle of the Pacific in the middle of World War II as the most fulfilling work of her very long career.

Thousands of soldiers fighting in the South Pacific—and a few Japanese prisoners—witnessed Anderson's excerpted Lady Macbeth by the end of World War II. Perhaps Naval Lieutenant Commander Richard Nixon saw Anderson play Lady Macbeth when he was stationed in the Pacific in New Caledonia from 1942 to 1946. He would have been a willing audience, for, before the war, as a college student in Whittier, California, he had himself participated in amateur theatre productions. And perhaps the young Marine intelligence officer, Joe McCarthy, stationed in the South Pacific with Scout Bombing Squadron 235, got to see Anderson perform Lady Macbeth to the troops. A line from *Macbeth* is the only Shakespeare he is known to have ever quoted, and he had his own theatrical flare and propensity for storytelling. For example, he made up a war record that later got him the Purple Heart for a leg injury from a fall down a flight of steps during a drunken Equator-crossing party aboard the seaplane *Chandeleur*, far away from any official hostilities.[19] At war's end, both Nixon and McCarthy launched political careers and became principal players in the witch-hunt to root out communists, a witch-hunt named after one of them—McCarthyism. Nixon was appointed to the House Un-American Activities Committee (HUAC) as a rookie Congressman from California in 1947. In his election campaign running against actress-turned-politician, Helen Gahagan Douglas, a veteran California liberal, Nixon won votes by calling her a "pinko" kind of Communist sympathizer. He followed up that victory by exploiting his HUAC affiliation to rise to power and make a name for himself hunting out other lefties in the entertainment industry. Just before World War II ended in 1945, the HUAC had been authorized to investigate any propaganda that attacked the principles of the American government. In 1947 the Truman administration went further by setting up Loyalty Review Boards to root out communists. Congressman Richard Nixon focused HUAC on the Hollywood film industry, claiming that communists were "producing propaganda films through a conspiratorial network of writers, directors, actors, and unions." The Committee called to account nineteen "unfriendly" witnesses, one actor, the rest writers and directors, establishing the Black List and destroying careers.[20]

While Margaret Webster came under suspicion for un-American activities, Judith Anderson stayed in the clear, focusing on her career and creating stage performances of two more "female monsters,"[21] in addition to Lady Macbeth. In 1947 Judith Anderson played Robinson Jeffers' *Medea* in New York in a sensational run at the National Theatre that lasted almost as long as her 1941 New York appearance in *Macbeth*. John Gielgud directed and played Jason, succeeded by Guthrie McClintock who acted Jason on tour. Following in Lady Macbeth's footsteps, Anderson's Medea went on a highly successful tour throughout the country and later appeared on television, as well as on a Decca sound recording. When in the 1950s the Eisenhower administration went looking for a performer to act as cultural ambassador at festivals in Berlin and Paris, Anderson was chosen to perform Medea. Medea superimposed on Lady Macbeth, a murderous female with knives in her hands, was first conjoined by Shakespeare when he appropriated Latin incantations from Seneca's *Medea* and adapted them for his Lady Macbeth.

The ambivalence of audiences toward Lady Macbeth—is she a monster or a woman to be pitied—is the same kind of ambivalence the poet Robinson Jeffers sought to project in his adaptation of Medea that he wrote expressly for Anderson to play. "Is she a proud and loving woman scorned who can topple the whole city of Corinth because of their masculine pride and prejudice?—Or is she an exciting monster, a deadly wild beast, and Jason and his friends merely normal unfortunate people?"[22] One may assume that the U.S. government officials who chose to send Anderson's Medea as representative of American culture would not have favored Jeffers's first interpretation of the play, which would have made their own "masculine pride and prejudice" suspect; but rather the second, which puts them in the position of identifying with "normal unfortunate people" victimized by an "exciting female monster." Anderson premiered her third "monster" wife role, Clytemnestra, another triumph, in 1950. Brooks Atkinson reasoned that what made Clytemnestra malefic and Fury-like on the stage was the actress herself. He all but says that the person of Judith Anderson is by instinct and temperament malefic and powerful. "Since Miss Anderson is playing, the character is malefic and powerful.... She is at home with the Furies. By instinct and temperament, she acts on their plane."[23]

The year 1950 was a seminal year. Joe McCarthy was elected to the U.S. Senate from his home state of Wisconsin and came out of the right-wing corner swinging at "Reds," "Pinkos," "Commies," lefties, socialists, liberals, and just plain Democrats, and aided by FBI director J. Edgar Hoover, the Justice Department, the CIA, the Internal Revenue Service, Passport and Immigration services, National Security Agency, the U.S. Post Office, and fellow Congressmen. This was also the year that the Russians exploded their first atomic bomb, China fell to Mao's communist armies, and Americans started fighting in Korea. It was a time when the loyalty review boards spread to state and local agencies, all of them acquiring "whatever material they could lay their hands on concerning people's lives, habits, beliefs, associations, relatives, etc., no one being above suspicion." What started as an effort to assure and reassure Americans' sense of security ended up having the opposite effect: "It heightened anxieties and thus invited promises of greater security, which in turn, further heightened the anxiety."[24]

A comic book reduction of Shakespeare's *Macbeth* came out in 1950, the year that Joe McCarthy delivered his famous Wheeling, West Virginia, speech that launched him on his witch-hunt. The next year, on the Senate floor, in his most "daring and seditious" speech, McCarthy opened his attack on President Truman's secretary of Defense as a "traitor and assassin" by reciting lines from *Macbeth*. Like putting speech in the cartoon bubble above a comic book character, McCarthy assigned Macbeth's words to the secretary of Defense as if to make them his confession of guilt. "I am in blood/ Steeped[25] in so far that should I wade no more / Returning were as tedious as go o'er." "These lines of Macbeth's seem to have been the only bit of Shakespeare McCarthy had ever heard of." One historian asks, "Was this in the deeper sense an allusion to himself?" and answers, "I suspect that in some very deep sense—too deep...to fathom—this may have been the case. At any rate, I know of no sinner so quick to attribute his own sins to others."[26] Three years later, McCarthy's role in the witch-hunt played itself out, reaching its climax and denouement in late spring of 1954 when the senator's demagoguery was exposed to millions of Americans watching him on television. During the hearings McCarthy used the same Macbeth lines that had worked for him before, this time to implicate a high-ranking army official. But this time McCarthy's rant produced outrage. His mendacity exposed, like a defeated and punch-drunk fighter, McCarthy had to leave the ring. Macbeth's lines had served to express his own course of action, and there was no turning back. Out of office, out of favor, he died a drunk.

But the *wives* were to blame for the hate and vituperation that came from McCarthy and his fellow witch-hunters, not their affable husbands. So said Senator Harry Cain, one of McCarthy's cronies. It was Cain's questioning at the hearings that was responsible for Charlie Chaplin leaving the United States. Chaplin defended Picasso, an "avowed Communist." Remembering the poker parties at McCarthy's home, Cain found McCarthy affable, even gentle. But while the senators were having a friendly game of cards, their wives harangued them about the ongoing hearings, goaded them to go after this one or that one. "When are you going to get this one or that one?" " Go get the son of a bitch!" Cain says they, the wives, were "the *real* haters," not the husbands.[27] Another television program during the year of the hearings backed up Cain's opinion of political wives and the argument, "She made me do it." Those millions of viewers who watched McCarthy on television in spring of 1954 had the opportunity to see Anderson's Lady Macbeth in the fall in a live broadcast from Brooklyn. Her Lady Macbeth was now a household image.

Arthur Miller, coming from the other end of the political spectrum, also blamed women for the witch-hunt in his 1952 play *The Crucible*. The playwright chose to dramatize the seventeenth-century Salem witch-hunt as parallel to McCarthyism. But in the play Miller has pushed the larger public actions into the background and pulled the more personal struggles of his principal character into the foreground. Fellow left-wing playwright Clifford Odets recognized this when he observed that the play is the history of a broken marriage.[28] Miller's play and the later film based on the play are mistakenly taken for a true historical documentation of the Salem witch trials. But the main plot is Miller's insertion of his own personal drama occurring simultaneously with his writing the play, his secret love affair with Marilyn Monroe and guilt at betraying his wife and children. Miller's description of his first wife, Mary, in his autobiography resembles John Proctor's wife Elizabeth, in *The Crucible*—cold, self-righteous, and sexually distant. The more public comparison would be Elizabeth Proctor as a stand-in for Ethel Rosenberg—stalwart wives to the bitter end. The play's sexually charged teenager, Abigail, who leads Proctor into adultery has Marilyn Monroe's allure. The historic Abigail, twelve years old at the time of the witch trials, had no sexual involvements with John Proctor or anyone else. Nor is there any basis for attributing to John Proctor extramarital affairs. Sex was not the issue in the Salem witch-hunt. Miller resolves Proctor's personal struggle with a noble ending: the character denounces his temptress Abigail and revives his lagging devotion to his wife, defending her from Abigail's accusations of witchcraft by making a true confession of his adultery in a public hearing. When faced with a choice between his death and a false confession of consorting with the devil, he refuses to put his good name to the false statement and exits to the gallows, a flawed but heroic martyr. Miller's own private predicament, while similar to Proctor's, resulted in a different outcome. He left his wife and married Marilyn Monroe in 1956, the same year he was subpoenaed to the hearings. That call was late in coming, four years after his colleagues Lillian Hellman, Clifford Odets, and Elia Kazan were called, and two years after McCarthy's humiliating censure and departure, after which the majority of Congress had little stomach for continuing the witch-hunt. Monroe claimed that her presence at the hearings got Miller off the hook, which may well have been true. The congressmen investigating Miller's politics showed far more interest in meeting and having their pictures taken with Miller's famous movie-star mistress during the hearing's recess, when Miller and Monroe announced their engagement to be married.[29] A few years later, Miller blamed the failure of this second marriage on Marilyn Monroe and turned it into another play, symbolically called *After the Fall* in which he explores the aftermath of Adam's loss of innocence and the self-destruction of temptress Eve. When the play opened at Lincoln Center in 1962 it reunited the playwright with his former director and friend Elia Kazan. Their association had been cut off when Kazan chose to be an informer and named forty names for the witch-hunters in 1952, just when Miller was heading for Salem to gather research for *The Crucible*. At this point in his autobiography, Miller explains that it was really Kazan's wife, Molly, " a rather moralistic woman," "a woman fighting for her husband's career,"[30] who was responsible for Kazan's cooperation with the McCarthy investigation—she made him do it. In these happier times of ten years later, Molly is out of the picture and Kazan has married the actress who plays Marilyn Monroe in *After the Fall*.

Leftist activists Yves Montand and Simone Signoret played the Proctors in a French version of *The Crucible* by Marcel Aymé, *Les Sorcières de Salem*, which opened in the Sarah Bernhardt Theatre in Paris in 1954. Aymé made the witch trials a struggle between the rich and the poor, and Salem like a Catholic provincial French village. In his private papers the playwright wrote that he found Miller's treatment of Abigail inhumane, that the American playwright had reduced her to a dramatic device that enshrines Proctor as a hero: Miller's Abigail is made a servant to the Proctor family, treated harshly by Mrs. Proctor, seduced by Mr. Proctor, and then driven from their house. Aymé's French version softens that treatment. Jean-Paul Sartre based his script for Raymond Rouleau's film of *Les Sorcières de Salem* on Aymé's play, with Montand and Signoret again appearing as the Proctors. The year the play premiered in Paris, Spanish-born Marie Casares performed Lady Macbeth in the Jean Vilar production of *Macbeth* at Avignon, the same year that the French war in Indochina ended and the war in Algeria began, and the year that Judith Anderson's Lady Macbeth was broadcast live on television, Americans finished fighting in Korea, and Congress censured Joe McCarthy.

But in 1953, as the New York premier of Miller's *Crucible* limped to a disappointing closure, the McCarthy hearings continued apace, convicted spy Ethel Rosenberg was executed, and *Macbeth*'s director Margaret Webster was called before the Senate Subcommittee. In the eyes of the witch-hunters, Ethel Rosenberg was a live stand-in for the monster wife roles Anderson was playing. And just as Lady Macbeth, Medea and Clytemnestra are killed or driven away as a form of purgation, so Ethel Rosenberg became a scapegoat for the plagues of war and the proliferation of nuclear weapons. Ethel Rosenberg was the second woman in American history to receive the death penalty from the federal government; the first was Mary Surratt implicated in the conspiracy to assassinate Abraham Lincoln in 1865, both scapegoats for the U.S. government and a fearful American populace. On the day Ethel was arrested, August 11, 1950, a U.S. Justice Department official gave a press conference and blamed her for the Korean War. The *New York Times* blamed Ethel Rosenberg for the spy ring that passed atomic secrets to Russia, running the headline "Atomic Spy Plot is Laid to Woman." Different from the popular 1950s wife image of the blond Doris Day, All-American-Girl type, Ethel Rosenberg was small in frame, dark haired, implacable and enigmatic in demeanor. "Ethel was Jewish, the daughter of immigrants, lower Eastside, poor, a labor activist and organizer in her shipping clerk union before her marriage, and a suspected communist."[31] Ethel's story continues to unfold. Many years after her execution, her brother David Greenglass came forward and confessed that he and his wife, Ruth, both of them spies, had set Ethel up to save themselves. That confession has not exonerated Ethel, however, for now historians are saying she should have spoken up on her own behalf, as everyone, they say, expected she would, instead of remaining silent in court in support of her husband and his communist ideology. "The threat of the electric chair was used as leverage to pry loose the names of all their accomplices. Instead the Rosenbergs 'called our bluff,' as one official said, virtually daring the government to pull the switch... Eisenhower's refusal to commute the death sentence ensured that the Rosenbergs would never be able to supply further information and provided an occasion for anti-American protests throughout the world."[32]

The Rosenberg trial began in March of 1951. Roy Cohn, McCarthy's aid, was lawyer for the prosecution. David and Ruth Greenglass served as witnesses for the prosecution. Ethel Rosenberg's silence was taken as a sign of her guilt, (just as Rebecca Nurse's silence condemned her as guilty in the Salem trial). Ethel's "refusal to demonstrate feeling was read as evidence of guilt in *a cold and unnatural woman*." In pronouncing the death sentence for both the husband and the wife, *the judge laid most of the guilt on the wife*, "Judge Kaufman singled out Ethel as... *a moral failure as a woman and a wife in not having deterred her husband from his ignoble cause*." During her three years of imprisonment, two in solitary confinement, right up until her execution, the FBI and the White House focused their blame on Ethel Rosenberg. An FBI agent wrote to J. Edgar Hoover *that Julius was the "slave" and Ethel his "master*."[33] These phrases became part of official reports and public statements, even appearing in Eisenhower's correspondence as he weighed and dismissed presidential clemency in the case.

Ethel Rosenberg was executed by electrocution on June 19, 1953. Thirty-five reporters watched. One described the "strange unearthly sound" emanating from her every pore, and his fearful sensation that she would somehow break her bonds "and come charging across the floor, wielding those tight little fists."[34] Julius Rosenberg's wife in her public death throes inspired fear, impressing on the onlooker an unearthly, unnatural creature who might break loose like a bound and hissing animal to attack him. She was cast out, gotten rid of, an "exciting monster" wife to the very end.

Margaret Webster was called before the Senate Subcommittee in May of 1953, one month before the execution of Ethel Rosenberg. An accomplished author as well as director and actor, Webster writes poignantly of that experience, and with shame, hardly warranted:

> The story that I shall try to tell... is personal and small; it took place only on the periphery of the main events; it is not a story of which I am proud. But I think it needs to be told, partly because it now [1972] seems so utterly

incredible, but even more because we need to be reminded that, incredible or no, it could happen again; not in the same framework or with the same weapons, but under the same pressures of insecurity, ambition, hatred, and above all—fear; always, and on both sides, fear.[35]

A telegram signed by Joseph R. McCarthy summoned Webster to Washington. José Ferrer had given her name in his testimony, and her name was on a list of theatre and radio artists used by the FBI called "Red Channels," a pamphlet published in 1950 by the right-wing journal *Counterattack*. Questioning went on for an hour and a half about her work in various theatre organizations and with artists known to have connections with communism, about her public statements defending blacklisted artists—she was asked about directing Paul Robeson in a production of *Othello*. Robeson, a known communist, was under severe censure. But in spite of Roy Cohn's badgering style of questioning, never letting Webster finish a sentence, and his stated intention of getting her for perjury if she didn't hang herself by taking the Fifth Amendment, the senators dismissed her. "Senator McCarthy told me they had decided I was an OK American after all and thank you very much.... McCarthy held out his hand. To my eternal regret, I took it."[36] But even after this dismissal the FBI continued to follow Webster and tap her phone. A year later, Webster was offered the job of directing the Shakespeare scenes in a movie about Edwin Booth starring Richard Burton. She told her agent that the studio better check on her blacklist status, and got this response, "you should know that they did check on your clearance and were informed that you are 'still active in associations that are on the Attorney General's subversive list.'" She advised that they instead hire her former partner and more politically conservative Eva Le Gallienne, and they did. "It turned out to be the American Legion which had supplied Twentieth-Century Fox with its completely inaccurate information. But the source didn't matter, neither did the accuracy. Once on the blacklist, you stayed there."[37] Webster acknowledges that in the fall out of the witch-hunt her career was somewhat undermined "if not ostensibly broken." But she grieved for losses beyond her own:

> I believe that no one touched the blacklist, witch-hunt pitch, without being lessened and to some degree defiled; neither those who were injured by the lists, nor those who compiled them, nor those who used them nor those who went along with them.... it did lasting damage to the United States and very few people emerged from it with any credit whatever, certainly I was not one of them—I mean, of course, in my own eyes.[38]

She derived some satisfaction from one of the consequences: "I got to know whom I'd like to be in a trench with and whom I'd just as soon not have on my side." And she concludes the story by standing up for liberals, shortly before her death in 1972:

> It is the fashion in the early Seventies to despise "liberals" and liberalism, whether you are a Black Panther or Vice President of the United States. Liberals have always been mown down by extremists from either side in any and every revolution; but they have somehow managed to get up again. There is plenty of justification for despising the "liberals" of twenty years ago. But we are tougher than we look. We shall still be around when a lot of the shouting and the shooting and the burning to the right and left of us has gone with the wind.[39]

While Webster dealt with the witch-hunt and as her career as a leading director of Shakespeare's plays on the American stage curtailed, she finished writing her book, *Shakespeare Today*. Her interpretation of *Macbeth* speaks directly to the events and tragedies she has just experienced, and those of World War II when she directed the play on Broadway. "All-pervasive" in the play and in the war "the power of evil" contaminates "like dry rot, or smog or the pollution of a river." She chooses to see the end of the play as the "ultimate defeat" of the power of evil, but is less certain about the outcome offstage, "more manifest in external circumstance than in events onstage." The play's pervasive "power of evil" acts as a "third protagonist," the power behind the thrones of both Macbeths. For Lady Macbeth, the power of evil comes to her at the very beginning when she invokes and invites it to come and possess her:

> *Come you spirits.... Come...you murdering ministers.... Come, thick night, /And pall thee in the dunnest smoke of hell....* And they come...They use her, possess her, just exactly as she had prayed them to do...they shroud the stars and charge the blackened night with terror. And, when the murder is once accomplished, Lady Macbeth is exhausted, used up.... Possessed...Lady Macbeth can no more reach or rescue her husband from evil's hold on him, a hold she initiated. She cannot unfasten what she fastened, undo what's been done, and the haunting hallucinations of reenacting what they've done drives her to an early grave.... Fear is in the ascendant, fear and hate, under whose banners evil has always triumphed.[40]

Lady Macbeth's suffering and death as poetic justice delivered upon an ambitious and overbearing wife appealed to the witch-hunters of the McCarthy era who were themselves filled with fear and hate—so, too,

those officials and journalist who feared and hated Ethel Rosenberg, per-
ceiving her as another "monster wife." Attempts were made to characterize First Lady Eleanor Roosevelt as a kind of Lady Macbeth having
undue influence over President Franklin Roosevelt's policies and actions.
Hunting season on, the three-term First Lady and later ambassador to the
United Nations lasted a long time, for Mrs. Roosevelt's career as a liberal public servant spanned over half the century. Where Edith Wilson
failed at the end of World War I to keep alive her husband's plan for an
international organization that would work for peace among the nations,
Eleanor Roosevelt became ambassador to the United Nations, a more lasting international organization that was formed during World War II. Mrs.
Roosevelt presented a largely visible if constantly moving target. Her support of blacks, women, immigrants, poor laborers, artists, and intellectuals
made her vulnerable to right-wing attacks. Her busy lecture circuit, weekly
news columns, national and international diplomatic missions, brought
on sobriquets of "Empress Eleanor" and "The Gab," coined by the nemesis who most persistently hounded her, right-wing journalist Westbrook
Pegler who, active on behalf of McCarthy and his henchmen, later became
a leader of the John Birch Society.[41]

The shadow of those McCarthy era witch-hunts that cast a pall over the
careers of so many theatre and film artists apparently never darkened
Judith Anderson's path just as the "mystery" Webster looked for in the part
of Lady Macbeth never became part of Anderson's performance. Was the
actress oblivious to the nightmare going on outside the theatre? Or did she
choose to ignore it, feeling as a British subject, that this was not her war to
fight? Or is it possible she was in sympathy with the witch-hunters? Her
very long, ghost-written and unpublished autobiography is noticeably silent
on the subject. The wars, witch-hunts, treason, spying, and assassination
that inform the play world of the Macbeths all occurred in the real world
of American history during Anderson's twenty plus years of performing
Lady Macbeth in America. How surprising it is then to go through the
materials on Judith Anderson's life and find nothing that reveals she had
any awareness or concern for her theatre and film colleagues who were
being adversely affected.

After her early expression of admiration for Eleanor Roosevelt when
she was invited to lunch at the White House in the late 1930s, Anderson
reserved her political enthusiasms for the British monarchy. As an Australian
descended from a Scottish father and English mother, her patriotic sentiments remained ever affixed to "their" royal family. In her autobiography,

she describes how she felt when touring in Australia she met a member of the British royal family:

> This would have been an honor and a joy for anyone, I think. But for me, who remembered from my childhood the very sound of the minister's voice intoning, "most heartily we beseech Thee with Thy favor to behold our most gracious sovereign...," who had never for a moment forgotten that I too, though born so far away and later working and making my home in a country that was not my own, was still a subject of the Crown, to learn that I was to be presented to members of the Royal Family was all but overwhelming. I had followed the developing lives of every member of it, like all Australians.... They were *our* family, the super-family; so it was with a combination of awe and joy and excitement, a glittering residue of fairy-tale glamour, that I entered the anteroom of the Royal Box.[42]

More "fairy tale glamour" followed. During the MGM filming of *Macbeth* "on location" in Scotland, Anderson took a day off from the shooting at Hermitage Castle to answer Queen Elizabeth's summons to Windsor Palace. There the Queen bestowed the title of "Dame" on the actress, an honor she considered the proudest moment of her career. After the ceremony, when Dame Judith arrived back on the film set in Scotland, a loudspeaker interrupted the sleepwalking scene with the song, "There is nothing like a dame!" and Anderson was swept up into a procession leading to a portrait of her as Lady Macbeth in her bright-red costume. Anderson kept that portrait prominently displayed in her California living room for the rest of her life, another thirty-five years.[43]

From the time she arrived in America in 1917, at the age of nineteen, until her death in 1992, at the age of ninety-four, Anderson chose to remain a resident alien working and owning property in America. Being apolitical was to her career's advantage at a time when theatre and film artists were being held suspect for disloyalty and lack of patriotism toward the United States. And being a resident alien could only enhance the sense of "otherness" of the scapegoat roles she played. But while an instinctive actor like Judith Anderson may have believed that she was staying out of the political fray, she was nevertheless used for political purposes of which she was either unaware or unconcerned. Other actors, her cohorts, wittingly allowed themselves to be used politically, none more ostentatiously than Ronald Reagan.[44] The U.S. government could show off Judith Anderson at international festivals as an example of talent fostered by America while at the same time hold up her "female monster" wife roles as lessons in what happens to women who are ambitious and meddlesome, the kind of woman that might be a communist spy like Ethel Rosenberg, or a liberal First Lady, like Eleanor Roosevelt. For, while Anderson herself may have been totally apolitical, her roles as Lady Macbeth and Medea projected personae with a political subtext. The government, in sending her to perform Medea in Berlin in 1951 and to Paris in 1956, had political control over the selections. In her autobiography Anderson admits, perhaps ingenuously, to being a little puzzled that she was selected to represent the U.S. government abroad when she herself was Australian born. Anderson's stage characters, heroines of evil deeds, chronicles of bad wives, spoke more decisively for the politics of the American government.

The struggles of becoming a successful actress, the sacrifices made, the losses in love, the gains in major roles, these form the subjects of Anderson's autobiography. Self-absorption is not unique to this actress. Perhaps narcissism is a necessary component of acting just as much as ambition and talent are. But for Anderson the struggle to succeed became more like an all-out war, and her rhetoric reflects this. She describes her striving as "warring" to become a successful actress, her career as a "battlefield," her own nature as "warring" with itself and "plaguing" her. "I know that if I had truly wanted domesticity and motherhood instead of the lone battleground that is a career woman's life, I would have had them. Instead I got what I asked for—as we all do, in one way or another.... But none of us are wholly what we are: there is always some vestigial warring other nature, asserting itself at intervals to plague us: in my case, the sudden, rather awful realization of loneliness, of unfulfillment, of being incompletely a woman—the cost I have had to pay for the drive to reach as near the top of my profession as I could get."[45] Even in her personal relationships, as revealed by her letters, she fights in a "white rage" and is compared to a "fire storm." The men who loved Judith Anderson wrote to her in searing language. Thornton Wilder's nephew, Kevin Wallace, a young man half Judith Anderson's age and in love with her during World War II, wrote: "You are wildfire burning over the cover of lonely coast hills; far fire restlessly investigating the crests of hills, that are not yet peopled. Some day you'll be scooped up in spite of all your smoking rage and put on a hearth with a cookpot hung over you; and I wish that I were the Lone Ranger who could do it."[46] Contrary to his wishes, she never did allow a "cookpot" to hang over her, neither Wallace's nor anyone else's. Her marriages lasted only a short time, her first to the U.C. Berkeley professor who introduced her to Robinson Jeffers. Anderson appears to have been adept at making men, and women such as Sally Bowles, desire her passionately, and then after a single or few passionate encounters, she would leave off fighting with them and devote her extraordinary energies to fighting career battles.

Motivation to be like her role model Sarah Bernhardt seems to have obsessed Anderson's inner as well as external life. That dream came closer to reality when in June of 1955, the U.S. government, under President Eisenhower and Vice President Nixon, sent Anderson to play Medea in Paris as the American entry in an international festival. She performed in the Sarah Bernhardt Theatre, where her idol had reigned, "the great French actress with whom I had always felt a presumptuous identification. There was something infinitely thrilling to me to dress in the lavish dressing room that had been hers, to walk on the stage where she had walked, to speak in the auditorium that had once vibrated to the whiplash of her voice." She was further delighted when one of the French critics referred to her as "the new Sarah Bernhardt." However Anderson's identification with Bernhardt, perhaps more of an imitation, could produce mixed results, "delightfully artifical" posing according to another critic.[47] Many years later, Anderson returned to Bernhardt when she saw Zoe Caldwell play Sarah Bernhardt on television, a performance that inspired Anderson to get up another production of *Medea* with Caldwell playing the principal role, and the eighty-five-year-old Anderson playing the Nurse. The "Story of Sarah Bernhardt" was to have been Judith Anderson's role. In the middle of World War II, after playing Lady Macbeth on the mainland and before touring her to the Pacific, Anderson was preoccupied with plans to play Sarah Bernhardt in a dramatized life of the French actress. The producer Ray Goetz lined up Moss Hart as the writer. Anderson remembers:

> Naturally, that resemblance to the great French tragedienne which, years before, I had dared to find, the identification with her that others had been kind enough to make, the hours I had spent reading about her, absorbing her, thinking about her, wishing I had ever seen her, and listening to the ghost of that passionate voice on archaic records speaking the mounting Alexandrines of Phèdre like chained lightning—all this combined to make me enthusiastic about Ray's idea.

After Moss Hart came on board as the writer, all kinds of complications arose with getting permission from Bernhardt's descendants. In the University of California Santa Barbara Judith Anderson archives there is a list of scenes for a play about Sarah Bernhardt, which may be by Moss Hart, but more likely by Bernhardt's son-in-law, Louis Verneuil, who had submitted to Anderson his own outline for the story, which Anderson found impracticable. Ultimately it was Anderson herself who torpedoed the project by refusing to go on without her own personal hairdresser, a vain demand that she would regret but could excuse herself for identifying too closely with her "imperious" idol: "It is possible that some of the great Bernhardt's own imperiousness, as I thought about her and made the first steps, even without a script, toward comprehending her, had rubbed off on me." Moss Hart had had enough, and that was the end of Anderson in the Sarah Bernhardt life story.[48]

The year 1961 that the Kennedy/Nixon "Great Debates" won an Emmy Award, Anderson received an Emmy for the MGM film version of her role in *Macbeth* shown on television soon after John F. Kennedy won the election.[49] Viewing Anderson's performance of Lady Macbeth on television, a *Time Magazine* critic reported seeing Judith Anderson "so evilly and essentially Lady Macbeth" that he could imagine her as the original, historic Queen of Scotland lying in wait the last nine hundred years. "With blood-red hair and blood-red voices as she told her hollow-hearted thane to screw his courage to the sticking place, Judith Anderson was so evilly and essentially Lady Macbeth that she seemed to have been waiting there among the Scottish battlements 900 years for NBC to come and shoot her" (November 28, 1960). What this critic failed to see is that Judith Anderson's essentially evil vampira Lady Macbeth embodied that ancient queen for twentieth-century Americans only, a Lady Macbeth for her times, not for the ages.

Conclusion ∽

The search to understand how Shakespeare's creation of Lady Macbeth came to haunt America's cultural memory and shape impressions of political wives began with the recent example of "Lady Macbeth Hillary Clinton," then goes back in time to see how Shakespeare transformed the historical figure of Gruoch, Queen of Scotland, into Lady Macbeth, and how that character arrived in America. At both ends of the time spectrum, twentieth century and eleventh century, wars and assassinations predominated—clashes between rival cultures, political parties, and religions. How obvious—*Macbeth* is a war play—with domestic, civil, international, and intercultural conflicts all at play. As the key players of Lady Macbeth have come into view, it can be seen that their prominence in the role coincided with America's major wars; at the same time as the women serving as First Ladies in the White House, while not all specifically called a Lady Macbeth, nevertheless suffered a similar nomenclature and for the same reasons—public anxiety about the conduct of the war and pressures on the commander in chief coming from an influential wife. "Her Highness" and "Petticoat Government" for Abigail Adams, "Her Grace" and "Hellcat" Mary Todd Lincoln, "Mrs. President" Edith Wilson, "Empress" Eleanor Roosevelt, and "Lady Macbeth" Hillary Clinton, all reflect that anxiety. Tags less imperial and more animalistic, comparisons to feline animals, the First Ladies shared with actors portraying Lady Macbeth on the stage: "pantheress" and "tigress," degenerating to the frequently used term—"monster."

Shakespeare puts the words "fiend-like queen" into Malcolm's assessment of Lady Macbeth at the end of the play; whether or not that was Shakespeare's opinion has proven debatable. Fiends did exist to the Puritans forming New World nationalism in New England, demons that along with monstrously intelligent women, needed to be driven out or destroyed. Believing in a devil that used the theatre as his playpen and employed religions other than theirs to enslave the world, the Puritans denied themselves theatre's potential for catharsis, and instead put their community in danger by staging real witch-hunts. And so began the haunting of America by Shakespeare's wayward and witch-like Lady Macbeth, a character that in the next century horrified President John Adams and that his wife found "detestable," but who nevertheless resembled her in the First Lady's conduct of another "Season of Witches." Putting to use whatever media was available to her, in addition to newsprint and church sermons, Abigail used the theatre as her bully pulpit to propagandize her idea of a national identity. She demonstrated Puritan exclusivity in demonizing immigrants "tainted" by origins other than English, especially Irish and French, and religions other than hers, especially Catholic—attitudes that have prevailed within America's more conservative parties for the past two hundred years. The Irish-Catholic actress performing Lady Macbeth when Abigail ruled as First Lady was no longer the gorgeous, young, and still a little awkward figure that she was when she premiered Lady Macbeth in Scotland and England in 1776, but a large and middle-aged American citizen teaching and performing a vast repertoire of roles in the United States. Charlotte Melmoth introduced to the young nation a Lady Macbeth born in the revolutionary period that bridged enlightenment with romanticism, neoclassical universality with passionate individuality, Irish nationalism with American nationalism.[1] Melmoth's Lady Macbeth reflected the largely liberal spirit represented by Jeffersonians and First Lady Dolley Madison. Lyrical and passionate in performance, Melmoth appealed to her audience not as a monstrous and fiendish Lady Macbeth, but as an intelligent, even "amiable" character. Working in an age that championed the actor's artistry and debated craft, intelligent and talented women like Melmoth could succeed in the theatre without depending on a husband for support and respect. However, opponents to such women drew from Lady Macbeth's opening speech the words "un-sex me," to condemn them as having destroyed their feminine nature and "proper" roles as wife and mother.[2] In tempering her own ambition and qualifying her lack of tenderness, Abigail Adams seems to have agreed; for even while she was asking her husband to "Remember the Ladies," she conceded, "my ambition will extend no further than reigning in the Heart of my Husband."[3]

A half century later, Charlotte Cushman personified the masculine, "unsexed," image of Lady Macbeth. Her audiences found her overbearing strength thrilling and horrifying at the same time. But she was no cartoon. She elicited pity as well as terror, especially in the sleepwalking scene. The obsession with the play *Macbeth* during the Civil War, made manifest in numerous productions, brought to American theatres on both coasts Verdi's opera that makes Lady Macbeth the dominating evil force, a revision of

Shakespeare's character that gives her stunning arias to sing but strips her of humanity. First Lady Mary Todd Lincoln suffered a similar fate, in that her detractors dismissed her as insane, of a diseased brain, inhuman, a "monster." Ellen Terry restored the feminine but not very smart Lady Macbeth, making her a wife who does everything to support her husband. Sarah Bernhardt restored the sensuality of a sexual woman to Lady Macbeth so successfully that Macbeth seemed to disappear into the backdrop. Margaret Webster restored intelligence to the character; but her nuanced interpretation paled next to Judith Anderson's "vampira" that dominated the twentieth-century Lady Macbeth in America.

Reviewing a production of *Macbeth* in the early 1960s, Mary McCarthy describes Lady Macbeth as a woman who has "'unsexed' herself, which makes her a monster by definition."[4] The execution of "monster" wife, Ethel Rosenberg, blamed for the Korean War and selling the secrets of the atomic bomb in the 1950s witch-hunt, played into Arthur Miller's *The Crucible* that dramatizes the Salem witch-hunt of the 1690s as a parallel to McCarthyism.[5] But despite Miller's leftist politics, he along with right-wing McCarthyists blamed the women, the wives, for the actions of the men, the husbands. Barbara Garson reversed the blame in her Macbeth parody, *MacBird*. Soon after John F. Kennedy's assassination, with the Vietnam War escalating, Garson did not choose to make her Lady-Macbeth-Lady-Bird character the one to blame for Vietnam. But in identifying Hillary Clinton with Lady Macbeth, that First Lady's enemies did blame her for President Clinton's actions, making her a witch-like "monster" wife, their image of Shakespeare's Lady Macbeth impressed upon them by Judith Anderson's "vampira" performances on stage, film, television, and sound recordings.

In showing how Shakespeare's Lady Macbeth has haunted America from the founding of the United States to the present, the two centuries intervening between Abigail Adams and Hillary Clinton seemed to contract when political enemies of the Clintons donned the mantle of the old Federalist Party and revised its partisan history to celebrate John Adams as the real father of the country, making Abigail Adams the mother. Having steered George W. Bush and Laura Bush into the White House, the neo-Federalists continued to rely on the vice president and his wife, Dick and Lynn Cheney, to lead their way back to the values of John and Abigail Adams, in both foreign and domestic policy. Anti-French and pro-English in forming their allies, echoing the Alien and Sedition Acts in formulating their anti-immigration walls and laws, the Cheneys and their neoconservative assistants pushed the country into war. Lynn Cheney wrote a children's book about Abigail Adams, and hosted dinner parties for her compatriot neoconservatives, complementing their revised looks at the Adams family in biographies and on television.

A production of *Macbeth* late in the Bush/Cheney second term reflected, as in a mirror darkly, the administration's actions. Set in "modern times," billed as "Stalinist," the postmodern assemblage of details from the present as well as the past provoked comparisons to Dick Cheney and his wife more than to Stalin. Starring a Shakespearean actor of television "Star Wars" fame, the play performance on the American stage in the first decade of the twenty-first century reflected images of America's wartime occupation of Iraq. Following sold-out performances at the Brooklyn Academy of Music, the production moved to Manhattan for an extended run. Drama critics may have disagreed on the "success" of the interpretation, but that had no effect on audience demand for tickets and the stunned and horrified attention paid to the performance. Patrick Stewart's Macbeth, aging and balding, a cold and calculating politician, his insatiable appetite for power equaled by gluttony and lust, commanded, ate, and sexually groped his way to the play's bitter end. The set, a kind of underground bunker, was fitted with a cage-like elevator upstage that took characters out and up, or down and into the cold, imprisoning space. Stainless steel gurneys rolled in and out to serve as a hospital deathbed, kitchen table, and counters, or to outfit an interrogation torture chamber. The role of hostess suited this Lady Macbeth best, a capable and attractive first lady, nervous, commandeered by her husband rather than commanding, more able to boss the servants in the Dunsinane kitchen where she was ultimately sidelined in her arguments with the constantly eating, blood-letting, devouring husband. The Witches dressed in charity-hospital nurse uniforms coldly turned off the life supports of the wounded soldier in the first act, and transformed into servants and spies for later scenes. The messenger, a spy-turned-informer by torture, was backed with projections of what looked like images of water boarding. The clanking of the metal elevator cage door, the butcher knives, the deep-freeze refrigerator in the relentlessly stainless-steel grey kitchen and butcher chamber, matched the world of the Bush/Cheney Iraq war with *Macbeth*'s, and the roles of Laura Bush and Lynne Cheney with an early twenty-first-century performance of Lady Macbeth.

"Our Shakespeare," says novelist Zadie Smith, "sees always both sides of a thing, he is black and white, male and female—he is everyman." In a lecture given at the New York Public Library in December of 2008 soon after the election of President Barack Obama, Zadie Smith drew a comparison between Obama's many voices expressed in his autobiography and

Shakespeare's in his plays, admiring them both for their "cultural contingency." Concerned that politicians are expected to adhere to specific dogmas, to be ideological, she contrasts the constraints imposed upon Obama in the political arena with the freedom to be beyond logic and dogma that Shakespeare enjoyed in the theatre. "It was a war of ideas that began for Will—as it began for Barack—in the dreams of his father." She explains that Shakespeare's father openly professed allegiance to the official Church of England, and of necessity secretly hid his Catholicism, which made him "a kind of equivocator." Fortunately for Shakespeare, she says, as an artist, "he had an outlet his father didn't have—the many-voiced theater.... In his plays he is woman, man, black, white, believer, heretic, Catholic, Protestant, Jew, Muslim." The theatre gave him the freedom to express "simultaneous truths," "irreducible multiplicity." "And he offers us freedom: to pin him down to a single identity would be an obvious diminishment, both for Shakespeare and for us."[6] In fostering such a comparison between President Barack Obama and playwright William Shakespeare, will the "many-voiced" theatre, with its freedom to express "simultaneous truths," foster an equally liberating comparison for the nation's First Lady that can exorcise the haunting figure of Lady Macbeth in the White House?

Just as Shakespeare's Lady Macbeth posed dramatic questions about women in power in his own time, the actors interpreting Lady Macbeth in America have reflected audiences' questions about powerful political wives in their times. Horrified by the character in performance, twentieth-century audiences have perceived certain wives with comparable anxiety and made them scapegoats for their fears. In previous centuries the actors inspired pity and even admiration for their Lady Macbeths, as well as horror and terror, confirming Shakespeare's power to create simultaneously juxtaposed reactions in the audience as well as simultaneous truths in the script. These lead players of Lady Macbeth in America, however different their costumes and scenery, their voices and shapes, all were able to disturb their audiences' attitudes regarding good wives and bad ones. The Calvinist firebrand, John Knox, asserted that "men subject to the counsel or empire of their wyves [are] unworthy of all public office" With Lady Macbeth, Shakespeare makes that assertion a question. Just as many of his plays explore leadership, as to what qualities and actions make for a strong or weak leader, his *Macbeth* questions the role of a wife in the leader's exercise of power. Shakespeare gave complexity to his Lady Macbeth, good qualities bent on self-serving deeds, her husband's political power ill-begotten, violence that breeds more violence, inhumanity that leads to inhumane governance. Shakespeare's plays, *Macbeth* his favorite, provided Abraham Lincoln with a study in leadership. He acknowledged that he was "a nobody" when he met and fell in love with Mary Todd, referring to his wife as his "partner of greatness," like Macbeth; and so might we ask whether the United States would be a union today had Lincoln not married Mary? Would slavery have been abolished had his abolitionist wife not rallied support? On the other hand, if Abigail Adams had held complete sway over her husband's decisions, the young republic would have gone to war with France, the country that had made it possible for the colonies to win their independence from England. As it was, "the politicianess" prevailed upon her husband to enact the draconian Alien and Sedition Acts. This play, *Macbeth*, that situates a married couple battling for position and power, has by virtue of strong actors in the role of Lady Macbeth, provided America with a fictive figure analogous to First Ladies in the White House, for better, for worse.

Notes ❧

INTRODUCTION

1. Brooks Anderson, "Queen of Tragedy," *New York Times*, December 10, 1950; reviewing Anderson in Robinson Jeffers' *Clytemnestra*.
2. Lorraine Helms, "Acts of Resistance," *The Weyward Sisters: Shakespeare and Feminist Politics* Dympha C. Callaghan, Lorraine Helms, and Jyotsna Singh (Oxford: Blackwell, 1994), 132, 137.
3. Catherine Belsey, "Subjectivity and the Soliloquy," *New Casebooks: Macbeth*, ed. Alan Sinfield (London: Macmillan, 1992), 85. Hereafter cited as Sinfield *New Casebooks*.
4. Drawing on J.E. Neale's observations. Phyllis Rackin, *Shakespeare and Women* (Oxford, New York: Oxford University Press, 2005), 30.
5. Cristina León Alfar, *Fantasies of Female Evil: The Dynamics of Gender and Power in Shakespearean Tragedy* (Newark: University of Delaware Press; London: Associated University Presses, 2003), Introduction.
6. Alan Sinfield, "'Macbeth': History, Ideology and Intellectuals," Sinfield *New Casebooks* 121, 132.
7. Sinfield *New Casebooks* 134.
8. J.L. Styan, *The Shakespeare Revolution: Criticism and Performance in the Twentieth Century* (Cambridge, London, New York: Cambridge University Press, 1977), 232, 237.

1. LADY MACBETH IN THE WHITE HOUSE

1. Barbara Garson, *MacBird* (Berkeley, New York: Grassy Knoll Press, 1966), 13. Hereafter cited as Garson. "'It wasn't an anti-Johnson play,' Garson says, though she did intend it as a broad critique of both Kennedy's and Johnson's approach to politics. 'It was the Johnson that Bill Moyers described...self-dramatizing, self-pitying, but also a true liberal, and unable to understand why these Kennedys, who did so little, really, were thought of as so beautiful.'" Garson quoted by Jane Horwitz, "She Hopes 'MacBird' Flies in a New Era," *Washington Post*, September 5, 2006; announcing the play's revival.
2. Garson 13.
3. Garson 29.

4. Garson 10.
5. Garson 11–12.
6. Daniel Wattenberg, "The Lady Macbeth of Little Rock," *American Spectator* 25(8) (August 1992): 25. Hereafter cited as Wattenberg. The title rhythmically parallels "Lady Macbeth of Mtsensk" a short story by Nikolai Leskov based on a famous crime in Russia committed by a wife who violently murders her husband to run off with her lover. The story is the basis for Shostakovitch's opera of the same title.
7. Joe Conason and Gene Lyons, *The Hunting of the President: The Ten-Year Campaign to Destroy Bill and Hillary Clinton* (New York: St. Martin's Press, 2000).
8. Wattenberg 26.
9. Quoted by Garry Wills in "Hating Hillary," *The New York Review of Books*, November 14, 1996.
10. "Truth to Power," *New York Times*, June 1, 2008.

2. FROM SHAKESPEARE'S STAGE TO AMERICA'S

1. Preferring the "absorption" of reading Shakespeare, Greenblatt has judged theatre, Shakespeare's as well, to be an institution compromised by commercial interests. Stephen Greenblatt, "Shakespeare and the Exorcists," *Shakespearean Negotiations: The Circulation of Social Energy in Renaissance England* (University of California: 1988; reprint, New York: Oxford University Press, 1997), 127–128.
2. Alan Sinfield gives a good argument for making Malcolm less than the hero who restores order at the end of the play; "there may be considerable overlap between the qualities of the tyrant and the true king." Sinfield *Casebook* 127.
3. Garry Wills, *Witches and Jesuits: Shakespeare's Macbeth* (New York: Oxford University Press, 1995), 77–89.
4. "[T]he misogynist Romans would have found in Cleopatra, the foreign queen, a useful scapegoat for the disasters of the wars. Just as Dido, Queen of Carthage, threatened to keep Rome's founding hero, Aeneas, away from the path of duty, so it was Cleopatra who led Antony and the others astray— their only crime being weakness of will in the face of a dangerously seductive, emasculating, immoral woman." Mary Beard, "The Truth about Cleopatra," *The New York Review of Books*, 56 (2) (February 2009): 44.
5. David Bevington, *Shakespeare's Ideas: More Things in Heaven and Earth* (Chichester: Wiley-Blackwell, 2008), 175, 188.
6. Turgot, *The Life of Saint Margaret, Queen of Scotland*, trans. William Forbes-Leith (Edinburgh: Floris, 1884, 1993).
7. One of her books, the gospels in a bejeweled binding, said to have been fished from the bottom of a river in miraculously good condition, reappeared as a

piece of evidence in the canonization of Saint Margaret—the only rich widow, mother of several kings, who died peacefully in her bed, to be made a saint.

8. Alvin Kernan, *Shakespeare, The King's Playwright: Theater in the Stuart Court, 1603–1613* (New Haven and London: Yale University Press, 1995), 71–88.

9. Stefan Zweig makes a case for identifying Queen Mary as an inspiration for Shakespeare's Lady Macbeth. See his biography, *Maria Stuart*, first published in German in 1935, and later translated into French and English. Sinfield compares Mary to Macbeth, Mary as "the lawful ruler *and* the tyrant.... To her are attributed many of the traits of Macbeth." Sinfield *Casebook* 127.

10. In addition to Garry Wills account in *Witches and Jesuits*, see Antonia Fraser's *Faith and Treason: The Story of the Gunpowder Plot* (New York: Nan A. Talese Doubleday, 1996) for full accounts and varying interpretations of the plot and the fate of its plotters.

11. See Clare Asquith's *Shadow Play: The Hidden Beliefs and Coded Politics of William Shakespeare* (New York: Public Affairs, Perseus Books, 2005); and for a more dispassionate analysis of Shakespeare's Catholic inheritance, see Stephen Greenblatt's *Will in the World: How Shakespeare Became Shakespeare* (New York and London: W.W. Norton, 2004), especially Chapter Three, "The Great Fear."

12. David Laing, ed., *The Works of John Knox* (Edinburgh: Bannaiyne Club, 1855), 4:373, 390, 395. Hereafter cited as Knox.

13. Knox 374.

14. Charles H. Shattuck, *Shakespeare on the American Stage: From the Hallams to Edwin Booth* (Washington, D.C.: Folger Shakespeare Library, 1976), 3.

15. Bruce C. Daniels, *Puritans at Play: Leisure and Recreation in Colonial New England* (New York: St. Martin's Griffin, 1995), 66–68. See also David Cressy, *Coming Over: Migration and Communication between England and New England in the Seventeenth Century* (Cambridge: Cambridge University Press, 1987).

16. Cotton Mather, *Magnalia Christi Americana, or the Ecclesiastical History of New England* (London: T. Parkhurst, 1702), 2:29.

17. Esther Cloudman Dunn, *Shakespeare in America* (New York: Macmillan, 1939), 24–25.

18. Simon Williams, "Taking Macbeth out of Himself: Davenant, Garrick, Schiller and Verdi," *Shakespeare Survey: An Annual Survey of Shakespeare Studies and Production, 57,* Macbeth *and its Afterlife*, ed. Peter Holland (Cambridge: Cambridge University Press, 2004), 55.

19. Quoted by George Winchester Stone, Jr., and George M. Kahrl, *David Garrick: A Critical Biography* (Carbondale: Southern Illinois University Press, 1979), 249. Hereafter cited as Stone and Kahrl.

20. From the 1623 First Folio, facsimile edition, *Mr. William Shakespeares Comedies, Histories, & Tragedies* (New Haven: Yale University Press, 1954), 724.

21. Joseph Roach, *Cities of the Dead: Circum-Atlantic Performance* (New York: Columbia University Press, 1996), 162, 169; Roach referencing Christopher Spencer, ed., *Davenant's Macbeth from the Yale Manuscript: An Edition, with a Discussion of the Relation of Davenant's Text to Shakespeare's* (New Haven: Yale University Press, 1961), 2–3.

22. Quoted in Rosamond Gilder, *Enter the Actress: The First Women in the Theatre* (London: George G. Harrap, 1931), 156.

23. Cotton Mather, "A Brand Pluck'd from the Burning," *Narratives of the Witchcraft Cases, 1648–1707*, ed. George Lincoln Burr (New York: Scribners, 1914), 282. Hereafter cited as Cotton Mather "Brand Pluck'd."

24. Cotton Mather "Brand Pluck'd" 283.

25. Nancy Armstrong, Leonard Tennenhouse, *The Imaginary Puritan: Literature, Intellectual Labor, and the Origins of Personal Life* (Berkeley: University of California Press, 1992), 204, 213.

26. The earliest Shakespeare play to appear in the libraries of colonial gentlemen in Virginia was also *Macbeth*. Edwin Eliott Willoughby, "The Reading of Shakespeare in Colonial America," *Biographical Society of America,* 6 (14) (June 23, 1937): 48, 49.

27. John Dunton, *Letters written from New England A.D. 1686* (London: 1705; Boston: 1867; Reprint New York: Burt Franklin, n.d.), 116; Willoughby 50.

28. Jonathan Bate, *Shakespearean Constitutions: Politics, Theatre, Criticism 1730–1830* (Oxford: Clarendon Press, 1989), 64. Hereafter cited as Bate.

29. Odai Johnson and William J. Burling, *The Colonial American Stage, 1665–1774: A Documentary Calendar* (Cranberry, New Jersey: Assoc. of University Presses, 2001), 196. Thomas Clark Pollock, *The Philadelphia Theatre in the Eighteenth Century* (Philadelphia: University of Pennsylvania Press, 1933), 414.

30. Robert J. Myers and Joyce Brodowski, "Rewriting the Hallams: Research in 18th Century British and American Theatre," *Theatre Survey* 41 (1) (May 2000): 11.

31. "[F]or three crucial years in his professional development Garrick was in love with Peg Woffington, and their love affair became public property for comment by all hack writers, rivals, and admirers." Stone and Kahrl 56.

32. Stone and Kahrl 52–57.

33. Kalman A. Burnim, *David Garrick Director* (Pittsburgh: University of Pittsburgh Press, 1961), 126.

34. Stone and Kahrl 249–251. "Hell drags me down. I sink, / I sink—Oh!—my soul is lost forever! / Oh! [He dies.]" Nigel Cliff, *The Shakespeare Riots* (New York: Random House, 2007), 101n*.. Hereafter cited as Cliff.

35. Dennis Bartholomeusz, *Macbeth and the Players* (Cambridge: University Press, 1969), 48–49.

36. Davies' *Life of Garrick* quoted in Bartholomeusz 49.

37. Marvin Rosenberg, *The Masks of Macbeth* (Newark: University of Delaware Press, 1978), 68. Hereafter cited as Rosenberg.

38. "Dr. Johnson found her not the conversationalist or intellect he found in Mrs. Woffington…" Johnson also "thought her acting, though good, somewhat mechanical and affected, as though she had some former player in mind which occasioned it." From Boswell's *Life of Johnson* in Stone and Kahrl 72, 555, 701 n35, 738 n78.
39. Stone and Kahrl 74–75.
40. Burnim 104.
41. Bartholomeusz 121, 279.
42. Mrs. Clement Parsons, *Garrick and His Circle* (New York: Putnam's; London: Methuen, 1906), 52.
43. Janet Dunbar, *Peg Woffington and her World* (Boston: Houghton Mifflin Company, 1968).
44. The "Patriots of Dublin," protesting the Lord Lieutenant's shutting down the Irish Parliament in 1754, rallied at the theatre to applaud *Mahomet*'s hero and the speech, "Power is a Curse when in a Tyrant's Hands," that led to a riot that all but destroyed the theatre and bankrupted Sheridan. For a full account see Christopher Morash, *A History of Irish Theatre 1601–2000* (Cambridge: Cambridge University Press, 2002), 58–66.
45. Rather than following the fashion of making Shylock a low comedy character, Macklin took him seriously. William Archer in *Actors and Actresses of Great Britain and the United States from the Days of David Garrick to the Present Time*, ed. Brander Mathews and Laurence Hutton (New York: Cassell, 1886), 9, 10. Hereafter cited as Mathews.
46. Allardyce Nicoll, *The Garrick Stage: Theatres and Audience in the Eighteenth Century* (Manchester: Manchester University Press, 1980), 170–172. Hereafter cited as Nicoll.
47. Macklin's note on the décor quoted in Bartholomeusz 90.
48. "The Harvard Theatre Collection has an extra illustrated copy of Kirkman's *Life of Macklin* containing two large double column pages of manuscript notes made by Macklin in preparation, obviously, for his celebrated production of *Macbeth* at Covent Garden in 1773." Arthur Colby Sprague, *Shakespeare and the Actors: The Stage Business in His Plays (1660–1905)* (Cambridge: Harvard University Press, 1944), 228.
49. Nichol 171.
50. The English government banned the wearing of traditional Scottish clothes in reaction to the Jacobean uprising in 1745 that attempted to restore the Stuart pretender to the throne, and led to the English massacre of Highlander Scots following the Battle of Culloden. John Prebble, *Culloden* (London: Penguin, 1961, 1996), 313–314.
51. From contemporary observations in Mathews, 164–165, 105, 110–111.
52. Sheridan quoted in Esther K. Sheldon, *Thomas Sheridan of Smock-Alley: Recording His Llife as Actor and Theater Manager in both Dublin and London; and Including a Smock-Alley Calendar for the Years of His Management* (Princeton: Princeton University Press, 1967), 305.

53. Sheldon. See also Beverly E. Schneller, "No 'Brave Irishman' Need Apply: Thomas Sheridan, Shakespeare and the Smock-Alley Theatre," *Shakespeare and Ireland: History, Politics, Culture*, ed. Mark Thornton Burnett and Ramona Wray (New York: St, Martin's Press, 1997), 175–192.

54. Ellen G. D'Oench, *"Copper into Gold," Prints by John Raphael Smith, 1751–1812* (New Haven and London: Yale University Press, 1999), 266–267.

55. The Royal Academy Catalogue for 1784 as annotated by Horace Walpole, Walpole Library, Yale University. "Lady Macbeth Walking in her Sleep."

56. Horace Walpole to Lady Ossory, December 25, 1782, in *Walpole Correspondence* 33:ii, 377. Like the Egyptians who erased the identity of former pharaohs from public art, the English reidentified images of former queens of tragedy as depictions of Siddons. For example, the picture of Siddons in Medea's costume, presumably a picture of the actress playing Medea, in actuality is her head on the body of actress Mary Ann Yates. Siddons never played Medea, a role almost exclusively belonging to Yates on the eighteenth-century English-speaking stage. J. Thomthwaite's 1792 illustration of Siddons for J. Bell's edition of Richard Glover's *Medea* came out twenty years after the original of Mrs. Yates.

57. "Siddons's fame rested more on nineteenth-century English standards of matronly respectability.... [S]he could embody a conception of duty to the nation, and thus defuse and tame the potentially radical Shakespeare." Her performance of Volumnia in *Coriolanus*, she made "about family values and a form of matriarchy that is in fact profoundly patriarchal.... conformable to the age of Queen Victoria." Bate 143.

58. *Henry Fuseli 1741–1825*, translation of Zurich catalogue by Sarah Twohig (London: Tate Gallery, 1975), 58–59. Stuart Sillars, *Painting Shakespeare: The Artist as Critic 1720–1820* (Cambridge: Cambridge University Press, 2006). Hereafter cited as Sillars. Sillars sees no eroticism in the Louvre's "Lady Macbeth Sleepwalking," rather an "ordinariness," "a combination of physical strength made greater by her otherwise very commonplace appearance," connecting what he sees as a lack of "sexual determinants" in the figure to Lady Macbeth's Act One invocation to spirits to "unsex her" (224–226). For Fuseli's Witch of Endor reference, see Sillars 104. For James Gillray's political caricature based on Fuseli's painting of "The Three Witches" see Bate 93.

3. "POLITICIANESS"

1. John Adams, reprinted in John Holroyd, Earl of Sheffield's *Observations of the Commerce of the American States with Europe and the West Indies* (Philadelphia: Robert Bell, 1783), 55. Early American Imprints, Series I.

2. L.H. Butterfield, ed., *Adams Family Correspondence* (Boston: Massachusetts Historical Society, 2007), 1:38. Hereafter cited as *Adams Family Correspondence*.

3. *Adams Family Correspondence* 1:318–319.
4. Letter to Benjamin Rush as quoted in Joseph J. Ellis, *Founding Brothers: The Revolutionary Generation* (New York: Knopf, 2001), 217. Hereafter cited as Ellis.
5. Stacy Schiff, *A Great Improvisation: Franklin, France, and the Birth of America* (New York: Henry Holt & Company, 2005), 235–236; William Howard Adams, *The Paris Years of Thomas Jefferson* (New Haven: Yale University Press, 1997), 76.
6. Ducis, like Shakespeare, drew on Plutarch and ancient Greek plays for material.
7. M. Ducis, *Macbeth* (Paris: Gueffier, 1790), vi [my translations].
8. My translation of Grimod de la Reynière, quoted in John Golder, *Shakespeare for the Age of Reason: the Earliest Stage Adaptations of Jean François Ducis, 1769–1792* (Oxford: Voltaire Foundation, 1992), 223. Hereafter cited as Golder.
9. Golder 218–220, in the *Macbeth* chapter 163–230.
10. Paul Albert, ed. and Introduction, *Lettres de Jean-François Ducis* (Paris: Jousset, 1879), lxxi, 118.
11. *Adams Family Correspondence* VI:185–186; VI:263, 25; VII:145.
12. *Adams Family Correspondence* VI:366–368.
13. Did Abigail read the reviews? Contrary to later opinions of Siddons' Lady Macbeth, her first season playing the role received a lackluster response from some, as, for example, John Taylor's review in the *Morning Post*, February 1785: "In the taper scene she was defective; her enunciation was too confined... the faces she made were horrid and even ugly, without being strictly just or expressive." Quoted in *No Turn Unstoned: The Worst Ever Theatrical Reviews* compiled by Diana Rigg (London: Arrow Books, 1982), 231. Contemporary actress, Mrs. Barry, observed that the school of acting of Siddons and her brother Kemble was "so full of paw and pause" that other actors on the stage "used frequently to prompt them." H.B. Irving, *Occasional Papers: Dramatic and Historical* (London: Bickers and Son, 1906), 59.
14. March 4, 1786, *Adams Family Correspondence*, VII:81.
15. William H. Drummond, ed., *Autobiography of Archibald Hamilton Rowan*, Introduction by R.B. McDowell (Shannon, Ireland: Irish University Press, 1972), 130, 135–136; quoting from memoir in *Monthly Repositories* for October and November 1812 soon after Ann Jebb's death.
16. Quoted in Anthony Page, *John Jebb and the Enlightenment Origins of British Radicalism* (Westport, CT: Praeger, 2003), 179, 254, 251–252. Hereafter cited as Page.
17. Phyllis Lee Levin, *Abigail Adams: A Biography* (New York: St. Martin's Griffin, 2001), 349, 364. Hereafter cited as Levin *AA*.
18. John Adams writing from Philadelphia to Abigail Adams, December 1, 1794.

19. Quoted in Richard N. Rosenfeld, *American Aurora: A Democratic-Republican Returns, the Suppressed History of our Nation's Beginnings and the Heroic Newspaper That Tried to Report It* (New York: St. Martin's Press, 1997), 47. Hereafter referred to as Rosenfeld.
20. Rosenfeld 64.
21. Rosenfeld 60.
22. Rosenfeld 76, 77, 83.
23. Rosenfeld 90.
24. Rosenfeld 94–95.
25. Quoted in David McCullough, *John Adams* (New York: Simon & Schuster, 2001), 500. Hereafter cited as McCullough.
26. Rosenfeld 87–88, 92.
27. Rosenfeld 109.
28. Rosenfeld 109–110.
29. Rosenfeld 110–111.
30. From Annals of Congress, Rosenfeld 112.
31. Polish writer Julien Niemcewicz, Rosenfeld 112.
32. *Porcupine's Gazette*, May 8, 1798, Rosenfeld 112.
33. Rosenfeld 115.
34. Rosenfeld 115.
35. Rosenfeld 116.
36. Rosenfeld 117.
37. Rosenfeld 119.
38. Rosenfeld 123.
39. Rosenfeld 151, 177.
40. William Dunlap, *Diary of William Dunlap (1766–1839): The Memoirs of a Dramatist, Theatrical Manager, Painter, Critic, Novelist, and Historian* (New York: New York Historical Society, 1930; Benjamin Blom, 1969), 312–315. Hereafter cited as Dunlap *Diary*.
41. McCullough 506–507.
42. Ellis 191.
43. Carl Sferrazza Anthony, *First Ladies: The Saga of the Presidents' Wives and Their Power 1789–1961* (New York: Harper Collins, Perennial, 2003; 1992), 69. Hereafter cited as Anthony.
44. Garry Wills, *Henry Adams and the Making of America* (Boston: Houghton Mifflin, 2005), 24–25.
45. John Quincy Adams, *Dermot MacMorrogh or the Conquest of Ireland: An Historical Tale of the Twelfth Century in Four Cantos* (Dublin: Maunsel, 2005), 18–19.
46. Anthony 69.
47. Quoted by William Seale, *The President's House: A History*, 2 vols. (Washington, D.C., White House Historical Assoc., National Geographic Society, and New York: Abrams, 1986) I:81. Hereafter cited as Seale.

4. PLAYING FOR REVOLUTIONARIES

1. Seale 1:81.

2. She appropriated the story of her partner's legitimate wife, Anne Larry, whom Samuel Jackson Pratt whisked away from a boarding school in England and hastily married in Scotland in 1767 or 1768. Anne died in 1805 in England, giving rise to the confusion of dates for Charlotte Melmoth's death in biographical dictionaries. C. Ruth Wright Hayre, "Samuel Jackson Pratt: Novelist and Poet (1747–1814)," (PhD diss., University of Pennsylvania, 1953), 3.

3. Another who judged her performance "very wild" was the Drury Lane prompter who noted it in his diary for that night. William Van Lennep, Emmett Langdon Avery, Arthur Hawley Scouten, Charles Beecher Hogan, and George Winchester Stone, *The London Stage 1660–1800: A Calendar of Plays, Entertainments & Afterpieces, Together with Casts, Box-receipts and Contemporary Comment* (Carbondale: Southern Illinois University Press, 1960–1970), 5:39. Hereafter cited as *London Stage*.

4. "Theatre Intelligence," [London] *Morning Chronicle*, November 26, 1776.

5. *Recollections of the Life of John O'Keeffe*, 2 vols. (London: Henry Colburn, 1826), II:125–26. Robert Hitchcock, *An Historical View of the Irish Stage; from the Earliest Period Down to the Close of the Season 1788*, 2 vols. (vol. 1 Dublin: Marchbank, 1788; vol. 2 Dublin: Wm Folds, 1794), 2:229–30.

6. The theatre would continue in use under new management and survives today in the framing of a games parlor for pool, pinball, and videos. In a financial bind from which he would never recover, Courtney's (Samuel Jackson Pratt's) reputation as a beggar and borrower who never pays back had begun.

7. The illustration of Charlotte Melmoth as Queen Elizabeth I appears in the Bell edition of the play, 1776. For listings of Charlotte Melmoth's roles in London, see *London Stage* vols. 4 and 5.

8. Emphasis mine. Anonymous, *Charles and Charlotte*, 2 vols. (London: Wm Lane, 1777), 1:86–91. Pratt's letter to Sheridan is in the Beinecke Rare Book and Manuscript Library, Yale University.

9. Fitzroy Maclean, *Scotland: A Concise History* (London and New York: Thames and Hudson, 1993, 1999), 200.

10. Hugh Blair, *Lectures on Rhetoric and Belles Lettres*, 3 vols. (Edinburgh: Creech, 1783, 1787), 3:349–350. Hereafter cited as Blair.

11. University English departments can trace their origin to Hugh Blair's appointment as the first professor of English language and literature and to his published lectures that became standard reading in schools in the United States for the next half-century. Blair 2:447. In the two-volume, fifth American edition taken "from the ninth and last London edition" and published in Brooklyn by Thomas Kirk in 1812, reference to Thomas Sheridan is deleted. American editors, mostly clergymen, shortened and changed Blair's *Lectures* into a series of questions and answers, as, for example, Rev. Marsh's *Blair's*

Lectures... Reduced to Question and Answer, Hartford, CT, 1820; Rev. Blake's *Abridgement* adapted for his Young Ladies' Literary School at Concord, New Hampshire, published in 1822. The language in these later editions waters down Blair's enthusiasm for Shakespeare's plays.

12. The *Edinburgh Evening Courant* and *Edinburgh Evening News* track more roles, January through April, 1776: Calista in Nicolas Rowe's *Fair Penitent*, Euphrasia in Arthur Murphy's *The Grecian Daughter*, Bellario in George Colman's *Philaster*, Mandane in John Banks *Cyrus*, Alicia in Nicholas Rowe's *Jane Shore*, Zara in William Congreve's *The Mourning Bride*, Marcia in Joseph Addison's *Cato*, Belvedira in Thomas Otway's *Venice Preserved*, Mrs. Belville in Hugh Kelly's *The School for Wives*, ending the season as Lady Randolph in John Home's *Douglas*. Norma Armstrong, "The Edinburgh Stage 1715–1820: A Bibliography" (Edinburgh: Central Library, 1968) culled from lists in a typescript (unique copy) assembled from the two leading Edinburgh newspapers by the librarian at Edinburgh's public library.

13. A handsome and graceful man, formal in style, grown portly with age, Digges, too, owed his start in the theatre to Thomas Sheridan in Dublin in 1749. The 1775–1776 Edinburgh season with Digges performing male leads to Charlotte's female ones would be repeated in Ireland, where they reprised their roles in *Macbeth* in 1782.

14. In Scotland with Charlotte, Pratt finished writing what would be his most popular novel, *Emma Corbett,* a story that reflects divided sympathies for the American Revolution. The spirited main character, one that resembles Charlotte Melmoth, cross-dresses to follow her beloved fighting in America on the English side, while her father and brother stand for the revolutionaries

15. Joseph R. Roach, *The Player's Passion: Studies in the Science of Acting* (Wilmington: University of Delaware, 1985; Ann Arbor: University of Michigan Press, 1993), 129.

16. For this and other correspondence of Charlotte and Courtney Melmoth with Ben Franklin see *The Papers of Ben Franklin*, ed. William B. Willcox, and Ellen R. Cohn (New Haven and London: Yale University Press, 1986), 25:249, 265, 430, 453, 466, 532–535, 544–546, 568, 580, 693, 725–726; 26:36–37, 114–115, 118, 131–136, 198–199, 198–199, 310, 330, 434–435, 671–672. Cohn notes that Paris police archives indicate Pratt was spying for the British secret service.

17. As quoted in A.T.Q. Stewart, *A Deeper Silence: The Hidden Origins of the United Irishmen* (Belfast: Blackstaff Press, 1993, 1998), 176. Hereafter cited as Stewart. He notes that Martha Harris Johnson was actually Franklin's niece.

18. Sparked most immediately by the English government recognizing the legitimacy of Catholics in Canada (by the Catholic Relief Act), the riots grew out of extremist Protestants' long-held fears that conceding any legitimacy to Catholics would threaten their political and economic as well as religious

supremacy in the British Commonwealth. Anthony Page, *John Jebb and the Enlightenment Origins of British Radicalism* (Westport, Connecticut: Praeger, 2003), 240.

19. John Bernard, *Retrospections of the Stage*, 2 vols. (London: Colburn and Bentley, 1830), 1:222.

20. There was more of a "rage" for Melmoth than for Kemble in their first appearances together in Smock Alley's 1782 summer tour of Cork and Limerick, when Melmoth played Kate to Kemble's Petruchio in Garrick's shortened version of *Taming of the Shrew*; Cleopatra to his Anthony in John Dryden's *All for Love*; Lady Allworth to his Sir Giles Overreach in *New Way to Play Old Debts*; Marcia to his Cato in Addison's *Cato*; Belvidera to his Jaffiere in Otway's *Venice Preserved*; Lady Touchwood to his Sir George Touchwood in Cowley's *Belle's Stratagem*. *Hibernian Chronicle* 1782–1783.

21. Marcus Tanner, *Ireland's Holy Wars: The Struggle for a Nation's Soul 1500–2000* (New Haven: Yale University Press, 2001, 2003). Hereafter cited as Tanner.

22. The *Dublin Evening Post* reports on November 7, 1780, that during the previous three years of the American Revolution, 6522 Irish emigrated to America: New York 1911, Philadelphia 2086, Charleston 966, New Jersey 326, Halifax 516, Newport RI 717; mostly young men fighting against England.

23. Tommasso Giordani founded the Opera Company and produced a dozen works, including Gay's *Beggar's Opera*, Handel's *Messiah*, Gluck's *Orfeo and Euridice*, and several of Giordani's own compositions. T.J. Walsh, *Opera in Dublin: 1705–1797: The Social Scene* (Dublin: Allen Figgis, 1973), 230, 231. Hereafter cited as Walsh. Melmoth's opera career continued later in the 1780s, singing with Michael Kelly, recently returned to Ireland from working with Mozart on the continent.

24. Quoted in John C. Greene, *Theatre in Belfast, 1736–1800* (Bethlehem, PA: Lehigh University Press, 2000), 248. Hereafter cited as Greene.

25. John T Gilbert, *A History of the City of Dublin*, 3 vols. (Dublin, 1854–1859; Shannon: Irish University Press, 1972), 1:294, 2:109, 3:26. Hereafter cited as Gilbert.

26. The newspaper was "bought by the administration for [Higgins'] secret service pension." R.F. Foster, *Modern Ireland, 1600–1972* (London, New York: Penguin, 1988, 1989), 239. Hereafter cited as Foster.

27. See the entry for Charlotte Melmoth in Philip H. Highfill, Jr., Kalman A. Burnim, and Edward A. Langhans, *A Biographical Dictionary of Actors, Actresses, Musicians, Dancers, Managers & Other Stage Personnel in London, 1660–1800* (Carbondale: Southern Illinois University Press, 1973–1993), 10:181–187. Hereafter cited as Highfill.

28. William Smith Clark, *The Irish Stage in the County Towns, 1720–1800* (Oxford: Clarendon Press, 1965), 52.

29. Gilbert 2:211–212. See also the entry for Richard Daly in Highfill.

30. Foster 177; Gilbert 1:45, 3:27.

31. In an open field adjoining Clonmell's estate close to Sea-point, Magee invited thousands of Dubliners for a full day of food, fun, and games. Lord Cloncurry attended the event and tells what happened: "A variety of sports were arranged...such as climbing poles for prizes, running in sacks, grinning through horse-collar, [asses and dancing dogs dressed up with wigs and scarlet robes as barristers],...until at length, when the crowd had obtained its maximum density, towards the afternoon, the grand scene of the day was produced. A number of active pigs, with their tails shaved and soaped, were let loose, and it was announced that each pig should become the property of any one who could catch and hold it by the slippery member. A scene impossible to describe immediately took place; the pigs, frightened and hemmed in by the crowd in all other directions, rushed through the hedge which then separated the grounds of Temple Hill from the open fields; forthwith all their pursuers followed in a body, and, continuing their chase over the shrubberies and parterres, soon revenged John Magee upon the noble owner." Gilbert 3:29–30.

32. The prompter's daughter, Miss Hitchcock, had received a most unflattering notice in Magee's paper for her performance in Beaumarchais's *The Barber of Seville*: "She sings somewhat out of tune and walks as if her legs were tyed together." Walsh 216–217.

33. William J. Fitzpatrick, *Sham Squire and the Informers of 1798* (London: Hotten, 1866), 60. Hereafter cited as Fitzpatrick.

34. *The Trial of John Magee, for Printing and Publishing a Slanderous and Defamatory Libel, against Richard Daly, Esq., Held before the Right Honourable Lord Viscount Clonmell, by a Special Jury of the City of Dublin, Monday, June 28, 1790* (Dublin: P. Byrne, 1790); Gilbert III:213–214.

35. "The traditions of Enlightenment debate were diffused through Belfast 'society.'" Foster 265.

36. Marianne Elliott, *Wolfe Tone: Prophet of Irish Independence* (New Haven and London: Yale University Press, 1989), 123. Hereafter cited as Elliott.

37. Stewart 155–160. Rowan *Autobiography* 153, 157–159. Richard Robert Madden, *The United Irishmen: Their Lives and Times* (New York: Catholic Publication Society, 1851, 1916), 5:240–241.

38. Bate 88–89. To Burke the Queen of France had appeared as a goddess; "surely never lighted on this orb, which she hardly seemed to touch, a more delightful vision....glittering like the morning-star, full of life, and splendour, and joy." Conor Cruise O'Brien, *Edmund Burke*, abridged by Jim McCue (Dublin: New Island Books, 1997; 1992), 218–220.

39. Stewart 147. Archibald Hamilton Rowan, a leader of the Volunteers and a founder of United Irishmen, elaborates on the "street performance" and its finale with pledges "to the health of benefactors Washington, Franklin, Grattan and to the memory of Locke, Mirabeau and Dr. Jebb." Rowan *Autobiography* 153.

40. Stewart 155.
41. "In Irish terms Freemasonry was important because it was almost the only sphere in which Catholics and Protestants could meet on equal terms. For Catholics it was a refuge from the penal laws, even after 1738, when Pope Clement XII's dramatic edict threatened excommunication to Catholics who became Masons.... the old asperities between protestants and Catholics seemed suddenly to melt, and both persuasions, especially in the North of Ireland, seemed eager to create a new Irish nationality. The coming together in a new sense of nationhood reached its highest point with the formation of the United Irishmen in 1791.... If the idea of brotherhood was in fact largely a Masonic inspiration, then much of the history of Ireland in this period needs to be rewritten." Stewart 177–178.
42. Jack Gallagher, "History of the Theatre in Derry," *The Derry Journal* Commemorative Edition 1972, Public Library, Derry, Ireland.
43. *The Derry Journal*, Bicentenary Supplement June 9, 1972. In 1847 Derry received famine relief of six hundred barrels of flour from Irish-Americans in Philadelphia.
44. Retired from the stage, Melmoth taught children of Irish immigrants (at least one from the Derry region), as well as children of the rich and famous families of the era.
45. *Belfast News-Letter*, No. 5659, November 1–November 4, 1791. Partially quoted in Clark 270; and W.J. Lawrence, "The Annals of 'the Old Belfast Stage,'" (unpublished typescript February 1897, Belfast: Linen Library), 150.
46. Thomas Holcroft, *The School for Arrogance* (London: Robinson, 1791), Preface.
47. In his *Memoirs of Thomas Holcroft*, Hazlitt quotes an entire scene between Lady Peckham and Count Conolly Villars, explaining that "Lady Peckham gives the author an opportunity... to expose the weaknesses of pride as it is founded on the prejudice either of wealth or ancestry." William Hazlitt, *Memoirs of the Late Thomas Holcroft, Written by Himself, and Continued to the Time of His Death, from His Diary, Notes, and Other Papers* (London: Longman, 1816; Oxford University Press, n.d.), 154–159, 149–150. Holcroft's play combines the class and spirit of Figaro and Suzanne in Beaumarchais's "revolutionary" *Marriage of Figaro*. For, Holcroft, upon hearing of *Figaro*'s triumphal run in Paris, pirated and translated it for an English production in 1784, renamed *Follies of the Day* with the help of his friend French friend Bonneville (mutual friend of Thomas Paine and father to the Bonneville who provided Washington Irving with his book on the American West). Holcroft reverses the satire of the English to become a satire of the French, but otherwise gives Figaro and Suzanne the same servant, middle-class critique of the aristocracy that caused monarchs to ban the play across the continent.
48. Quoted in Elliott 277.

49. *The Waterford Herald*, September 1792 issues.

50. Greene 29.

51. George C.D. Odell, *Annals of the New York Stage*, 15 vols. (New York: Columbia University Press, 1927–1949), I:332–333. Hereafter cited as Odell.

52. *The Life and Letters of Washington Irving*, Pierre M. Irving [nephew] (New York: Putnam, 1864) I:35. At nineteen in 1802, Washington wrote about the theatre in his brother's *Morning Chronicle*, the City's newspaper that consistently featured favorable reviews of Melmoth's Lady Macbeth. Writing under the name of Jonathan Oldstyle, Irving observed audience behavior as well as actors, such as a "brawny Irishman" in the gallery and a "little sharp-faced Frenchman dressed in a white coat and small cocked hat" in the benches, who, upon being hit by a missile from the galleries, "jumped upon his seat, shook his fist at the gallery, and swore violently in bad English. This was all nuts to his merry persecutors; their attention was wholly turned on him, and he formed their target for the rest of the evening." *Letters of Jonathan Oldstyle* (New York: Clayton, 1824), 24.

53. Her name appears in the 1800 population census for New York as head of household with a female child under the age of ten residing with her.

54. William Dunlap, *History of the American Theatre and Anecdotes of the Principal Actors* (1832; New York: Burt Franklin reprint, 1963), 202–205. Hereafter cited as Dunlap *History*. See also the new edition—with an index! (Urbana and Chicago: University of Illinois Press, 2005).

55. Dunlap *History* 203.

56. *New York Journal*, March 12, 1793, as quoted in Odell I:347.

57. James Hewitt's name, with its various spellings, appeared in the press notices for Melmoth's concerts as her accompanist, composer, and player of orchestral pieces. He continued to work with her for several more years as music director and conductor for the theatre. After having served as leader of the court orchestra of King George III, Hewitt left for America, purportedly protesting England's cruel treatment of conscripted sailors. See David Ewen, *American Composers* (New York: Putnam: 1982). Herman Melville set "Billy Budd" in this period and with England's conscripted sailors.

58. The politics of this piece did not appeal to Dunlap, a reformed Loyalist sympathetic to the Federalists. As a playwright manager he held himself apart from the actors, regarding them more as employees than colleagues, "I wish to keep my house free from visits which partake of the theatre." Dunlap refused to include actors' names for the boxes in the construction of the Park Street Theatre, permitting only the names of "dramatic Authors of Europe to the exclusion of the Actors." Dunlap *Diary* 55, 207.

59. Dunlap *History* 200–201, 209.

60. The Tammany Society, founded as a benevolent charity in New York City in 1787, incorporated Native American words such as "sachem" for their chief, and "wigwam" for their meeting place.

61. O.G. Sonneck, *Early Opera in America* (New York: Schirmer, 1915), 97.

62. Elise K. Kirk, *American Opera* (Urbana and Chicago: University of Illinois Press, 2001), 45–46. Kirk is in error when she says that after coming to New York from England, Hatton spent most of her professional life in the New World, for Siddons' sister returned to England soon after *Tammany* was performed in 1794. Back home she plagued her siblings, especially Sarah, publicly slandering her for her stinginess and staged a mock suicide as the destitute and abandoned sister of the more fortunate one.

63. Ann Julia Hatton, "Tammany…A Serious Opera" (New York: J. Harrison, n.d. [1794]). "Price one shilling. To be had at Harrison's, No. 3, Peck-slip, or, Mr. Faulkner at the Box office of the Theatre." Microfiche, Early American Imprints. Ironically, the son of *Tammany's* composer lived most of his life in Augusta, Georgia, and like his father became a musician and composer, but of Confederate and minstrel songs.

64. Originally from Milan, Ciceri was raised in Paris where he worked for the Paris Opera. His picaresque life reads like Candide's—shipwrecked, marooned on a deserted island, rescued by a fisherman, fortunes won and lost and won again. Dunlap *History* 209–213. When Thomas A. Cooper became manager, he fired Ciceri on the grounds that his elaborate designs had contributed to the theatre's bankruptcy. F. Arant Maginnes, *Thomas Abthorpe Cooper: Father of the American Stage, 1775–1849* (Jefferson, North Carolina, and London: McFarland, 2004), 137.

65. *Grecian Daughter* (November 20, 25, March 10), Widow Racket in *The Belle's Stratagem* (January 6, 8, 20), Calista in *The Fair Penitent* (January 24, February 12), Matilda in *The Carmelite* (February 1, April 4, 8), Zara in Congreve's *The Mourning Bride* (February 8), Lady Macbeth in *Macbeth* February 17, Marcia in *Cato* (February 24, 28), Portia in the first recorded New York production of *Julius Caesar* (March 14), Arpasia in *Tamerlane*, Emelia in *Othello* (April 7), Matilda, a new role, in Dunlap's *The Fatal Deception* (April 24), Lady Eleanor Irwin in Inchbald's comedy *Every One Has His Fault* (April 26 [another first production in America, a play that caused riots in Brighton in 1793 and Portsmouth, England in 1795]), Alexina in Cowley's comedy *Liberty Restored* (April 28), Isabella in Southerne's tragedy of that name (May 3), Alicia in *Jane Shore*, Mrs. Belleville in Kelly's *School for Wives*, Mrs. Beverley in *The Gamester* (May 28), Marina, Tell's wife, in Dunlap's new opera *William Tell* (June 4), and to end the season on June 7, Julia in R.B. Sheridan's *The Rivals*. See Odell vol. 1. by dates.

66. One translation asks the brown "Drimmin" "where are the strong ones?" She replies "they sleep beneath the cold turf, but that like leaves on the trees, new people will arise to chase the flint-hearted Saxon away." Fitzpatrick 61–62.

67. Odell 1:345.

68. *The New York Magazine* for January 1795, quoted in Odell 1:379; and Playbill, New York John St. Theatre, January 14, 1795, Harvard Theatre Collection, Houghton Library, Harvard University.

69. *Hamlet* II.2.512; III.2.21–22.

70. Dunlap *History* 2:20–22; Dunlap *Diary* 237. Odell 2:18. This is clearly a complicated bit of theatre history. In her biography of Cooper, Maginnes attributes Cooper's gesture to having been directed, and as a sign of being pro-British. Also, Maginnes credits Cooper with introducing Holcroft's plays to Dunlap, whereas Melmoth who had performed many of Holcroft's plays before coming to America in 1793 preceded Cooper in bringing them to the attention of Dunlap who may have acquired them himself without their help.

71. Contemporary description of theatre quoted in Odell 2:41–43; *Commercial Advertiser*, February 2, 1799, quoted in Odell 2:48–49.

72. Odell 2:73.

73. A letter Melmoth wrote to her public, printed in full in New York's *Commercial Advertiser*, July , 1802, gives her reasons for resigning from the Park company, and a glimpse of her self-expression, signing off as a "public servant."

74. Quoted in Odell 2:152.

75. Quoted in Odell 2:154.

76. *Morning Chronicle*, October 21, 1802. Writing for Peter Irving's newspaper, "L" cannot be easily identified by Dunlap's system. He names the critics as John Wells, Elias Hicks, Samuel Jones, William Cutting, Peter Irving (Washington Irving's older brother), and Charles Adams ("wastrel" son of Abigail and John Adams), who "by turns put down their remarks on the play of the evening, meeting next evening to criticize the critique, and give it passport to the press." "They signed with the initials of their names, the last letter being the actual writer. [But] finding that these initials led to the detection of the offenders against the liberty of murdering plays at will, they inserted other letters to mislead." Dunlap devotes a full chapter to these critics' savagery, noting how actresses received gentler treatment at their hands than male actors did. "The ladies, however, have the greater share in their praise, and we know they deserved it. Mrs. Melmoth's Alicia, and Mrs. Johnson's penitent Jane, were, the first full of *fiery passion*, the second of tender pathos" [emphasis mine]. Dunlap *History* 373–374, 378, 383.

77. Quoted in Odell 2:161–162.

78. *Ramblers' Magazine*, December 1809, 3:191. The Whitlocks returned home to Britain in 1806, but made a last visit to America 1812–1813, when Mrs. Whitlock played Lady Macbeth in Providence, Boston, and Philadelphia, and was regarded as much improved over her previous appearances in America, though grown quite corpulent.

79. Reese Davis James, *Cradle of Culture 1800–1810: The Philadelphia Stage* (Philadelphia: University of Pennsylvania Press, 1957), 52–53, 80.

80. *An Apology for the Life of James Fennell* (Philadelphia: Moses Thomas, 1814; New York: Blom reprint, 1969), 363, 367.

81. Odell 2:181–182.

82. Dunlap *History* 212.

83. Reese Davis James, *Cradle of Culture* 90.

84. Reese Davis James, *Old Drury of Philadelphia: The History of the Philadelphia Stage, 1800–1835* (Philadelphia: University of Pennsylvania Press, 1932), 9.

85. "Recollections of the Actors: A Passage in the Life of Mrs. Melmoth," *The New York Mirror: A Weekly Gazette of Literature and the Fine Arts* 16 (1): 5.

86. *Eighteenth-Century Women Dramatists* (Oxford, England: Oxford University Press, 2001), 232.

5. YANKEE

1. As one of the last to leave the White House, she had a servant hurriedly cut the canvas from its frame, roll it up, and whisk it out of the White House and into a farmer's wagon headed for New Jersey, just in time to escape the British soldiers entering the White house and setting it afire.

2. Like Cleopatra in other Shakespeare plays, *Julius Caesar* and *Antony and Cleopatra*, Dolley Madison was threatened with being taken hostage and paraded through the streets by the invading British admiral. Carl Sferrazza Anthony, *First Ladies: The Saga of the Presidents' Wives and Their Power 1789–1961* (New York: Harper Collins, Perennial, 1992, 2003), 81, 90, 108.

3. Henry Stiles, *A History of the City of Brooklyn* (Brooklyn, 1869; Facsimile Bowie, Maryland: Heritage Books, 1993), 156. Stiles says that Miss Butler assisted Melmoth with her school, the two of them served only by an old Dutch slave couple, a man and his wife, who milked the cows that, according to Dunlap, Melmoth kept to provide milk for market. What properties Julia Butler inherited from Melmoth and where she went after her friend's death remain unknown. Surely in addition to house and land and household items, there would have been the actress's costumes and Gilbert Stuart's paintings, maybe letters to and from her many friends and colleagues spanning the forty years of Melmoth's work in the theatre.

4. Geddeth Smith, *Thomas Abthorpe Cooper: America's Premier Tragedian* (Madison, London: Associated University Presses, 1996), 286. See Maginnes 192 for evidence of the friendship between Irving and Cooper's wife, Mary Fairlie, who, like Irving, was a member of a distinguished New York family, in correspondence that Maginnes, a direct descendant of Cooper and Fairlie, has in her family's archives.

5. From Irving's Letters, as quoted in Smith's *Cooper* 118.

6. Her husband, the southern plantation owner and musician in the theatre orchestra, Pierce Butler, inherited a vast plantation in Georgia with its hundreds of slaves. For several years, Fanny lived in Philadelphia, an unhappy wife chafing under her husband's mistreatment and recoiling at his extensive slave holdings. By the time she resumed her acting career a dozen years later, divorced and openly attacking slavery, she had lost her youthful looks

and magnetism, but succeeded in "platform readings" of Shakespeare's plays. With her voice, extraordinary in its range and tones, and her depth of understanding, Fanny Kemble could read the parts of all the characters in an entire play in one sitting to great effect, including *Macbeth*. Playing Lady Macbeth to William Charles Macready's Macbeth in London (February 1848) Fanny Kemble argued against his new way of staging the banquet scene on the premise that her way was Siddons' way. See Alan Seymour Downer, *The Eminent Tragedian William Charles Macready* (Cambridge: Harvard University Press, 1966), 283–285. Hereafter cited as Downer.

7. Jean H. Baker, *Mary Todd Lincoln: A Biography* (New York, London: W.W. Norton, 1987), 42–45. Hereafter cited as Baker *Mary Todd Lincoln*.

8. Joseph Leach, *Bright Particular Star: The Life and Times of Charlotte Cushman* (New Haven and London: Yale University Press, 1970), 44; and 38–39 for quotes from the *Bee*. Hereafter cited as Leach *Life of Cushman*.

9. By Gilbert Beckett, quoted in J.C. Trewin, *Mr Macready: A Nineteenth Century Tragedian and His Theatre* (London: Harrap, 1955), 212. Hereafter cited as Trewin.

10. From William Toynbee, ed., *The Diaries of William Charles Macready (1833–1851)*, 2 vols. (London: Chapman and Hall, 1912), 2:230; quoted in James Willis Yeater, "Charlotte Cushman, American Actress," (PhD Dissertation, University of Illinois, Urbana, 1959), 20. Hereafter cited as Yeater.

11. Nigel Cliff, *The Shakespeare Riots: Revenge, Drama, and Death in Nineteenth-Century America* (New York: Random House, 2007). Hereafter cited as Cliff.

12. Cliff 156–157.

13. Leach *Life of Cushman* 364. Eleanor Ruggles, *Prince of Players: Edwin Booth* (New York: Norton, 1953), 115–116. Hereafter cited as Ruggles. Faye E. Dudden, *Women in the American Theatre: Actresses and Audiences, 1790–1870* (New Haven: Yale University Press, 1994), 90. Hereafter cited as Dudden.

14. Yeater 62.

15. Charles Edgar Lewis Wingate, *Shakespeare's Heroines on the Stage* (New York and Boston: Thomas Crowell, 1895), 25. Hereafter cited as Wingate.

16. Cliff 133.

17. This included a financial war and international "repudiation" of the United States for not honoring their enormous debts to Britain's financial institutions. America was "'a confederation of public bankrupts' who had coolly refused to pay their debts, not from necessity but because it suited them not to. They were swindlers and scoundrels.... [having] 'no claim to ordinary credit or common courtesy'" Cliff 145–147.

18. The fact that Macready himself sprang from a struggling "working-class" Irish actor appears to have been ignored by the rioters and actors alike, and

especially by Macready who regarded the acting profession as beneath him, but a necessary evil. One of Macready's biographers, J.C. Trewin, writing from the vantage point of an Anglo-Saxon Englishman, states that Macready, being "half a Celt," "had certain racial traits: intolerance, a long memory, acute touchiness, a way of smouldering over ancient or fancied wrongs. But"—and here, is Trewin referring to the Celt or the English half?—"he was also affectionate and generous, loyal to his friends, creatively imaginative" Trewin 24. For a less partial biography of Macready see Downer.

19. Wingate 214. Richard Moody, *Astor Place Riot* (Bloomington: Indiana University Press, 1958). Hereafter cited as Moody.

20. *New York Daily Tribune*, May 11, 1849.

21. Lawrence W. Levine, *Highbrow/Lowbrow: The Emergence of Cultural Hierarchy in America* (Cambridge, MA: Harvard University Press, 1988), 63.

22. See Richard Barksdale Harwell, *Brief Candle: The Confederate Theatre* (Worcester: American Antiquarian Society, 1971). Hereafter cited as Harwell.

23. Asia Booth Clarke, *John Wilkes Booth: A Sister's Memoir*, ed. and intro. Terry Alford (Jackson: University Press of Mississippi, 1996), 50–51. Hereafter cited as Asia Booth.

24. My emphasis. Written on a leaf from Booth's diary and delivered to Stewart. John Rhodehamel and Louise Taper, ed., *"Right or Wrong, God Judge Me": The Writings of John Wilkes Booth* (Urbana: University of Illinois, 1997), 155, 159.

25. Gordon Samples, *Lust for Fame: The Stage Career of John Wilkes Booth* (Jefferson, North Carolina: McFarland, 1982), 78. Hereafter cited as Samples.

26. *Spirit of the Times*, March 1862, New York City, as quoted in Samples 83–84.

27. Her much older husband, an actor/manager and an abolitionist, provoked a riot in the Bowery Theatre in the 1830s for a remark he had made against Americans, a riot that spilled out into the streets with antiabolitionists attacking abolitionists and African Americans, one of many such riots presaging the most vicious attacks against abolitionists and blacks in New York City's Draft Riots of 1863.

28. Clara Morris, "I Stand between Lady Macbeth and Matrimony," *McClure's Magazine* 20 (3) (January 1903): 261.

29. Newspaper clipping dated March 1862 with no name of newspaper or critic; in one of the scrapbooks listed as "Players of the Past,".24:11; Beinecke Rare Book and Manuscript Library, Yale University.

30. Gene A. Smith, *American Gothic: The Story of America's Legendary Theatrical Family—Junius, Edwin and John Wilkes Booth* (New York: Simon and Schuster, 1992, 1993), 101. Hereafter cited as Gene Smith. *New York World*, April 19, 1865, quoted in David Rankin Barbee, "Mr. Lincoln Goes to the

Theater," in *Inside Lincoln's White House: the Complete Civil War Diary of John Hay*, ed Michael Burlingame and John R. Turner (Carbondale: Southern Illlinois University Press, 1997, 1999), 325–326, n271. This note 271 gives the source of David Rankin Barbee's "Mr. Lincoln Goes to the Theater," as Barbee MSS, Georgetown University, 44–48.

31. *New York Times*, July 16, 1863.
32. After the riot, the Astor Opera House hired Max Maretzak as its new director, a friend of French composer Berlioz. Three years later, the opera house, called the "English ARISTOCRATIC opera house" by the protesters, was converted to a library, a forerunner of the New York Public Library. Maretzak stayed on in New York City, producing opera during the Civil War. See his *Revelations of an Opera Manager in 19th-Century America: Crotchets and Quavers & Sharps and Flats* (New York: Dover, 1855, 1890, 1968).
33. Edwin Booth to Charlotte Cushman, September 3, 1863, Library of Congress, Charlotte Cushman Papers, vol. 9; quoted in Lisa Merrill, *When Romeo Was a Woman: Charlotte Cushman and Her Circle of Female Spectators* (Ann Arbor: University of Michigan, 1999), 229, 303 n103.
34. Leach *Life of Cushman* 305.
35. Adam Badeau, *The Vagabond* (New York: Rudd & Carleton, 1859), 247, 212. Albert Furtwangler, *Assassin on Stage: Brutus, Hamlet and the Death of Lincoln* (Urbana: University of Illinois Press, 1991), 126–127. Hereafter cited as Furtwangler.
36. Leach *Life of Cushman* 322–323.
37. Leach *Life of Cushman* 324; Gene Smith gives Booth and Odell gives Boniface.
38. *The Diary of George Templeton Strong*, 4 vols. (New York: Macmillan, 1952), 3:365, 367.
39. William Winter from *The Saturday Evening Post*, December 29, 1906, reprinted in his *Shadows of the Stage*, and reprinted again in Montrose Jonas Moses and John Mason Brown, *The American Theatre as Seen by Its Critics* (New York: W.W. Norton, 1934), 89.
40. For details of Cushman's farewell tour, see Clara Erskine Clement (Waters), *Charlotte Cushman* (Boston: Osgood, 1882), 126.

6. "HELLCAT"

1. Jonas Barish, "Madness, Hallucination, and Sleepwalking," *Verdi's* Macbeth: *A Sourcebook*, ed. David Rosen and Andrew Porter (New York: W.W. Norton, 1984), 154–155.
2. Baker *Mary Todd Lincoln* 147–148, 196.
3. Ruth Painter Randall, *Mary Lincoln: Biography of a Marriage* (Boston: Little, Brown, 1953), 56–57.

4. Letter to Charles Sumner, April 5, 1864 in Justin. G. Turner and Linda Levitt Turner, ed., *Mary Todd Lincoln: Her Life and Letters* (New York: Knopf, 1972), 174, 512. Hereafter cited as *Mary Todd Lincoln Letters*.

5. Baker *Mary Todd Lincoln* 197.

6. Margaret Leech, *Reveille in Washington, 1860–1865* (New York: Harper, 1941), 286. Hereafter cited as Leech *Reveille*.

7. My emphasis. *New York World*, in *New Haven Register*, September 14, 1863.

8. Mary Clemmer (Ames), *Men, Women, and Things* (Boston: Ticknor, 1886), 114–126. Carl Sandburg, *Mary Lincoln, Wife and Widow* (New York: Harcourt, Brace, 1932), 116–118. Hereafter cited as Sandburg.

9. *Mary Todd Lincoln Letters* 145.

10. Henry Villard, *Memoirs* (Boston: Houghton Mifflin, 1904), 1:157; quoted in Allison DeLarue, *The Chevalier Henry Wikoff: Impresario, 1840* (Princeton: Princeton University, 1948), 47–48.

11. Doris Kearns Goodwin, *Team of Rivals: The Political Genius of Abraham Lincoln* (New York: Simon & Schuster, 2005), 192–193, 364–365, 387–388.

12. Leech *Reveille* 311.

13. Quoted in *The Living Age* (New York) November 21, 1863, 347. See also Furtwangler 70–71 for the publication of the broadside.

14. Leech *Reveille* 278.

15. *Mary Todd Lincoln Letters* 207, 581–582.

16. Marquis Adolphe de Chambrun, *Impressions of Lincoln and the Civil War: A Foreigner's Account*, trans. General Aldebert de Chambrun (New York: Random House, 1952), 21–23. Hereafter cited as Chambrun.

17. Chambrun 100–102.

18. Chambrun 82–83; also partially quoted in Gene Smith *American Gothic* 129.

19. Michael Knox Beran, "Lincoln, Macbeth, and the Moral Imagination," *Humanitas* 11 (2) (1998), 4–21.

20. John S. Clarke "abhorred the 'secretiveness of the whole Booth race.' To his way of thinking it stamped them male and female Iagos. That may be in some measure a truth…but my observation has convinced me Mr. J. S. Clarke's mistakes, which are few, have been the result of a merry and over-indulged loquacity." Asia Booth 98–99.

21. Gene Smith 185.

22. Catherine Clinton, *Mrs. Lincoln: A Life* (New York: HarperCollins, 2009), 3. Hereafter cited as Clinton.

23. Baker *Mary Todd Lincoln* 268.

24. Joshua Shenk, *Lincoln's Melancholy: How Depression Challenged a President and Fueled His Greatness* (Boston: Houghton Mifflin, 2005), 221–243. For Shenk's analysis of the historical accounts of Lincoln's melancholy, see his "Afterword: 'What Everybody Knows': A Historiography of Lincoln's Melancholy."

25. Especially illuminating on Mary Lincoln's insanity case, containing Robert Todd Lincoln's letters and documentation, is Mark E. Neely, Jr., and R. Gerald McMurtry, *The Insanity File* (Carbondale: Southern Illinois University Press, 1986). Jean Baker's careful analysis had benefit of this published material.
26. See Clinton 321–325 for details of Mrs. Lincoln's four years in Pau, France.
27. *Mary Todd Lincoln Letters* 683–684.
28. *Mary Todd Lincoln Letters* 706–717.
29. Sandburg 83.
30. Sandburg 40, 77, 66; John Hay xvi.
31. Sandburg 64.
32. Marguerite Yourcenar, "La Symphonie héroique," *Essais et mémoires* (Paris: Gallimard, 1991, 1930), my translation.
33. Sandburg 78, 128–129.

7. "INNOCENT FLOWER" AND "SERPENT WITHIN"

1. Sarah Bernhardt, *Ma Double Vie: Mémoires de Sarah Bernhardt* (Paris: Charpentier, 1907), 464–465, my translation. Hereafter cited as Bernhardt *Mémoires*.
2. The newborn infant, Robert Markero, reintroduced himself to Sarah thirty-eight years later as she boarded a ship departing from New York in 1918 at the end of what would be her last tour to America as well as the end of World War I. By sad coincidence, Markero, too, like Bernhardt, had suffered a leg amputation, his, while serving with the U.S. Army in France. Lysiane Bernhardt, *Sarah Bernhardt: ma grand'mère* (Paris: du Pavois, 1945, 1947), 352–353, 188–190, my translation. Hereafter cited as Lysiane Bernhardt *ma grand'mère*.
3. New York *Sun*, October 28, 1880; an observation by Mrs. Lincoln's grandnephew who met her at the dock, quoted in *Mary Todd Lincoln Letters* 705.
4. Ernest Pronier, *Une Vie au théâtre: Sarah Bernhardt* (Geneva, A. Jullien, n.d., c. 1940), 71 n1. Hereafter cited as Pronier. Bernhardt relied upon the role of "Camille," actually named Marguerite—the character of a beautiful young courtesan who dies young of consumption and a broken heart—for surefire success throughout her long career, even recreating it for a silent film made in 1910 when the actress was sixty-six years old. A "hit" of the nineteenth century, the play provided the libretto, with changed names, for Verdi's opera, "La Traviata." In the 1930s Greta Garbo immortalized Camille on film.
5. Pronier 350.
6. Pronier 85.

7. "C'est elle, la petite vipère rousse, la saxonne perverse, qui est 'l'homme du ménage'.... Il, c'est un visionnaire...c'est lui, en vérité, qui est la femme de ce ménage." *l'Opinion*, April 6, 1914.

8. Pronier 85; Rosenberg *Masks of Macbeth* 573–574.

9. From the June 9, 1884, interview in Wilde's Paris hotel honeymoon suite with a reporter from England's *Morning News*. In Arthur Gold and Robert Fitzdale, *The Divine Sarah: A Life of Sarah Bernhardt* (New York: Knopf, 1991), 210; Elaine Showalter, *Sexual Anarchy: Gender and Culture at the Fin de Siècle* (New York: Penguin, 1990), 157.

10. Rosenberg 188, 190.

11. Emphasis mine. *Illustrated Sporting and Dramatic News*, July 1, 1885.

12. For a full account of the professional and personal partnership of Henry Irving and Ellen Terry, see Michael Holroyd, *A Strange Eventful History: The Dramatic Lives of Ellen Terry, Henry Irving, and Their Remarkable Families* (New York: Farrar, Straus and Giroux, 2008),specifically for Terry's premier of Lady Macbeth and subsequent tour to America see 193–201, 247–265.

13. Rosenberg 188.

14. Pamphlet in the Edward Gordon Craig papers, E.G.C. (Paris: Bibliothèque Nationale). Craig was Ellen Terry's son. Hereafter cited as E.G.C. BN.

15. George Fletcher's 1847 *Studies of Shakespeare*, quoted in H.H. Furness, ed., *Variorum, Macbeth* (London: Dent, 1873, 1898), 435; in E.G.C.papers with Gordon Craig's underlining and marginal notes. E.G.C., BN.

16. Ellen Terry, *Four Lectures on Shakespeare*, ed. Christopher St. John (London: Martin Hopkinson, 1932), 160.

17. Rosenberg 211.

18. Ellen Terry archives, library and museum, Smallhythe Cottage, Kent, England: E.T. 218, L888, annotated *Macbeth* script 43, 49, 50, 63. Hereafter cited as Smallhythe.

19. As observed by Terry's contemporary (Jacob) Jack Thomas Grein, the Dutch director of England's experimental Independent Theatre, quoted in Rosenberg 484.

20. Quoted in Tom Prideaux, *Love or Nothing: The Life and Times of Ellen Terry* (London: Millington, 1975), 181–182; as well as in Nina Auerbach, *Ellen Terry: Player in Her Time* (Philadelphia: University of Pennsylvania, 1987, 1997).

21. First Lady Edith Wilson relates in her memoir the story of Sargent's portrait of Woodrow Wilson painted in October of 1917: "Everyone knew Sargent's ability to find in human beings the counterpart of animals, and thus reveal some hidden beastly trait. Lodge [Henry Cabot, Wilson's political adversary] said that he knew there was something sinister hidden in Wilson which he looked to Sargent to reveal to the world." Evidently the Wilson portrait turned out much tamer than Lodge might have wished. Edith Bolling Wilson, *My Memoir* (New York: Bobbs-Merrill, 1938), 149. Hereafter cited as Edith Wilson *Memoir*.

22. Sillars 307.
23. To Sally Fairchild, May 14, 1889, Smallhythe Z2194.
24. Nina Auerbach gives a richly detailed account of Terry's Jubilee in the introduction to her biography.
25. Quoted in Arthur Jacobs, *Arthur Sullivan: A Victorian Musician* (New York: Oxford University Press, 1984), 279.
26. In a letter to her daughter, quoted in Rosenberg 185.
27. George Bernard Shaw, "Preface," *Ellen Terry and Bernard Shaw: A Correspondence*, ed. Christopher St. John (New York: Putnam, 1932), xxvi, xiii.
28. Eleanor Wilson McAdoo, ed., *The Priceless Gift: The Love Letters of Woodrow Wilson and Ellen Axson Wilson* (New York: McGraw-Hill, 1962), 88–89, 125–126, 126–127.
29. Edith Craig and Christopher St. John, *Ellen Terry's Memoirs* (London: Gollancz, 1933), 293.
30. Autumn Stephens, *Wild Women in the White House* (Berkeley, California: Conari Press, 1997), 73. Hereafter cited as Stephens.
31. Quoted in Phyllis Lee Levin, *Edith and Woodrow: The Wilson White House* (New York: Scribner, 2001), 75. Hereafter cited as Levin EW.
32. Stephens 72.
33. Edwin Tribble, ed., *A President in Love: The Courtship Letters of Woodrow Wilson and Edith Bolling Galt* (Boston: Houghton Mifflin, 1981), 200.
34. Styan *Shakespeare Revolution* 232–233.
35. Edith Wilson *Memoir* 36–37, 145.
36. Levin EW 585.
37. Louis Verneuil, *The Fabulous Life of Sarah Bernhardt*, trans. Ernest Boyd (New York: Harper, 1942), 286.
38. Gold and Fitzdale 320.
39. Ramon Hathorn, *Our Lady of the Snows: Sarah Bernhardt in Canada* (New York: Peter Lang, 1996), 217–218.
40. Lysiane Bernhardt *ma grand'mère* 351.
41. Edith Wilson *Memoir* 252–253.

8. VAMPIRA

1. "Untitled Autobiography" by Judith Anderson with Robert Wallsten (unpublished typescript, c. 1960), 270. Hereafter cited as Anderson Autobiography. By permission of Robert Wallsten and Special Collections, University of California, Santa Barbara.
2. H.H., *Observer* (n.d.), J.E. Sewall, *Daily Telegraph*, November 27, 1937, in the production files of the Theatre Museum, formerly Covent Garden, now in the Victoria and Albert Museum, London.

3. Judith Anderson Archive, Special Collections, University of California Santa Barbara Library.
4. Anderson Autobiography 388–391.
5. Quoted in Anderson Autobiography 378–379.
6. Anderson Autobiography 408.
7. Milly S. Barranger, *Margaret Webster: A Life in the Theater* (Ann Arbor: University of Michigan Press, 2004), 98. Hereafter cited as Barranger.
8. Program in my possession.
9. Barranger 126–127.
10. Quoted in Anderson Autobiography 38.
11. Anderson Autobiography 435–436.
12. Letter from Margaret Webster to Judith Anderson, quoted in Anderson Autobiography 434.
13. Margaret Webster, *Don't Put Your Daughter on the Stage* (New York: Knopf, 1972), 103. Hereafter cited as Webster *Daughter*.
14. Barranger 32, 48, 54–55.
15. London *Times*, February 1, 1934, quoted in Barranger 55, 316.
16. He does, however, propagate an historical error in attributing to the nineteenth-century American actor Edwin Booth the innovation in the banquet scene of having Banquo's Ghost exist only in Macbeth's imagination and not physically present on the stage. John Philip Kemble originated the practice in Ireland or England. In turn, Kemble received credit for being the first Macbeth to make the dagger invisible for the "Is this a dagger I see before me" soliloquy, whereas it was Macklin who did it before him.
17. The 1942 newspaper clipping is in the Judith Anderson folder of the Theatre Collection at the Free Library in Philadelphia, with no indication of precise date or publication source.
18. Webster *Daughter* 99.
19. Richard H. Rovère, *Senator Joe McCarthy* (New York: World Publishing, 1960, 1970), 94–95. Hereafter cited as Rovère.
20. Rovère 25.
21. Review of the film of *Macbeth* when it aired in 1960, *San Francisco Chronicle*, November 22, 1960.
22. Robinson Jeffers' "Notes" in the *Medea* Program for the 1948 national tour.
23. "Queen of Tragedy," *New York Times*, December 10, 1950.
24. Albert Fried, *McCarthyism: The Great American Red Scare, a Documentary History* (New York: Oxford University Press, 1997), 24–25.
25. "Stept" in the First Folio, and frequently edited as "stepped."
26. Michael Straight's question and answer in Rovère 170–171.
27. Arthur Miller, *Timebends: A Life* (New York: Grove Press, 1987), 454. Hereafter cited as Miller.
28. Miller 236.
29. Their brief and unhappy marriage Miller blamed on Monroe, her abuse of alcohol and drugs, and on Paula Strasberg. Paula and Lee Strasberg coached

Marilyn in method acting allegedly suffocating Monroe's instincts and spontaneity and exploiting her for her money right up until her death. Paula was still living in Marilyn Monroe's house on the day Monroe died.

30. Miller 334.

31. Virginia Carmichael, *Framing History: The Rosenberg Story and the Cold War* (Minneapolis: University of Minnesota Press, 1993), 96–106. Hereafter cited as Carmichael.

32. My emphases. Carmichael 96–106.

33. "Tessie Greenglass, [Ethel's mother] the family *matriarch*, and her two elder sons sided with David and Ruth Greenglass and cruelly isolated Ethel and Julius Rosenberg. *Ruth, the shrewdest* of all the principals, embarked on a public relations campaign to distinguish the gullible Greenglasses from the *bewitching Rosenbergs*, taking her case to the *Jewish Daily Forward*, a publication keen to dispel the widespread perception that communism was a 'Jewish problem.'" "'By martyring themselves,' Roberts says, the Rosenbergs 'contributed considerably more to the cause of world communism than they ever had as spies.' No doubt. But it is a strange martyrdom that conceals rather than declares its principles and embraces falsehood rather than truth." Sam Tanenhaus, "A Family Affair," in the review of *The Brother* by Sam Roberts and *The Man Behind the Rosenbergs* by Alexander Feklisov and Sergei Kostin, *The New York Review of Books* (March 26, 2001): 41–44. Emphasis mine.

34. Hearst reporter, Bob Considine, quoted in Carmichael 105.

35. Webster *Daughter* 243–244, 267. In Barranger's biography of Webster, Chapter Ten covers Webster's hearing before McCarthy and Cohn with detailed information unavailable to Webster during her lifetime. The sealed records opened to the public fifty years after the hearings.

36. Webster *Daughter* 270.

37. Webster *Daughter* 270.

38. Webster *Daughter* 273.

39. Webster *Daughter* 274.

40. Margaret Webster, *Shakespeare Today* (London: Dent, 1957), 99, 101, 227–228. Hereafter cited as Webster *Shakespeare*.

41. Doris Kearns Goodwin, *No Ordinary Time, Franklin & Eleanor Roosevelt: The Home Front in World War II* (New York: Touchstone, 1994), 204.

42. Anderson Autobiography 273.

43. Albert Goldberg, newspaper clipping, n.d., in Judith Anderson Archive, Special Collections, University of California, Santa Barbara.

44. Reagan was one of the actors who not only cooperated with the House witch-hunters, but as president of the Screen Actors' Guild led union attacks against its own liberal members.

45. Anderson Autobiography 272.

46. Letter sent from Tamalpais, Los Gatos, when he was an ensign in the Navy, before being shipped out to Pearl City, Oahu, in 1943, in the Judith Anderson Archive, Special Collections, University of California, Santa Barbara. Passionate letters from Anderson's producer Jed Harris are there as well.

47. For the play *Behold the Bridegroom*, the director wanted her to go up and over the top, gesticulating and mouthing from the wings, "Bernhardt! Bernhardt!" producing results that she regretted. She credits a critic for perceptively recognizing her excess: "As Miss Anderson passed away... in the flowing robes of an exotic invalid, her last words were almost as lute-like as those of Camille when spoken by Bernhardt's *vox celeste....* She is so delightfully artificial that if I had been the friendly old counselor in the play, I should have advised her to go on the stage." Anderson Autobiography 594.

48. Anderson Autobiography 445, 446-A.

49. The assassination of President Kennedy in 1963 coincided with the year Judith Anderson turned sixty-five and retired her Lady Macbeth, though not her career. At the age of seventy-two she performed Hamlet, again emulating Sarah Bernhardt, and in her eighties she was a regular, playing the *matriarch* on the television series "Santa Barbara."

CONCLUSION

1. The nationalism Charlotte Melmoth and Robert Owenson supported at their Fishamble Street Theatre in Dublin "had more in common with the cross-cultural, interdenominational nationalism of the United Irishmen than with the later Celtic and Catholic-identified nationalism of Yeats and Lady Gregory." Helen M. Burke, *Riotous Performances: The Struggle for Hegemony in the Irish Theater, 1712–1784* (Indiana: University of Notre Dame Press, 2003), 287.

2. "The Unsexed Females" is the title of a poem (1798) by Richard Polwhele, satirizing women of talent and intelligence, who wear the French fashion of thin gauze dresses he associates with radical ideas, a woman like Mary Wollstonecraft whom he characterizes as Satan. Paula Byrne, *Perdita: The Literary, Theatrical, Scandalous Life of Mary Robinson* (New York: Random House, 2004), 333.

3. Quoted in Lyndall Gordon, *Vindication: A Life of Mary Wollstonecraft* (New York: Harper Perennial, 2005, 2006), 153.

4. Quoted in Rackin 120.

5. The Salem witch-hunt had already appeared on the American stage in mid-nineteenth century, and then again as part of Hallie Flanagan's WPA theatre project in the 1930s. Bruce A. McConachie, *Melodramatic*

Formations: American Theatre & Society, 1820–1870 (Iowa City: University of Iowa Press, 1992), 77. The WPA script is in the Library of Congress.

6. She quotes Keats and Stephen Greenblatt on their recognition of Shakespeare's capability "of being in uncertainties... [in] doubts, without any irritable reaching after fact and reason" (Keats); and that of the "many forms of heroism in Shakespeare,... ideological heroism... is not one of them" (Greenblatt). Zadie Smith, "Speaking in Tongues," *The New York Review of Books* (February 26, 2009): 41–44.

Bibliography ✑

Adams, Abigail. *Adams Family Correspondence*, ed. L.H. Butterfield. Boston: Massachusetts Historical Society, 2007.

Adams, John. "Essay on Canon and Feudal Law," John Holroyd, Earl of Sheffield's *Observations of the Commerce of the American States with Europe and the West Indies*. Philadelphia: Robert Bell, 1765, 1783. Early American Imprints, Series I.

Adams, John Quincy. *Dermot MacMorrogh or the Conquest of Ireland: An Historical Tale of the Twelfth Century in Four* Cantos. Dublin: Maunsel, 2005.

Adams, William Howard. *The Paris Years of Thomas Jefferson*. New Haven and London: Yale University Press, 1997.

Albert, Paul, ed. *Lettres de Jean-François Ducis*. Paris: Jousset, 1879.

Alfar, Cristina León. *Fantasies of Female Evil: The Dynamics of Gender and Power in Shakespearean Tragedy*. Newark: University of Delaware Press; London: Associated University Presses, 2003.

Anderson, Judith, with Robert Wallsten. "Untitled Autobiography." c. 1960. By permission of Robert Wallsten and Special Collections, University of California, Santa Barbara.

Anthony, Carl Sferazza. *First Ladies: The Saga of the Presidents' Wives and Their Power 1789–1961*. New York: Harper Collins, Perennial, 1992, 2003.

Armstrong, Nancy, and Leonard Tennenhouse. *The Imaginary Puritan: Literature, Intellectual Labor, and the Origins of Personal Life*. Berkeley: University of California Press, 1992.

Armstrong, Norma. "The Edinburgh Stage 1715–1820: A Bibliography." Edinburgh: Central Library, 1968.

Asquith, Clare. *Shadow Play: The Hidden Beliefs and Coded Politics of William Shakespeare*. New York: Public Affairs, Perseus Books, 2005.

Auerbach, Nina. *Ellen Terry: Player in Her Time*. Philadelphia: University of Pennsylvania, 1987, 1997.

Badeau, Adam. *The Vagabond*. New York: Rudd & Carleton, 1859.

Baker, Jean H. *Mary Todd Lincoln: A Biography*. New York: W.W. Norton, 1987.

Barish, Jonas. *The Antitheatrical Prejudice*. Berkeley: University of California Press, 1981.

———. "Madness, Hallucination, and Sleepwalking." *Verdi's* Macbeth: *A Sourcebook*. Ed. David Rosen and Andrew Porter. New York: W.W. Norton, 1984.

Barranger, Milly S. *Margaret Webster: A Life in the Theater.* Ann Arbor: University of Michigan Press, 2004.

Bartholomeusz, Dennis. *Macbeth and the Players.* Cambridge: Cambridge University Press, 1969.

Bate, Jonathan. *Shakespearean Constitutions: Politics, Theatre, Criticism 1730–1830.* Oxford: Clarendon Press, 1989.

Beard, Mary. "The Truth about Cleopatra." *The New York Review of Books* (February 12, 2009).

Belsey, Catherine. "Subjectivity and the Soliloquy." *New Casebooks: Macbeth.* Ed. Alan Sinfield. London: Macmillan, 1992.

Beran, Michael Knox. "Lincoln, Macbeth, and the Moral Imagination." *Humanitas* 11 (2) (1998).

Bernard, John. *Retrospections of the Stage.* London: Colburn and Bentley, 1830.

Bernhardt, Lysiane. *Sarah Bernhardt: ma grand'mère.* Paris: du Pavois, 1945, 1947.

Bernhardt, Sarah. *Ma Double Vie: Mémoires de Sarah Bernhardt.* Paris: Charpentier, 1907.

Bevington, David. *Shakespeare's Ideas: More Things in Heaven and Earth.* Chichester: Wiley-Blackwell, 2008.

Blair, Hugh. *Lectures on Rhetoric and Belles Lettres.* London: Strahan, Cadell; Edinburgh Creech, 1783, 1787.

Booth, John Wilkes. *"Right or Wrong, God Judge Me": The Writings of John Wilkes Booth.* Ed. John Rhodehamel and Louise Taper. Urbana: University of Illinois, 1997.

Burke, Helen M. *Riotous Performances: The Struggle for Hegemony in the Irish Theater, 1712–1784.* Indiana: University of Notre Dame Press, 2003.

Burnim, Kalman A. *David Garrick Director.* Pittsburgh: University of Pittsburgh Press, 1961.

Byrne, Patrick. *The Trial of John Magee, for Printing and Publishing a Slanderous and Defamatory Libel, against Richard Daly, Esq., Held before the Right Honourable Lord Viscount Clonmell, by a Special Jury of the City of Dublin, Monday, June 28, 1790.* Dublin: P. Byrne, 1790.

Byrne, Paula. *Perdita: The Literary, Theatrical, Scandalous Life of Mary Robinson.* New York: Random House, 2004.

Carey, Mathew. *Autobiography. The New-England Magazine 1833–1834; 1837;* Brooklyn: Research Classics, 1942.

Carmichael, Virginia. *Framing History: The Rosenberg Story and the Cold War.* Minneapolis: University of Minnesota Press, 1993.

Chambrun, Marquis Adolphe de. *Impressions of Lincoln and the Civil War: A Foreigner's Account.* Trans. General Aldebert de Chambrun. New York: Random House, 1952.

Clark, William Smith. *The Irish Stage in the County Towns, 1720–1800.* Oxford: Clarendon Press, 1965.

Clarke, Asia Booth. *John Wilkes Booth: A Sister's Memoir.* Ed. Terry Alford. Jackson: University Press of Mississippi, 1996.

Clement, Clara Erskine. *Charlotte Cushman.* Boston: Osgood, 1882.

Clemmer, Mary (Ames). *Men, Women, and Things.* Boston: Ticknor, 1886.

Cliff, Nigel. *The Shakespeare Riots: Revenge, Drama, and Death in Nineteenth-Century America.* New York: Random House, 2007.

Clinton, Catherine. Mrs. *Lincoln: A Life.* New York: HarperCollins, 2009.

Conason, Joe, and Gene Lyons. *The Hunting of the President: The Ten-Year Campaign to Destroy Bill and Hillary Clinton.* New York: St. Martin's Press, 2000.

Cowley, Hannah. *The Belle's Stratagem. Eighteenth-Century Women Dramatists.* New York: Oxford University Press, 2001.

Craig, Edith, and Christopher St. John. *Ellen Terry's Memoirs.* London: Gollanca, 1933.

Craig, Edward Gordon. Archive E.G.C. 4 1155. Paris: Bibliothèque Nationale.

Cressy, David. *Coming Over: Migration and Communication between England and New England in the Seventeenth Century.* Cambridge: Cambridge University Press, 1987.

Daniels, Bruce C. *Puritans at Play: Leisure and Recreation in Colonial New England.* New York: St. Martin's Griffin, 1995.

DeLarue, Allison. *The Chevalier Henry Wikoff: Impresario, 1840.* Princeton: Princeton University Press, 1904.

Demos, John. *Entertaining Satan: Witchcraft and the Culture of Early New England.* New York: Oxford University Press, 2004.

D'Oench, Ellen G. *"Copper into Gold," Prints by John Raphael Smith, 1751–1812.* New Haven and London: Yale University Press, 1999.

Downer, Alan Seymour. *The Eminent Tragedian William Charles Macready.* Cambridge: Harvard University Press, 1966.

Ducis, Jean-François. *Lettres de Jean-François Ducis.* Ed. Paul Albert. Paris: Jousset, 1879.

———. *Macbeth.* Paris Gueffier, 1790.

Dudden, Faye E. *Women in the American Theatre: Actresses and Audiences, 1790–1870.* New Haven: Yale University Press, 1994.

Dunbar, Janet. *Peg Woffington and Her World.* Boston: Houghton Mifflin, 1968.

Dunlap, William. *André.* New York: The Dunlap Society, 1887.

———. *Diary of William Dunlap (1766–1839): The Memoirs of a Dramatist, Theatrical Manager, Painter, Critic, Novelist, and Historian.* New York: New-York Historical Society, 1930; Benjamin Blom, 1969.

———. *History of the American Theatre and Anecdotes of the Principal Actors.* 1832. Reprint, New York: Burt Franklin, 1963.

Dunn, Esther Cloudman. *Shakespeare in America.* New York: Macmillan, 1939.

Dunton, John. *Letters Written from New-England A.D. 1686.* London: 1705. Boston: 1867. Reprint New York: Burt Franklin, n.d.

Durey, Michael. *Transatlantic Radicals and the Early American Republic.* Lawrence: University of Kansas, 1997.

Eger, Elizabeth, and Lucy Peltz. *Brilliant Women: Eighteenth-Century Bluestockings.* New Haven and London: Yale University Press, 2008.

Elliott, Marianne. *Wolfe Tone: Prophet of Irish Independence.* New Haven: Yale University Press, 1989.

Ellis, Joseph J. *Founding Brothers: The Revolutionary Generation.* New York: Knopf, 2001.

Ewan, David. *American Composers.* New York: Putnam, 1982.

Fennell, James. *An Apology for the Life of James Fennell.* Philadelphia: Moses Thomas, 1814; New York: Blom reprint, 1969.

Fitzpatrick, William J. *Sham Squire and the Informers of 1798.* London: Hotten, 1866.

Foster, R.F. *Modern Ireland: 1600–1972.* London: Allen Lane, 1988; Penguin Books, 1989.

Franklin, Benjamin. *The Papers of Ben Franklin.* Ed. William B. Willcox and Ellen R. Cohn. New Haven and London: Yale University Press, 1986.

Fraser, Antonia. *Faith and Treason: The Story of the Gunpowder Plot.* New York: Nan A. Talese Doubleday, 1996.

Fried, Albert. *McCarthyism: The Great American Red Scare, a Documentary History.* New York: Oxford University Press, 1997.

Furness, H.H. Ed. *Variorum, Macbeth.* London: Dent, 1873, 1898.

Furtwangler, Albert. *Assassin on Stage: Brutus, Hamlet and the Death of Lincoln.* Urbana: University of Illinois Press, 1991.

Gallagher, Jack. "History of the Theatre in Derry." *The Derry Journal, Commemorative Edition.* Derry: Public Library, 1972.

Garson, Barbara. *MacBird.* Berkeley, New York: Grassy Knoll Press, 1966.

Gilder, Rosamond. *Enter the Actress: The First Women in the Theatre.* London: George G. Harrap, 1931.

Gilbert, John T. *A History of the City of Dublin.* Dublin 1854–1859; Shannon: Irish University Press, 1972.

Glover, Richard. *Medea.* London: J. Bell, 1792.

Gold, Arthur, and Robert Fitzdale. *The Divine Sarah: A Life of Sarah Bernhardt.* New York: Knopf, 1991.

Golder, John. *Shakespeare for the Age of Reason: the Earliest Stage Adaptations of Jean-François Ducis.* Oxford: Voltaire Foundation, 1992.

Gordon, Lyndall. *Vindication: A Life of Mary Wollstonecraft.* Great Britain: Little, Brown, 2005; New York: HarperCollins Perennial 2006.

Goodwin, Doris Kearns. *No Ordinary Time: Franklin & Eleanor Roosevelt: The Home Front in World War II.* New York: Touchstone, 1994.

———. *Team of Rivals: The Political Genius of Abraham Lincoln.* New York: Simon & Schuster, 2005.

Greenblatt, Stephen. *Shakespeare Negotiations*. New York: Oxford University Press, 1988, 1997.

————. *Will of the World: How Shakespeare Became Shakespeare*. New York: W.W. Norton, 2004.

Greene, John C. *Theatre in Belfast, 1736–1800*. Bethlehem, Pennsylvania: Lehigh University Press, 2000.

Harwell, Richard Barksdale. *Brief Candle: The Confederate Theatre*. Worcester: American Antiquarian Society, 1971.

Hathorn, Ramon. *Our Lady of the Snows: Sarah Bernhardt in Canada*. New York: Peter Lang, 1996.

Hatton, Ann Julia. *Tammany...A Serious Opera*. New York: J. Harrison, c. 1794. Early American Imprints.

Hay, John. *Inside Lincoln's White House: The Complete Civil War Diary of John Hay*. Ed. Michael Burlingame and John R. Turner. Carbondale: Southern Illinois University Press, 1997, 1999.

Hayre, C. Ruth Wright. "Samuel Jackson Pratt: Novelist and Poet (1747–1814)." PhD Dissertation. Philadelphia: University of Pennsylvania, 1953.

Hazlitt, William. *Memoirs of Thomas Holcroft: Written by Himself and Continued by William Hazlitt*. London: Humphrey Milford, 1816; Oxford University Press, 1926.

Helms, Lorraine. "Acts of Resistance." *The Weyward Sisters: Shakespeare and Feminist Politics*. Ed. Dympha C. Callaghan, Lorraine Helms, and Jyotsna Singh. Oxford: Blackwell, 1994.

Henry Fuseli, 1741–1825. Exhibition Catalogue, Kuntshaus, Zurich, translation Sarah Twohig. London: Tate Gallery, 1975.

Higgins, Francis. *Revolutionary Dublin: 1795–1801: The Letters of Francis Higgins to Dublin Castle*. Ed. Thomas Bartlett. Portland, Oregon: Four Courts Press, 2004.

Highfill, Philip H., Jr., Kalman A. Burnim, and Edward A. Langhans. *A Biographical Dictionary of Actors, Actresses, Musicians, Dancers, Managers & Other Stage Personnel in London, 1660–1800*. Carbondale: Southern Illinois University Press, 1973–1993.

Hitchcock, Robert. *An Historical View of the Irish Stage; from the Earliest Period Down to the Close of the Season, 1788*. Dublin: Marchbank, 1788.

Holcroft, Thomas. *The School for Arrogance*. London: Robinson, 1791.

Holland, Peter, ed. *Shakespeare Survey: An Annual Survey of Shakespeare Studies and Production: 57,* Macbeth *and Its Afterlife*. Cambridge: Cambridge University Press, 2004.

Holroyd, Michael. *A Strange Eventful History: The Dramatic Lives of Ellen Terry, Henry Irving, and Their Remarkable Families*. New York: Farrar, Straus and Giroux, 2008.

Irving, H.B. *Occasional Papers: Dramatic and Historical*. London: Bickers, 1906.

Irving, Washington. *Letters of Jonathan Oldstyle.* New York: Clayton, 1824.

———. *The Life and Letters of Washington Irving.* Ed. Pierre M. Irving. New York: Putnam, 1864.

Isaacson, Walter. *Benjamin Franklin: An American Life.* New York: Simon & Schuster, 2003.

Jacobs, Arthur. *Arthur Sullivan: A Victorian Musician.* New York: Oxford University Press, 1984.

James, Reese Davis. *Cradle of Culture, 1800–1810: The Philadelphia Stage.* Philadelphia: University of Pennsylvania Press, 1957.

———. *Old Drury of Philadelphia: The History of the Philadelphia Stage, 1800–1835.* Philadelphia: University of Pennsylvania Press, 1932.

Johnson, Odai. *Absence and Memory in Colonial American Theatre.* New York: Palgrave Macmillan, 2006.

Johnson, Odai, and William J. Burling. *The Colonial American Stage, 1665–1774: A Documentary Calendar.* Cranberry, New Jersey: Association of University Presses, 2001.

Kernan, Alvin. *Shakespeare, the King's Playwright: Theater in the Stuart Court, 1603–1613.* New Haven and London: Yale University Press, 1995.

Kirk, Elise K. *American Opera.* Urbana: University of Illinois Press, 2001.

Knox, John. "The First Blast of the Trumpet against the Monstrous Regiment of Women." *The Works of John Knox.* Ed. David Laing. Edinburgh: Bannaiyne Club, 1855.

Lawrence, W.J. "The Annals of 'the Old Belfast Stage.'" Unpublished Typescript, 1897. Belfast: Linen Library.

Leach, Joseph. *Bright Particular Star: The Life and Times of Charlotte Cushman.* New Haven and London: Yale University Press, 1970.

Leech, Margaret. *Reveille in Washington, 1860–1865.* New York: Harper, 1941.

Levin, Phyllis Lee. *Abigail Adams: a Biography.* New York: St. Martin's Griffin, 2001.

———. *Edith and Woodrow: The Wilson White House.* New York: Scribner, 2001.

Levine, Lawrence W. *Highbrow Lowbrow: The Emergence of Cultural Hierarchy in America.* Cambridge: Harvard University Press, 1988.

Lincoln, Mary Todd. *Mary Todd Lincoln: Her Life and Letters.* Ed. Justin G. Turner and Linda Levitt Turner. New York: Knopf, 1972.

Maclean, Fitzroy. *Scotland: A Concise History.* London and New York: Thames and Hudson, 1993, revised 1999.

Madden, Robert. *The United Irishmen: Their Lives and Times.* 1851. New York: Catholic Publication Society, 1916.

Maginnes, F. Arant. *Thomas Abthorpe Cooper: Father of the American Stage, 1775–1849.* Jefferson, North Carolina: McFarland, 2004.

Maretzak, Max. *Revelations of an Opera Manager in 19th Century America: Crotchets and Quavers & Sharps and Flats,* 2 vols. in 1. New York: Dover, 1968.

Mather, Cotton. "A Brand Pluck'd from the Burning." *Narratives of the Witchcraft Cases, 1648–1707.* Ed. George Lincoln Burr. New York: Scribners, 1914.

———. *Magnalia Christi Americana, or the Ecclesiastical History of New England.* London: T. Parkhurst, 1702.

Mathews, Brander, and Laurence Hutton, eds. *Actors and Actresses of Great Britain and the United States from the Days of David Garrick to the Present.* New York: Cassell, 1886.

McConachie, Bruce A. *Melodramatic Formations: American Theatre & Society, 1820–1870.* Iowa City: University of Iowa Press, 1992.

McCullough, David. *1776.* New York: Simon & Schuster, 2005.

———. *John Adams.* New York: Simon & Schuster, 2001.

McPherson, Sue, and Julia Swindells, eds. *Women's Theatrical Memoirs. Part II.* London: Pickering and Catto, 2008.

Merrill, Lisa. *When Romeo Was a Woman: Charlotte Cushman and Her Circle of Female Spectators.* Ann Arbor: University of Michigan, 1999.

Miller, Arthur. *The Crucible.* New York: Viking Press, 1953.

———. *Timebends.* New York: Grove Press, 1987.

Myers, Robert J., and Joyce Brodowski. "Rewriting the Hallams: Research in 18th Century British and American Theatre," *Theatre Survey* 41 (1) (May 2000): 1–22.

Moody, Richard. *Astor Place Riot.* Bloomington: Indiana University Press, 1958.

Morash, Christopher. *A History of Irish Theatre, 1601–2000.* Cambridge: Cambridge University Press, 2002.

Morris, Clara. "I Stand Between Lady Macbeth and Matrimony." *McClure's Magazine* 20 (3) (January 1903).

Moses, Jonas, and John Mason Brown. *The American Theatre as Seen by Its Critics.* New York: W.W. Norton, 1934.

Murray, Judith Sargent. 1798. *The Gleaner.* Schenectady, New York: Union College Press, 1992.

Neely, Mark E. Jr., and R. Gerald McMurtry. *The Insanity File.* Carbondale: Southern Illinois University Press, 1986.

Nathans, Heather S. *Early American Theatre from the Revolution to Thomas Jefferson.* England: Cambridge University Press, 2003.

Nicoll, Allardyce. *The Garrick Stage: Theatres and Audience in the Eighteenth Century.* Manchester: Manchester University Press, 1980.

O'Brien, Conor Cruise. *Edmund Burke.* 1992. Abridged. Dublin: New Island Books, 1997.

Odell, George C.D. *Annals of the New York Stage.* 15 vols. New York: Columbia University Press, 1927–1949.

O'Keeffe, John. *Recollections of the Life of John O'Keeffe.* London: Henry Colburn, 1826.

O'Toole, Fintan. *A Traitor's Kiss: The Life of Richard Brinsley Sheridan.* London: Granta Books, 1997.

Page, Anthony. *John Jebb and the Enlightenment Origins of British Radicalism.* Westport: Praeger, 2003.

Parsons, Mrs. Clement. *Garrick and His Circle.* New York: Putnam's, 1906.

Pollock, Thomas Clark. *The Philadelphia Theatre in the Eighteenth Century.* Philadelphia: University of Pennsylvania Press, 1933

Pratt, Samuel Jackson. *Charles and Charlotte.* London: 1777.

Prebble, John. *Culloden.* London: Martin Secker & Warburg, 1961; Penguin, 1996.

Prideaux, Tom. *Love or Nothing: The Life and Times of Ellen Terry.* London: Millington, 1975.

Pronier, Ernest. *Une Vie au théâtre: Sarah Bernhardt.* Geneva: A. Jullien, c. 1940.

Rackin, Phyllis. *Shakespeare and Women.* New York: Oxford University Press, 2005.

Randall, Ruth Painter. *Mary Lincoln: Biography of a Marriage.* Boston: Little, Brown, 1953.

Rawlings, Peter. *Americans on Shakespeare, 1776–1914.* Aldershot: Ashgate, 1999.

Richepin, Jean. *L'Opinion,* April 6, 1914.

Rigg, Diana. *No Turn Unstoned: The Worst Ever Theatrical Reviews.* London: Arrow Books, 1982.

Roach, Joseph R. *Cities of the Dead: Circum-Atlantic Performance.* New York: Columbia University Press, 1996.

————. *The Player's Passion: Studies in the Science of Acting.* Wilmington: University of Delaware, 1985; Ann Arbor: University of Michigan Press, 1999.

Rosenberg, Marvin. *The Masks of Macbeth.* Newark: University of Delaware Press, London: Associated University Presses, 1978.

Rosenfeld, Richard N. *American Aurora: Democratic-Republican Returns, the Suppressed History of our Nation's Beginnings and the Heroic Newspaper That Tried to Report It.* New York: St. Martin's Press, 1997.

Rovère, Richard H. *Senator Joe McCarthy.* New York: World Publishing, 1960.

Rowan, Archibald Hamilton. *Autobiography of Archibald Hamilton Rowan.* Ed. William H. Drummond. Shannon: Irish University Press, 1972.

Ruggles, Eleanor. *Prince of Players: Edwin Booth.* New York: Norton, 1953.

Russell, Gillian. *The Theatres of War: Performance, Politics, and Society, 1793–1815.* Oxford; Clarendon Press, 1995.

Sainsbury, John. *Disaffected Patriots: London Supporters of Revolutionary America, 1769–1782.* Kingston and Montreal: McGill University Press, 1987.

Samples, Gordon. *Lust for Fame: The Stage Career of John Wilkes Booth.* Jefferson, North Carolina: McFarland, 1982.

Sandburg, Carl. *Mary Lincoln, Wife and Widow.* New York: Harcourt, Brace, 1932.

Schiff, Stacy. *A Great Improvisation: Franklin, France, and the Birth of America.* New York: Henry Holt, 2005.

Schneller, Beverly E. "No 'Brave Irishman' Need Apply: Thomas Sheridan, Shakespeare and the Smock-Alley Theatre." *Shakespeare and Ireland: History, Politics, Culture.* Ed. Mark Thornton Burnett and Ramona Wray. Great Britain: Macmillan Press, New York: St. Martin's Press, 1997.

Seale, William. *The President's House: A History.* 2 vol. Washington, D.C., White House Historical Association, National Geographic Society; New York: Abrams, 1986.

Shakespeare in American Life. Exhibition Catalogue. Ed. Virginia Mason Vaughan and Alden T. Vaughan. Washington, D.C.: Folger Shakespeare Library, 2007.

Shakespeare, William. *Mr. William Shakespeares Comedies, Histories, & Tragedies.* First Folio 1623; Facsimile Edition, New Haven: Yale University Press, London: Oxford University Press, 1954.

Shaffer, Jason. *Performing Patriotism: National Identity in the Colonial and Revolutionary Theater.* Philadelphia: University of Pennsylvania, 2007.

Shattuck, Charles Harlen. *The Shakespeare Promptbooks: A Descriptive Catalogue.* Urbana: University of Illinois Press, 1965.

———. *Shakespeare on the American Stage: From the Hallams to Edwin Booth.* Washington, D.C.: Folger Shakespeare Library, 1976.

Shaw, George Bernard. *Ellen Terry and Bernard Shaw: A Correspondence.* Ed. Christopher St. John. New York: Putnam, 1932.

Shaughnessy, Nicola, and Robert Shaughnessy, eds. *Lives of Shakespearian Actors 1: David Garrick, Charles Macklin and Margaret Woffington.* London: Pickering & Chatto, 2008.

Sheldon, Esther K. *Thomas Sheridan of Smock-Alley: Recording His Life as Actor and Theater Manager in Both Dublin and London.* Princeton: Princeton University Press, 1967.

Sheridan, Thomas. *A Discourse: Being Introductory to His Course of Lectures on Elocution and the English Language.* 1759. University of California, Los Angeles: Augustan Reprint, William Andrews Clark Memorial Library, 1969.

Shenk, Joshua. *Lincoln's Melancholy: How Depression Challenged a President and Fueled His Greatness.* New York: Houghton Mifflin, 2005.

Showalter, Elaine. *Sexual Anarchy: Gender and Culture at the Fin de Siècle.* New York: Penguin, 1990.

Sinfield, Alan. "'Macbeth': History, Ideology and Intellectuals." *New Casebooks: Macbeth.* Ed. Alan Sinfield. London: Macmillan, 1992.

Smith, Geddeth. *Thomas Abthorpe Cooper: America's Premier Tragedian.* London: Associated University Presses, 1996.

Smith, Gene A. *American Gothic: The Story of America's Legendary Theatrical Family—Junius, Edwin and John Wilkes Booth.* New York: Simon and Schuster, 1992, 1993.

Smith, Zadie. "Speaking in Tongues." *The New York Review of Books* (February 26, 2009).

Sonneck, O.G. *Early Opera in America.* New York: Schirmer, 1915.

Sprague, Arthur Colby. *Shakespeare and the Actors: The Stage Business in His Plays (1660–1905).* Cambridge: Harvard University Press, 1944.

Stephens, Autumn. *Wild Women in the White House.* Berkeley, California: Conari Press, 1997.

Stewart, A.T.Q. *A Deeper Silence: The Hidden Origins of the United Irishmen.* Belfast: Blackstaff Press, 1993.

Stiles, Henry. *A History of the City of Brooklyn.* 1869. Maryland: Heritage Books, 1993.

Stone, George Winchester, Jr., and George M. Kahrl. *David Garrick: A Critical Biography.* Carbondale: Southern Illinois University Press, 1979.

Strong, George Templeton. *The Diary of George Templeton Strong.* New York: Macmillan, 1952.

Styan, J.L. *The Shakespeare Revolution: Criticism and Performance in the Twentieth Century.* Cambridge: Cambridge University Press, 1977, 1983.

Tanenhaus, Sam. "A Family Affair." Review of *The Brother* by Sam Roberts and *The Man Behind the Rosenbergs* by Alexander Feklisov and Sergei Kostin. *The New York Review of Books* (March 26, 2001): 41–44.

Tanner, Marcus. *Ireland's Holy Wars: The Struggle for a Nation's Soul, 1500–2000.* New Haven and London: Yale University Press, 2003.

Terry, Ellen. *Four Lectures on Shakespeare.* Ed. Christopher St. John. London: Martin Hopkinson, 1932.

———. Annotated "*Macbeth* Book." E.T. 218, L888. Smallhythe Cottage, Kent, England.

Trewin, J.C. *Mr Macready: A Nineteenth Century Tragedian and His Theatre.* London: Harrap, 1955.

Turgot. *Life of Saint Margaret, Queen of Scotland.* c. 1100. trans. William Forbes-Leith 1884. Edinburgh: Flories, 1993.

Van Lennep, William, Emmett Langdon Avery, Arthur Hawley Scouten, Charles Beecher Hogan, and George Winchester Stone. *The London Stage, 1660–1800: A Calendar of Plays, Entertainments & Afterpieces, Together with Casts, Box-receipts and Contemporary Comment.* Carbondale: Southern Illinois University Press, 1965.

Verneuil, Louis. *The Fabulous Life of Sarah Bernhardt.* Trans. Ernest Boyd. New York: Harper, 1942.

Walpole, Horace. *Walpole Correspondence.* Ed. W.S. Lewis, Grover Cronin, Jr., and Charles H. Bennett. New Haven: Yale University Press.

———. Annotated *Royal Academy Catalogue 1784.* Walpole Library, Yale University.

Walsh, T.J. *Opera in Dublin: 1705–1797: The Social Scene.* Dublin: Allen Figgis, 1973.

Wattenberg, Daniel. "The Lady Macbeth of Little Rock." *American Spectator* 25 (8) (August 1992).

Webster, Margaret. *Don't Put Your Daughter on the Stage.* New York: Knopf, 1972.

———. *Shakespeare Today.* London: Dent, 1957.

Williams, Simon. "Taking Macbeth out of Himself: Davenant, Garrick, Schiller and Verdi." *Shakespeare Survey: An Annual Survey of Shakespeare Studies and production, 57,* Macbeth *and its Afterlife.* Ed. Peter Holland. Cambridge: Cambridge University Press, 2004.

Willoughby, Edwin. "The Reading of Shakespeare in Colonial America." *Biographical Society of America* 6 (14) (June 1937): 45–56.

Wills, Garry. "Hating Hillary." *The New York Review of Books* (November 14, 1996).

———. *Henry Adams and the Making of America*. Boston: Houghton Mifflin, 2005.

———. *Witches and Jesuits: Shakespeare's Macbeth*. New York: Oxford University Press, 1995.

Wilson, David A. *United Irishmen, United States: Immigrant Radicals in the Early Republic*. Ithaca: Cornell University Press, 1998.

Wilson, Edith Bolling. *My Memoir*. New York: Bobbs-Merrill, 1938.

Wilson, Woodrow, and Edith Wilson. *A President in Love: The Courtship Letters of Woodrow Wilson and Edith Bolling Galt*. Ed. Edwin Tribble. Boston: Houghton Mifflin, 1981.

Wilson, Woodrow, and Ellen Axson. *The Priceless Gift: The Love Letters of Woodrow Wilson and Ellen Axson Wilson*. Ed. Eleanor Wilson McAdoo. New York: McGraw-Hill, 1962.

Wingate, Charles Edgar Lewis. *Shakespeare's Heroines on the Stage*. New York and Boston: Thomas Crowell, 1895.

Yeater, James Willis. "Charlotte Cushman, American Actress." PhD Dissertation. Urbana: University of Illinois, 1959.

Yourcenar, Marguerite. "La Symphonie héroique." *Essais et mémoires*. Paris: Gallimard, 1991.

Newspapers (All prefixed with "The")

Ireland

Belfast Newsletter
Derry Journal
Dublin Evening Post
Faulkner's Journal (Dublin)
Freeman's Journal (Dublin)
Hibernian Chronicle (Dublin)
Morning Post (Dublin)
Northern Star (Belfast)
Waterford Herald

London

Daily Telegraph
Illustrated Sporting and Dramatic News
Morning Chronicle

Observer
Times

New York

Commercial Advertiser
Morning Chronicle
New York Daily Tribune
New York Mirror
New York Times

Other

New Haven Register
San Francisco Chronicle
Washington Post

Index ❧

for instigating McCarthy era witch-
hunt and black list, 168; *see also*
Richard Nixon
Howe, Julia Ward, 109
Hutchinson, Anne, 25

Inchbald, Elizabeth, playwright,
novelist, actor, in company with
Charlotte Melmoth and John Philip
Kemble, 201n65
Iona, island sacred to Scots and Irish,
site of sixth century monastery
founded by Irish Saint Colmkill,
where Queen Gruoch Macbeth is
believed to be buried, 22
Irish Rebellion 1798, 59; *see also*
United Irishmen
Irving, Henry, Ellen Terry's long time
acting partner and Macbeth, 143–4,
150–1, 209n12
Irving, Washington, writer, on theatre
and Charlotte Melmoth, 79, 94, 95,
199n47, 200n52, 202n76

Jacobites, supporters of James II
(defeated by English at the Battle
of the Boyne 1690) and "Prince
Charlie" (defeated at Culloden,
Scotland, 1745), for Catholic
emancipation and parliamentary
reform, considered treasonous by the
English, 83, 191n50
James II, King of England, Scotland
and Ireland 1686–1688, grandson
of James I, last of Stuart line and
last Catholic monarch, succeeded by
Protestants William and Mary, 83;
see also Jacobites
James VI, King of Scotland
1567–1625, James I, King of
England 1603–1625, for whom
Shakespeare created Banquo in
Macbeth 1606, 2, 23; see
Daemonology

Jebb, Ann, "Priscilla," writer in
England, wife of John Jebb,
supporter of Irish Catholic
emancipation and French
Revolution, 50, 193n15
Jebb, John, Dubliner, scholar of
Classical and Arabic languages,
denied professorship in England
due to politics, pro-reform in Ireland,
physician, hosted Abigail and John
Adams in England, 50, 198n39
Jefferson, Thomas, President
1801–1809, 44, 46, 56, 59,
61, 62, 84, 94
Johnson, Lady Bird, First Lady
1963–1969, Chapter 1. Lady
Macbeth in the White House,
satirized as Lady Macbeth, 7–9
Johnson, Lyndon, President 1963–1969,
satirized as Macbeth, 7–9, 187n1
Johnson, Martha Harris, Ben Franklin's
niece and London connection, 71,
196n17
Johnson, Samuel, preference for Peg
Woffington over Mrs. Pritchard,
191n38
Jones, Robert Edmond, America's first
"modern" stage designer, 153
Julius Caesar, by Shakespeare, 44, 50,
64, 79, 93, 108, 201n65, 203n1

Kazan, Elia, stage and film
director, named names in McCarthy
era, 171
Kazan, Molly, wife to Elia, blamed for
husband's actions, 171
Keene, Laura, actress, manager, 138
Kelly, Hugh, author of *School for Wives*,
196n12, 201n65
Kelly, Michael, Mozart's Bardolfo in
premier of opera *Marriage of Figaro*;
performed opera in Ireland with
Charlotte Melmoth, 1787–1788,
197n23

CPSIA information can be obtained at www.ICGtesting.com
Printed in the USA
BVOW012048161211

278298BV00003B/17/P